Dreams and
Reconstruction

A Cultural History of British Theatre

1945-2006

Michael Prior

ISBN: 978-1-4303-0857-7

First published 2006

Revised: 2006

This book is dedicated to Buzz
Goodbody and to all her hopes for the
theatre and for the world

Dreams and Reconstruction

Contents

Introduction

Theatre in Britain occupies a central but often contradictory position in its national culture. It is and has been hugely successful in just about every way that can be defined. It is both popular and extremely prolific. Through the second half of the 1990s, it ran neck-and-neck with the cinema in terms of number of annual admissions though cinema outstripped it in the first years of the new century thanks to a number of popular blockbusting films.[1] There were also a very large number of individual productions. Aggregate national numbers are not collected but, as an example, in the Greater Manchester area[2] in 2004/2005 there were 645 separate theatrical productions performed by about 347 groups at 272 different venues. (Haworth) The number of venues is inflated by the performances of companies working mainly in schools but, even so, the size is imposing. For comparison purposes, there were, at that time, 18 cinemas in the same area with about 150 screens in all mostly showing the same films at any one time.[3] A rough estimate suggests that about 800 different films in a year were shown in Greater Manchester, broadly the same as theatrical productions. The scale of the drama productions ranged widely from the industrial level of *Miss Saigon*

---

[1] Keynote Reports on the Theatre and Cinema, various years

[2] This includes the cities and boroughs of Bolton, Bury, Manchester, Oldham, Rochdale, Salford, Stockport, Tameside, Trafford and Wigan, in effect the urban metropolis surrounding Manchester.

[3] These statistics are taken from the local listings publication, *City Life*. No accurate figures are available for the number of different films shown so the estimate here is only rough.

at the huge Palace Theatre to amateur shows in church halls. But they were all linked by the common purpose of putting on plays for a paying audience.

Theatre can also be extremely successful commercially. The most successful production of the last fifty years, perhaps the most successful entertainment ever devised, in these terms has been *Phantom of the Opera* which has attracted more revenue world-wide than the film, *Titanic,* often reported to be the most financially successful film ever made. This conclusion was reached in the Wyndham Report in 1998 which put the actual numbers as that, by 1998, *Phantom of the Opera* had grossed £1.73 billion, *Cats*, £1.14 billion and *Les Misérables*, £0.77 billion whilst *Titanic* had grossed £0.92 billion. *Titanic* is now well past its sell-buy date and by 2005, both *Phantom* and *Les Misérables* had grossed more than £1.5 billion and show no signs of stopping. *Miss Saigon* has also probably surpassed the billion-pound gross worldwide.

Finally, in Britain the theatre has been the most successful national cultural form of the last half-century using culture in its narrower artistic sense. Success in these terms is hard to establish but few would quarrel with the proposition that British theatre, beginning in the 1950s with dramatists such as Osborne and Wesker continuing through the Bond, Arden and Pinter generation to more recent writers such as Hare, has achieved an international reputation for excellence. Only British popular music, and then in a patchy way, has acquired an international cultural presence which matches that of the theatre. One way of illustrating this is that London is the only city in the world with the partial exception of New York where 'taking in a show' is part of the standard tourist package. In New York, a 'show on Broadway' means a lavish musical; in London, the 'West End' means choosing from a theatrical *smorgasbord* which ranges from equally lavish musicals through standard classics to new writing in venues like the Royal Court and the Almeida. The way in which the weight of this metropolitan presence affects theatre throughout Britain is something to which we will return. The point to be emphasised here is that the continuing success of West End theatre rests upon international cultural renown as much as commercial excellence.

Yet, despite this evidence of success, there is a continuing undercurrent of crisis. It is alleged that the big national companies are in a mess, both financially and in artistic terms, that regional theatres are facing bankruptcy, that the standard of new plays is poor and that theatre needs a 'new' audience to survive. Such complaints may be well-founded but it is also true that these complaints have been perennial throughout the past fifty years. In 1959 only three years after the alleged theatrical revolution of *Look Back in Anger* at the Royal Court, John Whiting could write " *The struggle at the Royal Court and elsewhere, it would seem, was for the theatre to take on a greater social and political responsibility. Crying 'Forward', it is dwindling from our sight. Plays are being produced which rely for their effect on a false naivety. The problems they present are being simplified to appoint of non-existence...Socially, the whole way of thinking is out of date. And, I say this without malice, out of touch.*" (Marovitz p.110) Fifteen years later, in 1974 when state-funding was probably expanding as fast as it had ever done, the Council of Regional Theatres, (CORT) estimated that of its twenty-six members, six faced immediate bankruptcy and all faced serious cutbacks in funding their programmes. (Elsom (1976) p.129) No change there then. In 1985, when the Arts Council of Great Britain produced a report surveying

British theatre, most contributors to it referred to a sense of crisis in the industry whilst in 2004, Arts Council England, as it had now become, also referred to a "crisis" in English theatre.

One of the themes of this book is that this sense of ongoing crisis has been a long-term feature of British theatre, something there effectively since its foundation, and which is probably one of the wellsprings of its cultural success. In a cultural form which is so ephemeral in terms of individual productions, it is surprising that in this as in several other features, there is so much historical continuity in the way in which the theatre has developed. This is not to suggest that the current problems of British theatre, such as they are, may not be genuine, possibly terminal in some cases. The point is that in theatre as in other walks of British life, there is a strong sense of repetition, a kind of circularity in which the same issues and contradictions constantly re-emerge and the same conflicts are engaged with but remain unresolved. This constant repetition is one reason why this survey of the last half of the twentieth century begins with a lengthy historical introduction. The key contradiction and one to which we will return several times is the problem of being both a popular and an elitist cultural form at one and the same time. This contradiction emerges in a number of ways, some of which are connected to the aesthetic of theatre, in the kind of play performed, how, where and to whom. It also emerges, however, in the more mundane though equally fundamental issue of money, who pays how much and to whom. Other artistic forms, notably music, visual art and, to a considerable degree, the novel, have long come to terms with the distinction between the popular and the elitist but, at least in the *British* theatre, no point of equilibrium has been nor, perhaps, ever will be found. An extension of this condition is that most other national theatres have to a considerable degree found such equilibrium with a clear distinction existing between highly-sponsored theatre, mostly public subsidy in Europe, mostly private in the U.S.A., and totally commercial theatre with a corresponding gap between the plays presented. British theatre has developed into a unique and uneasy unity between commercial and sponsored wings. The extent to which the specific dynamism and creativity of British theatre stems from this uneasy cultural position is something which cannot easily be defined but it almost certainly plays a part.

This is intended to be a cultural history of British theatre covering the last half of the twentieth century. Most of the words of this definition need some closer examination to avoid the most obvious accusations of bad faith or misrepresentation.

Culture

Culture is a notoriously difficult and slippery word. Raymond Williams famously offered three different definitions which ranged, effectively, from the narrow definition of culture related to general artistic activity through social manners and deportment to an almost anthropological definition covering just about all forms of social life. The difficulty with this approach is that usage of the word inevitably spills out along a spectrum covered by these definitions often without conforming precisely to any one of them. My use of the term is sometimes as guilty as any of this kind of general ambiguity for whilst I do not want to adhere to any one of these definitions neither do I want to exclude any. Certainly there is no intention here to write a cultural history in the narrow sense of the quality of dramatic texts or of particular productions or performances. In this perspective it may be interesting that there were four productions of

Macbeth and of *A Midsummer Night's Dream* in Greater Manchester in 2002 but only one of *Hamlet* insofar as this reflects upon an important relationship between the production of classic plays and their appearance as examination set texts but it is not particularly interesting to comment on their 'quality'. In the same vein, it is interesting that David Hare had a play running in the West End in 1974, the year before he helped found the Joint Stock touring company, and still in the early twenty-first century has plays running in the West End long after Joint Stock has disappeared. The relative artistic merits of *Knuckle* or *Fanshen* or *The Breath of Life* are not an issue here except in the way in which their form and content relates to the way in which writers have adapted to changing audience tastes or commercial pressures. We are interested in the things which say something about the way in which theatre relates to society, to its economics and to its politics as well as to its relations with other cultural forms.

Even so, at the same time it has to be acknowledged that, having tried to squeeze out judgements on artistic merit, they inevitably creep in by the back door. David Hare and Joint Stock are mentioned here rather than other possible exemplars of the shifts in the relationship between West End and touring theatre because they both matter in the narrow cultural history of British theatre. As a matter of personal judgement they both had artistic qualities which make them stand out from dozens of other writers and touring companies of the time. Such judgements form an inescapable part of any discussion about cultural issues however much one may seek to exclude them.

The problem here is that this book is concerned with the cultural aspects of a specific artistic activity. At one end of Williams' spectrum of definitions, this is virtually meaningless in the Arnoldian sense that culture is art and art is culture so all aspects of any art are cultural except, perhaps, how it is paid for. Aesthetics without the money if you like. It might also seem that the phrase becomes meaningless or at least extremely narrow at the opposite end of Williams' spectrum for if culture is concerned with specific aspects of social life, for example youth culture or rural culture, then it might appear that the best one might make of the 'culture of theatre' is an analysis of how audiences have shifted over the years. The culture of play-going in the same way that one might look at the culture of shopping in which shops played a more or less active role in stimulating their customers. Audiences without the aesthetics would be the easy summary.

The intention here is to consider the relations between theatre and British society; how the way in which the latter is organised, socially, economically and politically, has affected the theatre and how or indeed whether any reciprocal impact can be seen. There is a sense in which theatre treated in this way is indeed just one organ of social life along with, for example, football or shopping malls and it requires a very narrow cultural frame not to accept that one feature of modern theatre is that it has had to adapt to a big social shift in what is seen as popular entertainment. The venue for Manchester United FC at Old Trafford is sometimes called the 'Theatre of Dreams' by those who market its wide range of consumer products and there is a degree of resemblance between its star players and star actors. There is nothing new about theatre competing with a range of alternative entertainments and sport. One source of Elizabethan theatre was the bull and bear-baiting pits and the manners and customs of the patrons of some venues as well as their physical design reflected this. There is also nothing very new about an alignment between shopping, entertainment and various kinds of street theatre. The great Bartholomew's Fair held annually at Smithfield, just outside London's walls, was celebrated in just this way by Ben Jonson who would, probably, have been delighted by its reincarnation in various shopping malls in December.

 It makes very little sense to ignore this link between theatre as a cultural commodity and other forms of mass entertainment. This would be true even if one wishes to confine one attention to a narrowly aesthetic focus. In the 1970s and 80s, the Royal Shakespeare Company (RSC) was the sponsor and home for some of the most important new work in British theatre. Writers like Edgar, Bond and Barker were produced, names which continue to figure prominently in literary dramatic history. At the same time, the same company, directors and actors effectively created in *Les Misérables* the particular genre of blockbuster musical which has sustained London commercial theatre ever since. This is not so prominently displayed in such history but even the aesthetic development of the RSC is difficult to understand unless one includes the sometimes despised musical. However, most critical reviews of British theatre refuse to acknowledge that it exists as a form of mass popular entertainment and prefer to concentrate on a narrow dramatic aesthetic largely driven by the texts of playwrights and the work of a handful of directors. It is common, for example, for any survey of British theatre in the 1950s to devote pages to the production in 1955 at the Arts Theatre of *Waiting for Godot* with barely a mention for the most ground-breaking productions of the whole period, the American musicals. In his thoughtful survey of post-war theatre, Elsom includes the first of these, *Oklahoma!*, in a list of other major musicals of the 1950s and notes *"No other theatre genre since the war*

*has achieved the same degree of mass popularity. For
every teenager who was attracted to the theatre by an
Old Vic production, there must have been a thousand
who were hypnotised by these great show-business
spectaculars.*" (Elsom p.15) Having accepted the
musical as a theatrical genre, it is then banished in
favour of proper drama, that is the spoken 'serious'
form and *Oklahoma!* along with all other musicals
disappear from Elsom's history.

There is a practical critical reason for this kind of
emphasis, one which the author acknowledges[4], that it
is very easy to reduce any survey of the theatre to the
surviving written text plus some contemporary critical
reviews. The text of a play is certainly of interest. It
often, though far from invariably, provides the main
vehicle for the central theme of the play and it is the
basic substrata for any subsequent performance.
However focus on the text has several great
drawbacks. One of these is the obvious problem that
all the other elements of a play—music, movement,
light, sound, costume—are reduced to, at best,
ancillary components. Plays in which such elements
dominate or have equal status are necessarily reduced
in critical stature, sometimes to the point of
invisibility. In this form of literary analysis, the reason
why Davies in Pinter's *The Caretaker* is so anxious to
find comfortable shoes for a trip to Sidcup can occupy
pages whilst *Oh! What a Lovely War* can be
summarised, quite reasonably, as sentimental songs
from the First World War in an anti-war setting. It is
reasonable because from a literary point of view that is
just about that can or needs to be said.

The other great problem with this form of critical
review is that it has nothing to say about context. In a

---

[4] See Chambers and Prior, *Playwright's Progress*

sense, the fundamental assumption made is that all plays are put on in a setting close to that of an Edwardian theatre in which the curtain rises, the lights are dimmed and the audience is silenced, in other words the context of 'missing wall' theatre in which every effort is made to persuade individuals in the audience that they have the privilege of being solitary eavesdroppers on the 'real' world of the stage. It will be part of the argument of this book that one of the major shifts in British theatre over the past fifty years has been precisely a move away from this assumption, to make the audience aware of themselves and of the context in which they are watching a play. Sometimes this shift *can* be seen in purely literary terms, for example in Bond's *The Bundle* when Basho effectively asks the audience whether or not he should drown an abandoned baby. But often this is impossible. It reduces the work of, for example, the performance group Welfare State, who are both non-verbal and work outdoors, to sparse footnotes if they are mentioned at all. Sometimes, context is almost everything whatever the literary content of the work. When Gay Sweatshop performed in the 1970s, they were part of the cutting edge of a movement for gay rights which placed them, along with their audience, in possible physical danger when they took their shows on the road. Their work transcended the purely literary value of the plays which they presented. It also needs to be emphasised that both of these groups were profoundly influential within the theatre of their time leaving aside any wider social impact which they may have had. It is impossible to understand the change in the plays presented on the big stages of the National Theatre or the Royal Exchange in Manchester without knowing something of what these 'fringe' groups did.

The main reason why this kind of critical gap exists is that the dominant critical mode for looking at the theatre remains that of the late-Victorian and Edwardian period in which, for the first time in British theatre, spoken prose drama emerged as its defining genre with other forms relegated to a secondary place. Up to that point, texts had been largely manipulated artefacts like props, costumes or scenery whatever its potential literary 'quality'. In the eighteenth century, Shakespeare was normally rewritten to taste as a matter of course. The great Garrick himself, sometimes regarded as the champion of classical theatre compared with his rivals, provided *King Lear* with a happy ending[5] and limited the number of deaths at the end of *Hamlet*. This was done in full knowledge of the existence of carefully edited complete versions of the originals. Only at the end of the nineteenth century, with productions of plays by Chekhov, Ibsen, Shaw, Wilde, Pinero and so on, did the text emerge as the unchanging lynchpin of theatre along with the commercial concept that the text was the property of the author. These writers remain, along with Shakespeare, as the critical gold standard of British drama alongside which contemporary writing is judged. The emergence of playwrights as independent artists, retaining the copyright to their work and being paid a share of the box-office, was entirely in keeping with the general cultural spirit of the times. But, as we shall see, this style of drama was also entirely congruent with the needs of London commercial management of the time and the continuing status, down to the present day, of this form of drama continues to be linked with commercial necessity though of a subtly different kind. It is no coincidence that just as a new kind of 'public' theatre was emerging in the 1960s supported by state subsidy, one

---

[5] Lear survives and sees Cordelia marry Edgar to become joint rulers before he retires to a monastery.

of the first major productions of this new theatre involved a reversion to the eighteenth century idea of using the original Shakespearean text as just a starting point for the final script.

If it is impossible to analyse modern theatre except as a cultural commodity, it is also impossible to consider it as *just* a cultural commodity. Essentially, we need to pay attention to a specific cultural role which theatre has. In 1958, Raymond Williams in the seminal work of modern cultural history wrote:

> *A culture, while it is being lived, is always in part unknown, in part unrealised. The making of a community is always an exploration, for consciousness cannot precede creation, and there is no formula for unknown experience. A good community, a living culture, will, because of this, not only make room for but actively encourage all and any who can contribute to the advance in consciousness which is the common need...We need to consider every attachment, every value, with our whole attention; for we do not know the future, we may never be certain of what may enrich it.*
>
> *(Williams p.315)*

In this conception of what Williams termed a common culture, society is continually shifting those values which are underpinned by social awareness of such matters as its relations with the outside world, how social minorities are regarded, various forms of sexuality, the weight given to particular kinds of individual achievement and how its history is regarded. Just how this process takes place is complex and often rather mysterious but it is certain that some part, possibly rather a large part, takes place through telling stories. In Sinfield's words:

Stories, then, transmit power: they are structured into the social order and the criteria of plausibility define, or seem to define, the scope of feasible political change. Most societies retain their current shape not because subversives are infiltrated, penalized or neutralized, though they are, but because many people believe that things have to take more or less their present form—that they cannot, realistically, be improved upon, at least through the methods to hand. In other words, the prevailing stories are believed to be the most plausible ones.

(Sinfield p.29)

If one is to isolate one common feature of human social life which appears to be a constant back before recorded history it is this: that humans tell each other stories. The theatre is, primarily, a vehicle for stories, some of which reinforce, some of which alter Williams' common culture. It is, of course, only one of many such vehicles. It is obvious that one of the defining cultural features of recent decades has been the growth in the number of vehicles for stories including computer games and advertisements as well as multiple television and radio channels. Even so, it likely that in some respects, notably its potential for diversity and immediate impact as well as its accessibility, the theatre offers one of the best channel available for telling stories which alter or for that matter sustain social perceptions. This is particularly true for subversive stories, those which in some dimension seek to stretch what Sinfield calls the plausibility of the ideas they offer. Actors in plays are required to work hard to convince their audiences of the validity, if not precisely the reality, of the story they are presenting and, conversely, audiences have to work hard to understand what actors are doing. What both do is fundamentally different to the way in which a story is presented in either film or the television and how the viewer reacts. In these the reality of the story is largely created by the medium itself; the fact that fiction can reproduce documentary footage to any required degree and that in both cases the viewer is an identical homogenised voyeur. This is impossible in the theatre, even missing-wall theatre, however hard the production strives for realism. This is not to suggest that films or television do not act to alter or sustain the common culture, just that the theatre has the inherent flexibility, not to mention financial cheapness, to explore and to illuminate social alternatives as well as social stereotypes. In a very particular way, theatre makes people think precisely because they know that what they are seeing is not real in any immediate sense but may, nevertheless, be true. When actors mimed throwing stones into an empty pram on the stage of the Royal Court theatre the audience knew that what they were seeing was not real but the representation was still shocking because it was true. (Though, interestingly, some of the hysterical reviews and comment which greeted *Saved* and called for its censoring described the performance as though actual stones were thrown and that there really was a baby on the stage). Its truth lay not in an assertion that babies were often, or indeed ever, stoned to death in Hackney parks but that British society as a whole was moving closer towards such deeds. It may be that a play in this sense comes close to justifying Wittgenstein's rather mystical assertion that what is true can be shown though not spoken though he preferred to see this in poetry rather than the theatre.

One other distinguishing feature of theatre, already noted, is the importance of context, that is of the circumstances and conditions under which a theatrical performance is seen by any particular audience which both add to and in some ways define the particular story which is being told. Consider two, rather extreme examples of this. An audience going to one of the newly defined Edwardian theatres[6] did so in a rigidly stratified social context which, quite literally, reversed the class system by placing the higher in the stalls and the lower in the gallery. All aspects of theatrical management down to the way in which tickets were sold were designed to achieve this result. A few writers and directors of the time attempted to present socially subversive plays within this context, Shaw for example or Granville Barker. In purely literary terms their success can be argued but there can be little doubt that success in terms of shifting the common story of the times was, to say the least, compromised by the stiffly confined social context in which their plays were presented. In another time, Bill Bryden's production, *The Ship*, which enacted the construction and launching of a ship was almost defined by its context; a disused Govan shipyard. At the end, when the physically unsegregated audience watched a mock ship slide down and into the dark whilst that actors sang "Only remember", there were tears shed precisely because the audience could remember when real ships were launched from that place. In the roughly four hundred and fifty years in which theatre in its modern form has existed, both the physical setting and the social context in which drama has been performed have shifted very widely and, in unison with this shifting, so has the way in which theatre has either reinforced or subverted the common story of the time.

A common criticism of some forms of political theatre, so-called agit-prop, is that it 'preaches' to the

---

[6] The precise sense in which these theatres were 'newly' defined will be discussed at some length below.

converted and, presumably, thereby loses some of its dramatic credentials. In fact virtually all theatre 'preaches' to the converted in the sense that the stories presented are plausible within the social context of the audience. If they lack such plausibility then they fail dramatically in both senses of the word. Shaw, for example, was acutely aware that, even when he wanted to show some solidarity with working class agitation of the day, he believed that he could only do this indirectly though middle-class characters. He rationalised this by arguing that ordinary working-class conversation was too inarticulate to allow for the interplay of ideas which characterise his drama. Lawrence resisted this assumption, knowing it to be false, and wrote plays which were unpresentable for fifty years when they were discovered to be gems of realist drama. Shaw attempted to be subversive within the bounds of the social context within which he believed his plays had to be presented. A key aspect of theatre in the first half of the last century is that even though there were many theatre workers—writers, directors and actors—who were acutely aware that the social context of the theatre within which they worked was unable to cope with the shifts in the common culture of their time, they often worked to reinforce rather than subvert this society. They were unable to break out of the theatrical forms which smothered them. A summary of the work of the few who tried to alter these forms is part of the following chapters.

One result of the acute and direct relationship between physical and social context and the stories which theatre presents is that it is plausible that theatre functions in its most creative way when society is for some reason shifting its social values in new directions or at an unusual pace. The evidence for this from British theatrical history is simple: that the three periods of greatest dramatic fecundity, the

Elizabethan/Jacobean, the late Victorian/Edwardian and the last half of the twentieth century were also the periods when fundamental social values were also shifting rather fast. We will return to this possibly controversial proposition later but it needs to be noted here that any cultural history of theatre of the last fifty years has to include the fact that many of its most active practitioners believed that their theatre was one of positive social engagement, that biting back at consumers became a priority rather than an optional extra. It is, of course, difficult to measure the impact of this in any direct way particularly in relation to specific plays. To take one of the most obvious examples, it is impossible to measure just what part Littlewood's Theatre Workshop production of *Oh! What a Lovely War* shifted social perceptions of the Great War from a historical event to which polite attention was paid on Armistice Day to being a charnel house controlled by madmen. The specific production was part of a much wider social shift in the perception of war. Even so, it is impossible to ignore the fact that for a large part of the period considered here, the theatre was seen by many of its practitioners as a vehicle for shifting fundamental social and cultural values. As Howard Brenton put it: "*My generation shares an idea that theatre not only describes but actually shows new possibilities*" (Craig p.97) Inevitably, this means that a cultural history has to shift its focus quite sharply at times from money to ideals and back again.

There is one other usage of the word 'culture' which needs to be considered because, as noted above, it poses particular problems for the theatre—the common distinction made between 'high' or elitist culture and 'low' or popular culture which is otherwise known as entertainment. In the first part of the book, we will look at the historical tensions which have existed in British theatre around this perceived difference ever since the time of Shakespeare. In particular, we will look at the climactic efforts made at the end of the nineteenth century to claim theatre as a specifically class-based cultural pursuit with most elements of popular culture removed from it. This period also saw the development of a gap between high and popular culture in most other types of artistic activity, a gap created under both social and aesthetic pressures though the former largely preceded the latter.

This gap has existed ever since in most fields. Classical music and popular music have diverged almost completely to the extent that to write a cultural history of the music of the past fifty years which included both genres would be pointless. This would not be true, certainly not to the same extent, even fifty years ago after a period in which many 'classical' composers had been interested in fusing folk music into their compositions. In 1945, Keynes, someone whose support of 'high' culture was almost notorious, in writing about the new state-support for the Royal Opera House hoped that it would put on for at least one month every year, productions of Gilbert and Sullivan operas. The mental effort required to envisage the present board of the ROH proposing this emphasises the gulf which has widened between classical and popular music. Efforts are made to bridge the divide with opera excerpts at pop music festivals and some musicals being absorbed into the opera canon but these mainly serve to emphasise the gulf.

The same situation exists within fiction and, though the distinction seems even more artificial than in music, it is just as rigidly applied in critical appraisal. A body of fiction is produced which can loosely be called potential Booker Prize nominees, another which hopes to appear in the paper-back bestseller charts. In the former, entire ranges of fiction including historical, crime, science-fiction and romance are excluded except in disguise in an effort to preserve an elitist cultural form. An objective observer may fail to see any significant differences between these modes but it is nevertheless a distinction which is in practice rigidly applied, for example, in the book review pages of the British broadsheet press. Much the same gap in cultural perception exists in the visual arts with elitist work, whether conceptual or abstract, being differentiated from popular, mostly representational to some degree.

The interesting feature of British theatre is the way in which this distinction, despite being continually reinforced in a number of ways, has broadly speaking also continually broken down. The way in which this process has occurred is really the central focus of this book and it can be approached from a number of different angles. One possible entry point to this does centre around personalities and individual plays. An example, intriguing precisely because it is so personal, is the way in which the two key British theatre directors of the first part of our fifty year span, Littlewood and Brook, both ended up effectively in artistic exile in France at the end of the 1960s, both despising the British theatrical scene, yet both managing in quite different ways to break decisively the moribund theatrical world which they had entered a couple of decades before. Another is the 'Deep Throat' route, to follow the money as it has ebbed and flowed around British theatres. This, which in its crudest form (which hopefully will be avoided here) might be seen as an old Marxist base and superstructure analysis, nevertheless provides essential insights into just why cultural segregation along the lines of music has been a persistent, though never entirely successful, tendency in the British theatre.

Theatre

The second word in the title that needs some clarification is 'theatre', the use of which has already been partly defined: that it is a cultural form focussed on a place where stories are told by one group of people to another. Even so, this still leaves quite a wide area in a shadow. Even in the 1950s, it was possible to draw a quite clear line between, for example, a variety show and a play even though individual performers, particularly comedians, could win respect for the dramatic content of their acts. John Osborne, for example, describes Max Miller in just these terms (Osborne p.203) and, perceptively, contrasts the danger and the unexpectedness of Miller with the perfectly constructed but totally predictable play by Pinero or Rattigan. Such a clear division was, as we shall see, a product of a deliberate process within theatrical management in the last quarter of the nineteenth century.

However, in succeeding years, some divisions which had come to seem quite obvious began to break down so that by the 1990s, it became more and more difficult, for example, to distinguish a one- or even multi-person play from stand-up comedy, a trend particularly identified with shifts in the Edinburgh Festival fringe. A number of overlapping genres of live performance, notably music-hall, variety shows and revues, even to a degree circus, have almost entirely disappeared and have been partially absorbed into a more general definition of 'theatre'.[7] It is now difficult to draw any clear distinction between 'comedy shows' and 'theatre' except insofar as most

---

[7] In 2005, an Arts Council of England report on its priorities for the funding of theatre singled out support for circus.

major cities tend to have venues which describe themselves as one or the other.

There has also been an expansion of theatre along a musical axis. The extreme cultural rigidity of the form of opera has meant that it has resisted this kind of incorporation though at the expense of effective cultural stagnation. However, the most popular extensions in Britain of the operatic form[8] have in fact come from within the theatre and achieved huge international presence whilst the use of music and singing within plays has been part of the general breakdown of the rigid formalism of realist theatre.

Along another axis, that of the visual arts, there has also a occurred a less obvious but just as influential partial merging of previously separate artistic forms. It is customary, for example, to include the Welfare State company under the broad heading 'theatre' even though most critical reviews find it difficult to cope with a theatrical form which has no words and usually works in the open air. Welfare State's founders came from art rather than drama schools and the only way in which their work can really be distinguished from many conceptual artists is that they involve several people working together. Just where the boundaries are drawn is largely irrelevant so long as one appreciates that Joseph Beuys' 'performances' in Edinburgh in 1968, still perpetuated in ghostly form in a couple of blackboards with chalk markings reverentially preserved in Edinburgh's Museum of Modern Art, are as much part of theatrical history as anything performed in the same year at, say, the

---

[8] That is stories told by songs with no spoken text. This does of course put into question categorising *The Magic Flute* as an opera and indeed this was originally described as a *singspiele* This is another reminder that most current categories of live entertainment are of quite recent origin.

Traverse Theatre in Edinburgh and almost certainly more influential.

Much of these changes in the nature of the cultural form once called theatre can be summed up by the fact that 'theatre' is no longer seen solely in a 'theatre'. In a long-term historical perspective, theatres in the usage current around 1950 had only really existed before then for about a hundred years, ever since the Theatre Licensing Act had offered up a precise definition of such and precipitated a huge decline in the number of places offering live entertainment. Licensed premises for *'theatres, music halls and pleasure gardens'* in the area of the London County Council declined from a peak of just over 400 in 1860 to about 120 by 1900 whilst the numbers of licensed theatres rose slightly to about 50. (Almost exactly the number as still operate). Theatres *senso stricto*, that is as Shaw would have understood the term, clearly still exist today and, commonly though not entirely, they show 'theatre' but they are accompanied by an array of venues which, more or less frequently, put on theatre as well as other things. Occasionally these venues may include such various sites as public streets, blocks of flats, disused shipyards or tube-trains. In Edinburgh in August, it may be hard to find a place which is not acting as a theatre. This convergence of theatrical form and divergence of venue might be seen as achieving its final consecration in the National Theatre's collaboration with Shunt in 2005; one proscenium arch auditorium, one open stage, one flexible studio and some railway arches underneath Waterloo Station. It is common for theatrical venues to include schools but often they are called arts or leisure centres. As noted above, in Greater Manchester in 2005, they numbered at least 272. This proliferation of venue is not just an indication of how geographically widespread is the cultural form, it is also an indication of how diverse it has become.

History

The third word is 'history', a subject which has in recent decades has discovered just how much can be concealed by the procedure of regarding the past as a set of written records. Theatre history is as prone to this as any other area of history perhaps more so than many. The main record of theatre productions is the published text, a source whose apparent certainty conceals the fact that it says very little about the play as it was performed. In the 'golden age' of British drama, say from 1580 to 1640, there seem to have been about 2400 new plays performed. Only a small fraction of these survives, perhaps less than 10%, and despite a huge amount of scholarly work, very little is known about how these plays were actually performed in all the various venues, only some of which resembled the famous Globe. And even this small volume of knowledge looms large compared to what is known about the production of classical Greek drama. The same is true of relatively recent periods, in particular the decades in the nineteenth century when theatre was arguably at its most popular. The blanket term of 'melodrama' is used to cover the fact that probably a smaller fraction of the texts of plays performed in this period have actually survived than from Elizabethan and Jacobean theatre. Nor do we know very much more about how plays were actually presented then outside the big London theatres which were increasingly equipped with stage machinery beyond the reach of smaller provincial theatres.

It might be thought that the last fifty years are different from these periods, that the records are better. This is true though only to a degree. The indefatigable record of Greater Manchester theatre shows that 484 separate plays were performed in 2000/01. A rough estimate is that less than half of these, possibly a lot less, would have existed in any permanent form and even fewer as commercial play-scripts. This core of commercially published plays forms the circulating basis of theatrical production, slowly accreting and dropping plays, but existing on top of a larger mass of theatrical productions which effectively disappear from history. Thus of the twenty-three plays whose title began with G in the Manchester directory, some eight are certainly inside this canon of record including *Gameplan* (Alan Ayckbourn), *Ghosts* (Henrik Ibsen), *The Glass Menagerie* (Tennessee Williams) *Godspell* (Stephen Schwartz), *The Good Woman of Setzuan*, (Bertolt Brecht), *The Government Inspector* (Nikolai Gogol), *Grease* (Jim Jacobs), and *Guys and Dolls* (Damon Runyon). Would some historian a hundred years hence find this an odd selection? Dead white men in force, two contemporary plays, two musicals, over half from abroad; is this a true reflection of British theatre at the beginning of the third millennium? It is of course possible that within the fifteen plays not mentioned here, one or two will emerge into the world of the published play but the chances are that they will sink into the same forgotten limbo as those two thousand odd Jacobean pieces and the uncounted thousands of nineteenth century plays.

The literary voice finds this process of sieving to be not just inevitable but beneficial. The emergence of plays preserved in print and performed again and again is seen as the hallmark of good theatre. As distinguished a director as Richard Eyre, who ran the National Theatre for a decade, refers to a period of almost two-hundred and fifty years from 1640 as *"A time so blank and unsettling that we prefer to forget all about it"* (Eyre p.59) entirely because of the lack of many enduring plays written by British authors. The fact that throughout this period, dramatic theatre was an expanding, profitable and hugely popular cultural form counts for nothing. However, within a wider cultural focus, this emphasis leaves a lot out. Clearly one cannot ignore the continuing popularity of certain plays, for example these eight, as this says a good deal about the nature of the culture within which they are perpetuated. But to elevate them to a particular prominence above the other fifteen means that a good deal is missed about the cultural place of theatre at that moment in time. Just how much is missed is, of course, something which cannot be easily specified. *Groovy Date*, performed by the Wigan Pier Theatre Company in 2001 as one of a range of short plays inside the Museum of Memories of the Twentieth Century, might or might not provide the future historian with more cultural clues about late twentieth century society than any performance of *Ghosts*. It has, however, probably now ceased to exist except as an archive note.

Similarly, a performance of *Frankenstein*, a classic of early nineteenth century theatre, as produced at the Palace Theatre, Camberwell in 1954 and succinctly described by John Osborne in his brief residence there, (Osborne p.246) with its *"noisy and inattentive"* (but perhaps quite numerous) audience and its *"defeated"* actors might tell more about British theatre of the time than any West End production. If, that is, it could be rescued from total historical oblivion which is unlikely.

The first decades of the period reviewed here are already almost as remote in terms of historical record as Victorian melodrama. The situation improves as one moves through the century in part because the increase in public funding moves some aspects of theatrical finances out of the shadows in which it has traditionally resided and partly because many more of its active participants are still alive. Even so, the evanescent nature of theatrical production means that a great deal is lost. The Museum of Theatre History in London has an archive of recorded live performances which continues to expand but it dates only from the early 1990s. For earlier performances one is obliged to rely upon a few chance recordings such as that made by the BBC of the RSC production *War of the Roses*. This book does no more than scratch the surface of the problem of how cultural history of transient cultural performance can be constructed but it does attempt at least to acknowledge that its core lies as much within that which is apparently lost as that which is recorded.

The structure of the book is as follows. The first section, the Prologue, summarises the path of British theatre from Elizabethan times to about 1950. This is presented as a continuous historical narrative though with the emphasis upon a set of themes which are developed within the initial summary of the early Elizabethan and Jacobean theatre. Much of this section deals with familiar topics and is based entirely on secondary sources. It is included here not because it is contains much in the way of original comment but because this kind of historical context is required to understand what comes after. The second part contains an extended historical narrative of the second half of the twentieth century into the twenty-first, setting the changes in the cultural aesthetic of the theatre into a social and political context interspersed with sections which deal with a some specific topics—theatre in education, amateur theatre—which cut across this narrative. There is an extended bibliography at the end.

Prologue: Shakespeare to Shaw

The abiding myth: Elizabethan theatre

Elizabethan[9] theatre hangs over all subsequent British theatre as its abiding myth. Shakespeare, our national literary icon, is the one cultural artefact to which all school-children are required to be exposed by the National Curriculum. The vitality and alleged popularity of theatre in the period stretching, roughly, from 1580 to the closure of theatres in 1642 is commonly seen as a high-point of British cultural life. Stratford-on-Avon, though it may never have seen a performance of a Shakespeare play until nearly one hundred and fifty years after the playwright's death, is said to be the second most popular international tourist destination in England after London, all drawn by the legend of the world's most popular playwright. The plays of Shakespeare are seen not only as containing something universal about human behaviour but also something specific about Britain, specifically England. Any major production of *Henry IV* or *V* is always seen as a particular statement about the state of the nation, patriotic, pacifist, fascist to taste.

There is, of course, a great deal about the myth which is true. The first fixed theatre in Britain was built in 1576 effectively creating a new profession out of a previously largely amateur pastime. By the time the theatres were closed in 1642 as many as 2500 plays had been presented. Most are lost or are now known only by title as, until well into the seventeenth century, they were not regarded as lasting literature being originally written in a single manuscript copy with individual parts written out separately. The position of Shakespeare even amongst his contemporaries is demonstrated by the unusually early efforts made to preserve his plays in print. The core of the

---

[9] Jacobean and Caroline drama are included in this portmanteau word.

Elizabethan/Jacobean canon now consists of less than 100 plays which are performed today; most of Shakespeare along with Marlowe, Jonson, Fletcher and a handful of others. These are, however, only a small part of the flood of productions seen in London in this period of barely 70 years. (Even so, these numbers are not huge by contemporary European standards. The Spanish playwright, Lope de Vega, part of the so-called Golden Age of Spanish theatre is said to have written over 800 plays. Most plays of the time seem to have been written more quickly than the average soap-opera script.) In terms of literary interest, Shakespeare dominates but the period has continued to fascinate as one in which theatre may have been a genuinely popular medium. There has been some controversy about this claim, as will be discussed below, but whatever its truth, the era continues to exert its hold over contemporary theatre.

Elizabethan theatre is also of interest here because it introduces a set of themes which have continued to dominate the historical development of theatre in Britain. Some of these are inevitable consequences of the theatrical business, the 'technology' of theatre as one might say, others are factors peculiar to Britain and to the historical period in which theatre emerged but which have nevertheless continued to exert themselves down to the present day. In either case, the Elizabethan theatre has been so exhaustively studied that it forms a useful point to begin these dominant themes.

Theatre in Britain appears was invented almost overnight. In the first half of the sixteenth century, there is an incoherent parade of travelling entertainers, musicians, jugglers, dancers and the rest distinct from the scholastic study of Roman theatre, such as the comedies of Plautus and Terence and the tragedies of

Seneca, which was undertaken in schools and universities. The former still retained on occasion the forms of the Mystery Plays, formally banned since shortly after the Reformation though still performed subsequently in towns such as Coventry, but mostly they existed as various kinds of public pageant of which the annual Lord Mayor's Show in London is a faint current echo. The latter included various home-grown versions of the classical models: *Ralph, Roister Doister* was written in rhyming couplets in 1550 by the Headmaster of Eton; the first English tragedy is believed to have been performed in the Inner Temple before law students in 1561 just before Shakespeare's birth. The gap between the public performance, usually staged in inn-yards, and the private, usually in academic venues or noble houses was vast in both form and content. The form of Elizabethan theatre and a perpetual tension in British theatre since was set by the apparently contingent fusion of the two which took place in roughly forty years from 1560.

Harbage's heroic compendium of all known named English plays from 975 to 1700 lists thirteen pieces in 1560, nine known only by titles, of which six were court masques, three were interludes performed at great banquets, whilst only one is in the extant category of 'Tragedy'. (Harbage p.39) In 1600, he can list thirty-five pieces, only nine by anonymous authors and of these six can be cautiously attributed. Only three are described in terms of now unknown dramatic forms — 'jig', 'masque' and 'allegorical history'. What happened in these forty years was not just the invention of a profession but also a crystallisation of forms which have continued to define drama for four hundred years.

This transformation is all the more remarkable since public performance deeply alarmed Elizabethan authority. The period was one of rapid population growth (the population of England probably doubled between the 1520s and the 1640s) and great social mobility. The mercantile adventures of such as the East India Company and the sale of Church lands after the Reformation created a new class of rich gentry. Enclosure and population growth created a new underclass, the vagabonds and 'undeserving poor', who floated around the country creating an often justified fear of crime. Although reliable statistics were scarce, it is probable that, within this growing population, income differentials widened whilst the sources of this income, for example from land speculation and mercantile adventures, sat uneasily with that from accustomed lines such as rents, small retailers or bringing in the harvest. All this can be found in Shakespeare. It was probably quite reasonable at the time (and wholly in keeping with the future reputation of actors) to associate the growing number of vagabonds with the performances on village greens and inn-yards which formed the basis of public entertainment. In 1572, as part of an Act for the Punishment of Vagabondes, the government required that every performing company be authorised by one noble or two magistrates, usually the former. The result was to transform strolling players, or at least a superior set of them, into authorised groups under the nominal patronage of a patron. This patronage went beyond the formal in some cases—the Earl of Leicester took his players with him on a military expedition to Flanders in 1585—but in most cases, the association quickly moved on from aristocratic patronage to a more nominal authorisation though one which could prove handy when trouble loomed. The turning point was in 1576 when Burbage built the Theatre in Shoreditch just outside the boundaries of the City of London as an independent commercial enterprise. The surprise and the oddity of Elizabethan theatre essentially arises from these two socio-political factors; the desire of Elizabethan authorities to control potentially riotous public performance in a time of social turmoil and the emergence of a new form of business enterprise, commercial entertainment.

The way in which Shakespeare and his contemporaries are now performed tends to hide the odd and rather hybrid nature of the performances which were given in the new theatres (insofar as we know much about them). What marks out Elizabethan drama from, for example, the Spanish and French plays of Calderon or Corneille, and what gives them their great universality is the blend of the formal and the commonplace. Courtly wit and poetic digression mix with extreme physicality, sexual and violent. Some of the work is tightly narrative but musical interludes and dancing enter into many pieces, probably extended at the time well beyond the off-stage background music often used today. Bradbrook comments that *"The theatre of the Elizabethans, in its social atmosphere, was less like the modern theatre than it was like a funfair...Merriment, jigs and toys followed the performance; songs, dumb shows, clowns' acts were interlaced"* (Bradbrook p.97) There was a rapid evolution in playwriting as the audiences became more demanding and also more separate with different venues offering different styles. Even so, the origins of theatre in raucous inn-yard performance were never quite lost until the late-nineteenth century. One of the underlying themes of recent British theatre is the efforts to return to a form of performance seen as much closer to the Elizabethan and to make theatres something like Joan Littlewood's ideal 'fun-palaces'.

The 1572 Act was, so far as can be seen, a measure adopted purely in the interests of public order by a central bureaucracy which had little interest in cultural development. It is probable that the intent of the new authorisation process was to reduce the scope of travelling companies to create disorder simply by reducing their number and their ability to draw large crowds. It was the first attempt to make theatre more respectable by putting it under the control of responsible agents and, to a degree, it may have achieved this aim. But it also provided a unique business opportunity by allowing a semi-monopoly in a commodity, entertainment, for which there was a growing market at least in London. The monopoly allowed financial risk-taking which in turn encouraged artistic risk-taking. Shakespeare's extraordinary development and exploration of the artistic form essentially required the mobilisation of both capital and artistic talent in a concentration which effectively required some form of commercial monopoly.

Elizabethan theatre was the first commercial entertainment business organised on recognisably modern lines. The speed with which this happened is in its way as astonishing as the speed with which drama as a cultural form was invented and there can be little doubt that the two are linked. Two public amphitheatres for entertainment in the form of bear and bull-baiting existed in London before Burbage built the Theatre in Shoreditch and presumably the travelling entertainers of the early part of the century were paid in some way for their efforts. The most organised part of the entertainment business was the companies maintained by nobles and at the court. These performed various types of entertainment ranging from song and dance to simple morality pieces called interludes which were performed during banquets. The scale of these was relatively small however; Henry VIII maintained two companies totalling eight men (women were excluded from acting at this time) in all and there is no reason to believe that other nobles or the City livery companies maintained companies which were much larger. The Mystery plays had been financed sometimes at considerable cost by a town's livery companies but had been largely suppressed by the mid-16th century.

Burbage's innovation changed this situation totally. The heart of the system as it developed was a group of men who jointly took shares in a common stock comprising costumes, properties and, also, plays for these were owned literally by the company that possessed the manuscripts of the parts, there being no copyright system. The company would rent or lease one of the new theatres and hire a peripheral set of men to perform, manage the theatre and look after backstage. There would also be an impresario[10] who put up working capital and took a share of the takings. The form of the joint stock company was not invented by theatrical entrepreneurs but they were amongst the earliest to take advantage of its commercial possibilities and the theatrical name has been taken over by all such capitalist enterprises. The scale of these enterprises varied greatly but the largest, for example the Admiral's and Chamberlain's Men who had a duopoly of theatre inside London[11] from 1598, were able to employ dozens of men and to finance a level of investment in new theatres which was enormous for the time. The Fortune theatre in 1597 cost £520 to build at a time when working men were paid perhaps 8 pence a day.

---

[10] 'The money' as the film *Shakespeare in Love* perceptively called him.
[11] There was a great difference between performing inside the City limits and outside with the former requiring some degree of Court protection.

One of the key points about this was the absence of any kind of state or municipal subsidy. It was common for plays to be performed by the new companies at the court or in private houses but these were paid for on a commercial basis. The paid patronage of nobles or the municipal livery companies disappeared to be replaced by a very commercially-orientated set of theatre managers competing for audiences. This can be contrasted with the situation in continental Europe where court, municipal or aristocratic patronage continued and was transformed into the system of subsidy alongside commercial enterprise which so marked out Continental from British cultural systems and which continues to this day.

Elizabethan theatre is often lauded for the equalitarian nature of its audiences from penny apprentices to Queen Elizabeth and court aristocrats. Although this is true to some degree the actual situation was much more complex. Cook has gone so far as to claim that the Elizabethan theatre audience *"while not denying the presence of plebeians among the audiences, indicates that they probably attended in smaller numbers and with less frequency than has been supposed. Moreover, far from reflecting a cross-section of society, the spectators came chiefly from the upper levels of the social order."* (Cook p.8) The reality seems to have been that as the range of venues available to audiences after 1600 grew at least in London, they performed to audiences which differed quite widely. Just how widely is something which, in the absence of contemporary audience surveys, remains to speculative in great measure though it is likely that they contained very few of the poorest (of whom there were many). However, there is no doubt that audiences became more socially separated as venues proliferated.

Theatres were organised as commercial ventures with management anxious to maximise profit. This could be done, broadly, by one of three strategies. The first, based mainly on those theatres which were converted from the inns such as the Red Bull in Clerkenwell which had formed the initial base of public entertainment, went for the 'cheap and cheerful', plays in which drama was interpreted in its broadest sense and the entertainment came in part from the brothels which surrounded the theatres. Rather few of the original texts of these plays are extant. The Red Bull is believed to have been the venue where women first performed on the stage, something which probably fitted its general ambience. Interestingly, later in the seventeenth century, the same venue was known for its performance of plays which contained more than a whiff of political dissent.

The second was to move up market using small, enclosed theatres with high seat prices and presenting relatively intimate drama. This was probably the dominant trend after 1600 in the new 'private'[12] theatres such as the Blackfriars. Hall calls these "*the sixteenth century equivalent of Covent Garden or Glynebourne.*" (Hall p.144) Such theatres were quite small—about 500 or so—and charged high prices. The price range at the Blackfriars was 6d-2s6d, according to Harbage, who comments "*no more effective means could have been devised for excluding utterly the great majority of the former audience*" (Harbage (1941) p.64)

The third and most famous strategy was that seemingly tried at the great amphitheatres constructed in Southwark, first by Burbage in 1598 when his

---

[12] 'Private' here really means enclosed and roofed though they might have had what a club would now call a 'door policy' equivalent to no jeans or trainers.

company physically transported the timbers of the Theatre in Shoreditch over the Thames to form part of the Globe, to be followed by the Swan and the Rose. These venues were huge even by modern standards; their capacity was estimated by contemporaries at about 3000[13] partly standing in the open arena and partly seated in the surrounding galleries. It was in these venues that the legend of Elizabethan theatre was really born; huge audiences drawn from all levels of society watching epic drama drawn on the widest canvas. Howard Brenton once made the distinction between plays set outside and those set inside; whereas the private theatres increasingly showed 'inside' plays of private violence and revenge, the Globe showed the original 'outside' plays; battles, shipwreck, blasted heaths and all. The characters who walked, swam or exited pursued by bears in these plays largely mirrored their audience in coming from all ranks even though the best lines usually went to the aristocrats. They also told stories of social change and epic history in unprecedented ways.

Entrance to the Globe was, famously, set at a penny but the better seats in the galleries cost much more, up to 12d. A penny was affordable for the poorest of those in regular work. Harbage estimates that the real price of the Globe was much the same as a movie ticket in the USA in the 1940s. Of course, a significant part of the population were not in regular work and the fact that performances took place in the afternoon would have been a barrier to most workers. Even so, Harbage (Harbage (1941) p.65) estimates, admittedly on meagre statistics, that about 13% of the population

---

[13] Harbage (p.22) notes the incredulity with which this estimate is treated by some scholars but careful analysis of available evidence still supports it.

of London went to the theatre once a week.[14] This is some way from a truly mass audience. In the 1940s, when Harbage wrote, 65% of Americans went to the movies once a week though this can be seen as the high-tide of mass entertainment. Even so, given that this was time of little leisure, it suggests that Elizabethan theatre had moved across the divide from occasional and exceptional entertainment into regular and unexceptional practice. These numbers show that an audience existed for the new drama but what is much less well understood is just what were the underlying economics of the three strategies. The evidence of theatre building suggests that, although it was possible to make good profits from popular plays at the big venues like the Globe, the smaller, enclosed theatres stood to make more money week on week. There are various reasons which can be advanced for this of which three stand out.

First, it is exceedingly difficult to write plays for such huge venues for audiences wanting to see something of everything, some farce and some music and some romance and some tragedy, all sprawling over four or five hours. Shakespeare, of course, and, perhaps, Jonson managed it but the other names from the Jacobean period all seem to be moving towards a more intimate and enclosed drama, full of mayhem and sex but on a smaller canvas. Jonson, in Gurr's (Gurr p.1) opinion, may have left Shakespeare's company at the Globe in 1599 and moved to the smaller hall theatre, Blackfriars, to get a more attentive and better educated audience.

Second, commercial practice means that getting an audience willing to pay ten times as much for entrance is better even if it is one-tenth the size, given that the

---

[14] Interestingly, much the same proportion of the British population are currently reported to be regular theatre-goers.

fixed costs of smaller venues are always less than for large. The alternative is low cost, 'pack-them-in' entertainment, in which the prostitutes are as much on display as the actors and in which the profits from drink and food may compensate for the costs of the entertainment.

Thirdly, and reinforcing this, is the fact that audiences may be willing to pay a premium for social segregation, of seeing and being seen by the 'right' sort of people. In one of the later plays of the period, *Jack Drum's Entertainment*, Marston refers to the audience at one of the 'private' theatres

> *...A man shall not be choked*
> *With the stench of Garlick, nor be pasted*
> *To the barmy jacket of a beer-brewer.*

The audience reaction to these lines might have told one much about Jacobean social attitudes to the theatre and just how popular a mass theatre really was amongst those who paid top price.

This provokes a question about Elizabethan drama which is seldom raised because it is by now virtually impossible to answer: that is what exactly did audiences make of the various plays they saw? To present-day eyes, most extant plays of the period are hard to understand; school children need special tuition in Shakespeare's language and even then find many passages tough going. Some of this is down to corruption of the original text but there is no denying that much of the language of many Elizabethan and Jacobean plays is dense, allusive and full of double-meanings and obscure metaphor. It is common to assume that the audiences at the Globe, largely illiterate and without formal education, took this all in their stride living in a period when ordinary language was also complex and ambiguous. The problem is that we have real way of knowing this. It is accepted that Shakespeare's plays get tougher to understand as he matures and this is usually ascribed to a development of his own art, that he himself wanted to develop a more complex language. But is just as possible that Shakespeare's audiences shifted in character over time and that his later plays were presented to a more select, wealthy and, therefore, more formally educated sector of society and that Shakespeare was responding to this by writing plays which were less accessible.

The splitting of venues between the Red Bull and the Blackfriars modes almost certainly meant a splitting of the kind of play presented and the audience at the latter may have had the same view of those who went to the former as, today, an audience at the Almeida[15] has of those who go to see *Phantom of the Opera*. 'Was Shakespeare Always Tough Going and Marlowe Unpresentable?' is a great unwritten Ph.D. and doubtless will always remain so in the same way that we can never really know the original cultural status of classical Greek drama. There is a strong desire to believe that, once, cultural and aesthetic unities could exist across all society. Unfortunately, there is barely a scrap of evidence for this.

The pace and scale of development in the theatre at the end of the sixteenth century had a further far-reaching consequence; metropolitan concentration. London was by far the largest British city in this period. Although population data is scanty, London probably had a population of around 200,000 in 1600 and was expanding fast compared with the next largest cities such as Bristol or Norwich with less than a tenth of this number. It also had a concentration of the wealthiest plus a court which by now had set up in

---

[15] A small London theatre popular with a local, largely graduate, audience.

virtually permanent residence at palaces around London. (Cook pp. 52-96) It was inevitable that theatres would be built here first. What is perhaps less obvious is that the dominance would become so complete to the point that when London had about seventeen theatres (though not all in use simultaneously) there seems not to have been one permanent theatre in any other town. The London companies did travel outside the capital, sometimes because plague closed the London theatres, sometimes to play at special occasions, sometimes because of commercial pressures. But nothing original seems to have been created except in the capital.

The main reason for this has to be money. The financial risk associated with the scale of the new plays was such that only London could provide some assurance of the necessary audience. However it remains surprising that at least some of the larger cities could not have provided at least a secondary circuit for theatre. This failure is in some ways all the more surprising given that it was mostly in northern towns, such as Coventry and York, that the Mystery Plays were created and carried on the longest. It is believed, for example, that Shakespeare in his childhood could have seen a Mystery Play in Coventry. The city livery companies in such places were prepared to provide considerable resources to these and should have been able to finance some form of theatrical venture. However the merchant bourgeoisie, who dominated the main provincial centres, were often deeply hostile to the theatre. In London, the City merchants fought several battles to limit or even close the theatres before their ultimate success in 1642. It was protection from the Court which ensured a sometimes precarious survival. There is no real evidence either way but one might conjecture that in provincial cities such as York or

Norwich, where the merchants were comparatively more dominant, establishing permanent theatres would have been impossible.

It is one of the oddities of Elizabethan theatre, the most radical cultural form of the time, that the most politically radical elements in society were hostile to it. The reasons why the Puritans were so bitterly opposed to the theatre are complex but a recent survey of them by O'Connell makes it clear that the fundamental objection was to what was seen as idolatrous representation and not to the general dislike of public entertainment which has become, erroneously, attached to them. Politically, plays and popery went together. The Puritans had no problems with plays as texts, it was not that they contained obscenity or heresy; it was performance as such which aroused their ire — the image not the word. Ironically, when they came to power and closed the theatres in 1642, it was a turn towards publishing theatre scripts which preserved many of those Jacobean plays which survive. The religious difficulty with performance was the insistence on corporality which characterises Elizabethan and Jacobean theatre. In classical drama most of the action was described whilst Shakespeare *et al* put it all on-stage; the eyes came out whilst you watched. This all seemed too much like the wine actually turning into blood and the bread into real flesh for the Protestant faithful.

It was not always thus. O'Connell records the activities of John Bale (O'Connell p.93), a Protestant reformer in the first half of the sixteenth century who wrote some twenty-four plays which were performed by his own company before he fled England in 1540 to escape religious persecution. Bale was in direct descent from the provincial Mystery plays and was himself a provincial, born in East Anglia. But his work ended at much the same time as the Mystery cycles were suppressed ending the tradition of civic as against professional drama in England for more than four hundred years. O'Connell notes in reference to the disappearance of the Mysteries

> *For most people who saw it [the Mysteries],*
> *it was the only theater they witnessed in their*
> *lives. Its loss was a local and regional loss,*
> *an impoverishment of the life of provincial*
> *centers. In this, as in so many other elements*
> *of English Reformation culture, a centripetal*
> *force was at work, moving authority and*
> *control away from the regions and towards*
> *the capital. But—and this is perhaps*
> *strange—its disappearance had little direct*
> *consequence for the new London theatre. The*
> *indirect consequence, especially in the self-*
> *definition of the London theater, is of course*
> *another matter*
>
> *(O'Connell p.92)*

The obverse to Court protection was Court control. The Master of the Revels, a post regularised in 1578, was not just a patron—he organised court entertainment which could be lucrative for theatre companies—but also a censor. All new plays had to be submitted to him and a fee paid for the privilege. The Court was notoriously suspicious of any play which appeared to criticise the prerogatives of royalty and very little appeared on the stage which might be seen as subversive. It is of course possible to see in many plays, tensions and under-currents which are a reflection of social change. But there is no real evidence that Shakespeare or his contemporaries were politically radical in the sense of, say, Milton. Shakespeare is usually regarded as rather socially conservative with his emphasis on the dangers of social disorder following from breakdown of authority. Some of the later authors, such as Marston, are sometimes seen as more radical given their emphasis on the corruption and decadence of high society. However, only in the final years before 1642 does some kind of explicit political tension seem to have worked its way into theatrical performance. This, according to Gurr, reflected a growing gap between the poorer audiences of the amphitheatres and converted inns and the more socially select enclosed theatres. (Gurr pp. 191-193) In 1639, a huge fine of £1,000 was levied on the Red Bull players for making fun of High Church rituals in the performance of a revived play whilst, later in the same year, the same company put on a play which was alleged in the Privy Council to be an attack on taxes. Such incidents were rare however though, again, it has to be emphasised just how little is known about what was actually seen on stage particularly at the popular venues.

However, if not overtly politically radical, the new plays were almost required to include some reflection of the fact that these were rough times, the very middle of what Kamen has called the Iron Century stretching in his survey from 1550 to 1660.

> This is the Iron Age, wherin iniquitie hath the upper hand; and all conditions and estates of men seeke to live by their wittes, and he is counted the wisest that hath the deepest insight into the getting of gaines.
>
> Robert Greene, *Defence of Conny Catching* (1592)
>
> (Kamen, frontispiece)

There is considerable controversy as to just what was the extent of social crisis in this period. What is undisputable is that the problem of vagrancy and the dispossessed poor was widespread throughout Europe linked, partly, to changes in land ownership and partly to a series of appalling harvests. It is also clear that there were widespread popular rebellions which peaked in the 1590s, again throughout Europe as far east as Hungary though limited in England. It is also certain that a new form of social organisation, capitalism, was growing though exactly what, why and where remains controversial. What is clear is that there was a lot of money being made and lost and that social differentiation was growing. The Counter Reformation against Luther's Protestant version of Christianity was resulting in murderous warfare throughout the continent. In England, there was little warfare or popular uprising but there was a growing level of political dissent which was to culminate in the civil wars between 1640 and 1650.

There is one linkage between theatre and this social crisis which has already been mentioned, the law that acting companies be authorised by nobles, a requirement which, paradoxically, led directly to the formation of professional actors grouped into commercial companies separate from direct patronage or control. It is also clear that the growth in the economy, however one-sided in its wealth distribution, led to the development of a large group of people at least in London with enough spare cash and leisure to go to the new theatres.

What is less clear, indeed is inevitably no more than speculation, is the extent to which a context of social upheaval and political unrest led to the flowering of the new dramatic writing. The political undercurrents which permeate Shakespeare's plays are often noted, whilst many of many of the lesser plays also have a strong political flavour. They are not radical nor subversive; the dramatists of the time were not in that sense like those in the 1960s and 70s in Britain. It is possible that this lack of overt political radicalism was a result of the strong censorship of the time. Every new played performed had first to be licensed by the Master of the Revels, a court official, who seems to have carried out his duties quite strictly. A fee of seven shillings a play probably encouraged this. However, the strong sense of social movement, of changes in political structure and, after 1610, the growing conflict between King and Parliament, must have contributed to the free-wheeling structures and dramatic inventiveness which characterise the plays of this period. As Weimann puts it *"It is the dramatic integration of varied social values and cultural elements that, as Shakespeare progresses from his early work, makes the structure of the plays so balanced and the poetic perspective of experience so satisfying."* (Weimann p. 175) It is also, of course, the feature which makes it possible for every generation to have its own Shakespeare rather for than for the plays to be locked into their own time. Even so, there is little evidence of any direct links between the political radicals of the first half of the seventeenth century and the playwrights. In his search for the roots of the political beliefs of one overtly radical British writer of the Caroline period, John Milton, Christopher Hill, himself a political radical well-versed in the period's archives, makes no mention at all of the theatre, preferring to make some rather strained links with a poetic tradition of Jonson. This despite the fact that Milton's first commissioned work was dramatic, *Comus*, albeit in an almost discarded form, the masque.

There is a crucial generation gap between the Jacobean playwrights and, say, Milton, born in 1608, who could, when a child, have passed Shakespeare in the streets of London. Milton came to maturity in a time when radical, secular politics and politicians in the modern sense were emerging from the complex mixture of court and church intrigues which characterised politics in Shakespeare's time. The story which Shakespeare told in *Hamlet* and *Lear* as much as in the history plays was of an old order dying. The new order struggling to be born was still an embryo. (One can see this is Bond's *Bingo*, a modern attempt to understand the roots of Shakespeare's creativity. Only one character, and that a young man, seems aware of the basic social revolution just over the horizon). Names like Lilburne, Cromwell or Rainsborough lie three or four decades on. Even in the 1620s, radical talk was more of flight to the American colonies than of any form of secular resistance to the governing power. The Elizabethan, playwrights need to be seen as participants in a process to create modern politics, a process which, ironically, would lead to the closure of theatres and one of which they could hardly be expected to be aware.

Yet, is it entirely coincidence that the three periods of greatest activity and talent in British playwriting— 1590-1620, 1890-1915 and 1960-1980—were also times of major political and social shifts and turmoil? This is not a question which can be simply answered for it lacks any specificity. But it is an intriguing footnote to why Elizabethan theatre remains so resonant in the modern period.

Mayhem and manners

The period between 1660, when the London theatres reopened following the restoration of the monarchy, and the last quarter of the 19th century is a curious one for British theatre. As already noted, one commentator, a distinguished director, has described it as a 250-year coma, *"A time so blank and unsettling that we prefer to forget all about it."* (Eyre p.59) What Richard Eyre means by this is that, in this period, there were written relatively few plays which remain part of the modern repertoire in comparison with those from the scant forty years of the Elizabethan and Jacobean period. Those which are still regarded with some favour are, he notes, almost entirely written by a succession of Anglo-Irish incomers—Farquhar, Goldsmith, Sheridan, Boucicault—rather than any native English authors. One might quarrel with the emphasis of this. After all, the late-Victorian and Edwardian theatre in England is also studded with Anglo-Irish rather than English playwrights; Wilde, Shaw, Yeats and Synge for example. But the major problem with this kind of assessment is that during this period of 'coma', the number of theatres in Britain grew by leaps and bounds so that Pick can state that *"By the end of the [18th] century almost every town of more than 750 inhabitants had its theatre, and more than half of the population must have gone two or three times a year to see some kind of theatrical performance"* (Pick (1985) p.1) These are rough estimates on insecure data but it is clear that in these two visions, one of coma, the other of dynamic growth, are encapsulated quite different views as to what the theatre means.

In 1660, when Charles II came to the throne a tighter grip than before 1642 was thrown over the opening of theatres. The new king permitted spoken plays to be performed only in theatres that held patents awarded by the Crown. The previous policy of authorisation by aristocrats, which had become rather nominal, was replaced by centralised licence. Just two of these patents were initially given, both to close supporters of the king when in exile and both in London. This move should not be seen, necessarily, as one of exerting political control. As noted above, although there had been some small amount of overt political content to at least a couple of plays presented in the 1630s, overall the stage had been largely free of any explicit political flavour. The duopoly set up in 1660 needs to be seen primarily as an economic act, awarding monopoly rights to theatrical production just as they were commonly awarded in many other areas of trade or commerce at the time. It was a mercantilist age in which the award of economic monopolies was seen as both a legitimate way of raising revenue or rewarding political support and as the proper way to conduct economic business. In the following two centuries, the London theatre patents were to be traded as commodities, sub-divided amongst individuals who were free to sell on their portion at the market rate. It is true that the duopoly continued the measures undertaken in Elizabethan times to limit the number of companies located inside the City walls but it took another seventy-seven years for explicit censorship to be introduced.

The London patents were, in time, added to at various provincial theatres (Norwich and Bath in 1768, Liverpool 1771, Manchester, 1775 and Newcastle, 1788) but for over a century, in principle, spoken drama was limited to those two theatres whose owners possessed the patents which, after a few decades, became Drury Lane and Covent Garden (plus the Haymarket in summer). A distinction was made between 'legitimate', literally legal, theatre and 'illegitimate', a distinction still loosely in use in the

USA to refer to spoken as distinct from musical theatre. Illegitimate theatre was allowed to present music, dance and other live acts provided they steered clear of spoken drama. In 1737, the Theatre Licensing Act, reinforced this duopoly and required that all new plays be submitted for license to the Lord Chamberlain, a legal requirement which was in active force until 1968. The explicit censorship imposed for the first time probably arose because some overt political comment had begun to creep into the productions of Henry Fielding at Drury Lane following the extraordinary success of Gay's *The Beggar's Opera* in 1727 whose successor, *Polly*, was actually banned. These plays should not be seen as particularly radical; they were attacks on Walpole's Whig administration from the Tory side. However the perceived need to introduce overt censorship illustrates the sensitivity of live theatrical performance.

The period immediately after Charles II accession is unique in British theatre in that it is given a specific historical label and is associated with a single genre. 'Restoration comedy' refers simultaneously to a form and to a time. The fifty years of performance before 1642 was not forgotten; it scarcely could be after a gap of only eleven years during which publication in printed form of many pre-Civil War plays had proceeded apace. But there is no doubt that the repertoire of the two patent theatres shifted fundamentally away from the diversity of Jacobean theatre and into a new genre, the comedy of manners, in particular sexual manners. There are several reasons for this rather extraordinary shift. One is that the times immediately after the restoration of the monarchy were extremely sensitive politically not say dangerous. The surviving signatories of Charles I's death warrant either fled the country or were arraigned and executed.

The bodies of dead regicides were dug up and ritually dismembered. Milton, who passed close to prosecution, went into a kind of internal exile whilst other writers hastened to distance themselves from the republican regime. Gaiety in the theatres was the order of the day in part because it was potentially dangerous not to appear carefree and frivolous.

Another reason for the adoption of a hitherto unknown genre was that it appealed to the taste of a Court which had spent years in exile in France where this form was established. Finally, rather intimate and contemporary comedies suited the elitist and relatively small theatres of the Restoration period. The two patent theatres together originally seated around a thousand people and were designed to promote a hitherto largely unknown degree of physical intimacy between audience and actors. As Shepherd and Womack note, commenting on the huge thrust-stage of Wren's Drury Lane, built in 1676,

> *On the forestage, the actors are very obviously in the same room as the spectators. We see them amongst us as we see one another, lit by the same candles, audible within the same acoustic, communicating within the same gestural repertoire. There is even a sense in which they compete with the other spectators for our attention. Take, for example, the moment when Lord Foppington [in **The Relapse**] excuses the pains he takes with his appearance by remarking that 'a man must endeavour to look wholesome, lest he makes so nauseous a figure in the side-box, the ladies should be compelled to turn their eyes upon the stage'. The actor, Colley Cibber, says this standing a few feet from the side-boxes themselves, which form the side walls of the forestage, so that the gentlemen*

actually sitting in them are effectively part of the décor.

(Shepherd and Womack p.124)

This deep physical intimacy is linked to the equally deep social intimacy of the plays themselves in which an audience drawn from a relatively narrow social strata watched characters much like themselves in the contemporary context of London or familiar provincial towns. The strangeness of much Jacobean drama whether in place, time or social behaviour is banished in favour of a familiar if exaggerated social life centring around sexual or social transgression.

Restoration theatre established a new dramatic genre which has lasted to the present day, one of the most successful of forms, the 'boulevard' comedy in which laughter comes from the actions of a group of recognisable contemporary characters placed under some kind of social stress in which they strive to maintain social decorum. Ayckbourn is the most successful recent proponent of the style which ultimately rests upon the clear and complicit knowledge of an audience drawn from a fairly homogeneous social background. This kind of work requires suppression of emotions and activities which lie outside the social behaviour of its audience though it constantly teeters on its outer edges. Indeed much of the success of such plays lies precisely in the closeness to which they can approach genuine transgression of the rules without irreparably breaching them. The need for the theatre of the time to accommodate this can be seen in its efforts to retain Shakespeare as the great English writer but also to eliminate as much as possible of his social dissonance. Thus *King Lear* is rewritten to allow Lear to survive to see Cordelia ascend the throne married to Edgar and then retire to a monk's cell whilst Hamlet's mother and Laertes are spared at Hamlet's dying command. The difficulty with the boulevard comedy lies in precisely this complicity between playwright and audience; once the norms of social decorum shift so does audience's acceptance of particular kinds of stress. The sexual licentiousness on which Restoration comedy is based was, at least in public terms, quite transitory. David Garrick rewrote *The Relapse* to become *A Trip to Scarborough*, and *The Country Wife*, which became *The Country Girl*, to accommodate the social norms of the mid-eighteenth century but Restoration comedy had become by the mid-nineteenth century "*a disgrace to our language and national character*" and "*The Nadir of national taste and morality*" according to Lord Macaulay, a distinguished historian and arbiter of national standards at the time. Even so, Restoration comedy was the seed from which naturalism developed transcending at times the original's rigid boundaries of social behaviour but always carrying the fatal flaw of being the reflection, albeit distorted, of its audience's social rules. The point of Restoration comedy, the point it was forced to make in the context of its time, was that even though social conventions could be stretched, ultimately they would not break. The breakdown of civil society presented in various ways by the Jacobeans could not be allowed. Once a king had lost his head the implications of such breakdown were all too apparent.

Spoken drama had evolved with staggering speed from around 1580 up to the closure of theatres in 1642. New genres—tragedy, comedy, history—had developed or been refined way beyond their antecedents. But also a good deal had been abandoned, in particular the inclusive use of music and dance within drama. There was probably a good deal of music in Elizabethan theatre; one can see glimpses of this in many of Shakespeare's plays particularly those like *Twelfth*

Night written for court rather than public performance. But in the Jacobean period, musical elements were increasingly abandoned, perhaps under the constraints of the small 'private' theatres in which they were performed but also because that was the direction of artistic invention, towards tighter dramatisation. In Restoration theatre, this tradition of spoken drama was preserved and formalised in the distinction between legitimate and illegitimate theatre, the former being the only one where spoken, which had come to mean in some way 'higher' or 'respectable', drama could be seen.

Yet despite this distinction, by the early 18th century, the Patent Theatres themselves were turning to musical drama, indeed to so-called English opera, as well as to musical and speciality acts such as juggling performed in the intervals between the acts of classical drama. There was also the common use made of the double-bill in which a main piece, comedy or tragedy is played with an afterpiece of music, dancing or comedy. The origins of this lie in the desire of illegitimate theatres to circumvent the law by providing a musical entertainment for which admission was charged followed by a 'free' spoken drama. The Patent Theatres picked up this format by reversing it. A main piece, usually a spoken drama, was followed by an afterpiece. The reason for this pattern was clearly commercial. Admission to the main play at full-price was followed by allowing half-price admission after the third act and for the following afterpiece; a neat way of maximising revenue if the theatre was not filled at the regular price. However the inevitable result of this was a gradual dilution of any rigid difference between the two forms of drama. The greatest hit of the 18th century was *The Beggars Opera* in which music played a large part and was put on at a Patent Theatre.

As noted above, *The Beggars' Opera* was not radical in its fundamental politics but it was highly satirical and, in this sense, subversive. Ever since, as the Brecht/Weil collaborations illustrate, satire has tended to be framed by music.

The so-called Garrick Years attempted to hold back this trend at least in the citadel of his own Patent theatre, partly by an emphasis on the classics and partly by hiving-off music and dance into entirely separate genres such as opera and ballet based largely upon imported work. (Shepherd & Womack p.192) It was also possible to satisfy popular taste within the London theatre by the adaptation of such forms as the pantomime into a separate style which could be played as separate performances. David Garrick personified most of the problematic of eighteenth century theatre. In some respects he can be seen as the progenitor of 'modern' theatre. As the first major actor to come from the ranks of the gentry, albeit a somewhat hard-pressed branch, he was concerned to raise the social standing of actors and of theatre in general. He clearly wanted to shift acting styles away from rhetorical declamation in which the main characters simply planted themselves centre stage and emoted. He introduced innovations such as rehearsals which were actually attended by the main actors. He also attempted to withdraw the acting area away from the audience, partly by physically reducing the thrust of the stage, partly by banning the custom of having some of the audience actually onstage, and partly by innovations such as the use of side-lighting of the back part of the stage rather than relying on the same overhead lighting as the general auditorium. In this overall desire to withdraw into a separate 'room' with a missing fourth wall, he has been seen as the precursor to late-nineteenth century naturalism and even Stanislavski. At the same time, Garrick was a showman with a considerable desire to make money, an endeavour in which he succeeded handsomely, dying a multi-millionaire in modern terms. Even so, despite this personal success, making money in eighteenth century theatre was a chancy business particularly for the London Patent Theatres which were increasingly trapped by an apparently inexorable rise in costs and a very sticky ability to raise seat prices.

The arbitrary assignment of Royal Warrants in 1660 effectively banned drama productions outside London and the Licensing Act of 1737 placed this on an even firmer footing. Even so, throughout the 17th century, particularly in the second half, the number of provincial theatres grew rapidly even before the first grant of a patent to Bath in 1768. Pick (Pick (1985) p.2) gives the example of Retford where a theatre holding nearly 500 people was built in 1789. This was at a time when the town's population was 1034. The gallery cost one shilling and a box seat, three, almost half the weekly wage of an agricultural labourer. Even at these prices the theatre ran at a profit for more than fifty years. These theatres gave permanent residence to companies which regularly toured throughout the provinces. There was also a growth of theatres around the periphery of the growing urban mass of London which, forbidden to present spoken drama, and much more closely monitored for patent transgressions than the provincial theatres, presented various composite performances.

The turning point according to Rosenfeld, whose work though sixty years old remains the only general account of 18th century theatre outside London, came *"During the decade 1755-65"* when *"new and imposing theatres were being built."* (Rosenfeld p.1)These theatres seem to have become the focus of the various travelling fit-up companies which had operated throughout the country and production circuits developed in which the same company moved around a number of theatres in a geographical region. This process was solidified in 1788, after a number of Patents had been granted to provincial theatres, when an Act was passed allowing the performance of plays previously put on at a Patent theatre for up to sixty days provided the places were *"well outside London, Edinburgh, the King's residence or the Universities"* (Rosenfeld p.2) These circuits were quite large and profitable with several theatres in a region being linked often with one dominant theatre, possibly with a Patent, being the main originator of productions.

It is not clear exactly what was performed in these circuits let alone by the travelling companies which still existed alongside these more commercially developed enterprises. The only documentary evidence which remains is that of playbills and some references in local newspapers and these are necessarily haphazard and, apparently, little researched. One may surmise that the entertainment offered was very mixed, that it involved both spoken drama and music and that it may have involved specifically local characteristics. Probably, the plays moved gradually into that wide genre which is now called melodrama, the main dramatic form of the nineteenth century. What is clear is that theatre grew rapidly and developed as the main form of popular entertainment.

Mayhem uncontrolled: melodrama

Melodrama has undoubtedly received the worst critical press of any theatrical genre. In reviewing a production of *Cymbeline*, Shaw described it as *"stagey trash of the lowest melodramatic order"* (Shepherd & Womack p.219) and, a hundred years later, we still know what he meant. The word itself has moved away from the theatre and into a general description of anything that is false and over-emoted. As Shepherd and Womack point out a number of other words— sensationalist, escapist, hack, stock, claptrap—which have also moved out of purely theatrical use into wider pejorative use all originate in critiques of theatrical melodrama. It is common for the entire period from the end of the 18th century, when melodrama is usually placed as emerging as separate dramatic form, until around the 1870s to be dismissed as an artistic desert, the deepest sleep in Eyre's coma.

> That time is generally understood to be one of the low points in the history of English drama. It's not that no plays were being done. Indeed there were probably more performances in more theatres seen by more people than at any other period, including the present. But next to none of it seems to be either natural or proper—as if the English theatre was under occupation by an alien culture.
>
> (Shepherd & Womack p.219)

There are several problems with this widely held view.

The first is that the critical dismissal of melodrama is based on very little evidence as to what was actually presented and is also suspiciously biased. Very few critics would now dismiss the Gothic novel, so popular in the early 19th century, as an artistic desert and, for example, Mary Shelley's *Frankenstein* as beneath contempt. Yet it is hard to describe the Gothic novel in terms much different to that used, contemptuously, to describe dramatic melodrama. The two forms were, culturally, quite closely linked. Shelley's novel, first published in a small edition of only five hundred, only became widely popular after a stage adaptation of the work. Secondly, it is clear that melodrama existed in a variety of forms, some quite domestic, others quite grandiose. The form that Boucicault, sometimes picked out as one of the few playwrights of any consequence in the period, presented at the London Patent theatres can hardly be described as anything other than large-scale melodrama. On the other hand, *Maria Marten or Murder in the Red Barn*, one of the few melodramas which, largely by chance, has survived, is a very domestic piece which can be played relatively 'straight'. Melodrama is often associated as much with a style of presentation as with its content. If nowadays a critic calls a production 'melodramatic', they probably mean that the actors shouted too much and used too much body movement. Yet in terms of the necessities of the theatres of the period, when a rebuilt Drury Lane held at least 3500 and the Britannia, Hoxton about 2500, a lot of shouting and gesturing was needed as much by the un-miked Garrick and Kean as by the lesser lights of non-Patent melodrama.

Finally and crucially, melodrama was, as Eyre concedes, very popular. This was a time when the theatre was a genuinely popular form of culture, possibly the only time, apart from Elizabethan and Jacobean London when this claim could be made, certainly the only time when it could be applied nationally. "*It must be remembered that the period 1800-1870 was one of genuinely popular theatre, which is probably why no dramatic masterpieces were produced*". The people "*occupied the pit and gallery at the patent theatres and more sophisticated audiences did not return to the theatre until about the 1860s and 1870's"* (Booth (1965) p.56) The point hardly needs to be laboured that there is a massive critical assumption here, that the popular is incompatible with the good. Montague Slater, one of the few enthusiasts for melodrama is more positive. *"After 1780, there began to develop in different quarters of London, what one might call, in spite of its communist ring, 'Theatres of the People... They were illegal; they were democratic; they were the oddest places imaginable"* (Slater p.11)

Slater illustrates this by the claim that in the two Whitechapel theatres, there was always a kindly Jew in the production to reflect the demands of the largely Jewish local population. One of these, the Pavilion in Mile End Road, went on to become the Yiddish Theatre. The oddity of the times is often illustrated by the well-known act consisting of a man standing on a galloping horse in a circus ring reciting speeches from *Richard III.* This is certainly an unusual, if skilful, way of presenting Shakespeare but there is a point here so obvious that it is often overlooked; the horseman-actor recited Shakespeare rather than some humorous doggerel. There is, indeed, some evidence that in the nineteenth century, Shakespeare was more popular amongst the working-class than with Booth's sophisticates. Rose notes that *"Drama critics reported on Shakespeare productions where the boxes and stalls were half-sold, while the pit and gallery were filled with enthusiastic audiences who loudly commented on the performance and even prompted the actors"* (Rose p.122) He adds that *"For many of them, Shakespeare was a proletarian hero who spoke directly to working people. One weaver's son made that point by translating The Merchant of Venice into Lancashire dialect".*

If one takes such apparently risible examples as Shakespeare on a horse and adds in the conventional view of melodrama as villains with curly moustaches being hissed by the audience then it is easy enough to accept that the conventional critique of melodrama. However, Shepherd and Womack have analysed the aesthetic of melodrama much more sympathetically than most previous writers. They conclude, specifically referring to one well-known melodrama, *The Dumb Man of Manchester*[16]:

> The fact of **Dumb Man**'s commercial success at Astley's—that half-theatre, half-circus—could be taken to indicate the debased, lower-class nature of melodrama. But that should not conceal from us another fact: in its easy assimilation of modes of performing and spectating from well outside dialogue drama, **The Dumb Man** is telling us that a new theatrical language has already come into being.

(Shepherd & Womack p.199)

These authors also hint at the possibility that, as the century progressed, at least some melodrama took on the politically more radical flavour of the time. In 1848, the Lord Chamberlain refused a licence to a play by George Dibdin Pitt, probably the most prolific writer of melodramas, provocatively called *The Revolution at Paris*. There is also *The Factory Lad*, an obviously class-conscious melodrama about industrial unrest about which Smith sniffily comments:

> Protest melodrama speaks exclusively to the converted; **The Factory Lad** was played for six nights only to an audience of workers on the seamy side of London... Such plays may

---

[16] The central actor in this piece was the afore-mentioned equestrian Richard.

> *focus discontent, fire public feeling and*
> *congratulate their audience on siding with*
> *the angels, but they are too vehemently*
> *partisan and facile in denunciation, to*
> *persuade the uncommitted man of even*
> *moderate intelligence that their black and*
> *white world is the grey one he knows.*

> *(Smith p.10&74)*

So no newspaper sale there then. But, of course, Smith has no idea whether or not *The Factory Lad was* only played for six nights at the Surrey Theatre or whether it went round other venues particularly those outside London let alone possessing any detailed knowledge of the IQ's of such audiences. This remains a crucial problem with evaluating melodrama, the fact that so little is known about what was actually performed in the mass of theatres then operating throughout the country and just what constituted their audience. But what comes over clearly from Smith's criticism is that, in his view, *The Factory Lad* could have little aesthetic or cultural value precisely because it played *"only to an audience of workers on the seamy side of London"*. That is, it never played to a middle-class audience in the West End and thus, by definition, cannot claim any merit.

But whatever the role of melodrama or the value of its aesthetic, one thing is clear, in the second half of the 19th century, English theatre was out of control in a number of different ways; financially, aesthetically, possibly even politically to some degree.

Mayhem back to manners

Melodrama had to go, or at the very least, be confined. This seemed to be the universal conclusion of both dramatists and theatre managers as well as most critics of the time. It is possible to approach this shift from a number of different angles; the aesthetic, the social, the political, possibly even the geographical in terms of the relationship between London and the provinces. However the best starting point is the ever-present and central concern of the London theatre managers—how to make money from their fixed capital, the theatre. This had been a preoccupation since the building of the Theatre but in the second half of the 19th century it became clear that a complete change of strategy was required following the final collapse of the Patent system in 1843.

The Patent system had been set up on the basis of a royal monopoly under the patronage of nobles and the gentry. The two London theatres had had no restrictions on their audience but they were clearly aimed at a fashionable social sector. No doubt there was some degree of social mixing but this mattered very little in an age when a lord's son would come to the theatre drunk and in search of a whore just like anyone else. Nell Gwynne sold oranges in the intervals of the performance and her body as well. Her best-known capture was the king. The system functioned well enough through the 18th century but there are indications that by the beginning of the 19th, the reputation of the London theatre was such that it was beginning to lose an important slice of its market.

The centre-piece of one of Austen's manuals of decent middle-class behaviour, *Mansfield Park*, is a private theatrical. The rehearsals for the play, entered into with enthusiasm by most of the young people in the house (though naturally the heroine resists), are

69

interrupted by the unforeseen return of the head of the house who abruptly terminates the whole endeavour as immoral. Ultimately the eldest daughter goes off to London, where she sees too many plays and eventually runs off with a married man to her ruin. (The playgoing is an invention, elaborating on Austen's endless ellipsis.) The underlying message is clear: in 1813, the London theatre has become tinged with a social disrepute,[17] a state which intensifies as the century progresses until by 1850, it is accepted that 'decent' folk do not go to a theatre which has been largely taken over by the masses. Such was Dickens' view in his observation that:

> *Heavily taxed, wholly unassisted by the State, deserted by the gentry, and quite unrecognised as a means of public instruction, the higher English Drama has declined. Those who would live to please Mr Whelks, must please Mr Whelks to live.*

> *(Shepherd & Womack p.223)*

Mr Whelks, naturally, was a member of the lower orders, decent enough but lacking both education and the desire for self-improvement.

The *Theatre Licensing Act* in 1843 in principle allowed the theatre to flourish under new conditions of free competition. In practice, those with ambitions in this direction were hampered by the problem of making profit from new theatres when the audience was largely lower-class and incapable of paying high prices. Moreover, the demands of melodrama were insatiable in terms of new material. Runs were very short, repeats in other theatres in the provinces provided no revenue, whilst the 'effects' required to

---

[17] The message in *Mansfield Park* is clear enough even though Austen herself is known to have gone to the theatre regularly.

provide the sensation on which large-scale melodrama thrived were very expensive. Melodrama was killing the theatre in an almost classic Marxist fashion in which its very popularity was drawing in new entrants who competed more and more ferociously, driving down profit margins whilst striving to maximise their share of the market.

The strategy adopted to counter this essentially involved creating a new form of theatre and, in the process, creating for the first time clear class segregation in terms of audience. Pick's view of this process is that:

> *After 1865, the ordinary folk who had, for a short time, enjoyed the new populist theatre, did not choose to take their pleasures elsewhere; they were, by a series of deliberate managerial decisions, excluded from the new respectable theatre of the later Victorian age.*
>
> *(Pick (1983) p.11)*

This is a very instrumental view of the process but there is good deal of evidence to support this idea of a conscious strategy by the London theatre owners. The initial move towards respectability was famously undertaken when Squire Bancroft and Marie Wilton transformed the venue colloquially called the Dust Bowl into the Prince of Wales Theatre, its very name suggesting its respectability. One of their many innovations was to place antimacassars on the stalls' seats put in to replace the benches of the pit. The success of this venture was soon copied by other West End theatres. Squire Bancroft became the second theatrical knight after Irving and he retired in 1885 with a net personal fortune of £180,000. As early as 1859, a contemporary observer was able to comment with some surprise on audiences in these new venues, that *"they sit, for the most part, in silent admiration"* (Trussler p.234) and by 1870, 'they' were able to do this in the new and aptly named 'dress circles' which had supplanted the galleries. The stalls had become the most expensive seats replacing the old, almost Shakespearean 'pit' whilst the cheap seats were high up and approached by separate entrances, often round the corner from the grand foyers of the stalls and dress circle. In these new stalls the audiences behaved with a proper decorum as they might in their homes with none of the raucous noise associated with the old pit. Nowadays, only audience behaviour in a pantomime, a theatrical form resolutely old-fashioned, remains similar to that which would have been normal before Bancroft initiated his changes.

The techniques of making higher profits by moving upmarket extended to the kind of refreshments sold (chocolate boxes, ice-creams, drinks at the interval in segregated bars were all invented in this period), illustrated programmes and even to the style of ticket. Oscar Wilde complained about the quality of the tickets and in the 1890's, one of the most fashionable theatres, St. James, began to print tickets on stiff card as to a ball. Up to this point, theatre tickets were never pre-booked. One queued on the night in a social mix. However under the new regime, tickets were sold in advance from selected places which often only opened in the hours convenient those with a certain amount of leisure.

The Edwardian theatre developed this class basis almost to a point of parody. As Kennedy notes:

> *Evening dress was regularly worn in the stalls and dress circle everywhere... Perhaps it is hard for us, with our culture of prodigious informality, to imagine the strict protocol this imposed on the audience in*

> *Victorian and Edwardian England. The resolute distinctions between classes, plainly marked by their degrees of dress, separated the audience into discrete areas of the auditorium. (Booth (1996) p. 143)*

He goes on, referring to Alexander, the manager of the St James theatre:

> *He wanted a stage world that reflected the manners and dress of his leading spectators, one in which they could see themselves righteously manipulating the status quo. The wealthy members of the audience and the actors portraying wealthy figures on the stage were engaged in a reciprocal semiosis, in which their dress was the leading signifier. Even the advertisements in the programmes reinforced this mentality. In 1913, they were dominated by elegant clothiers; Furs from Revillon Freres of Regent Street, 'French Model Gowns' from the Elite Company of Grosvenor Mansions, Paquin designs, theatre gowns from Liberty's*

In a much more elaborate, profitable and, naturally, decorous way, Alexander was re-creating the Restoration theatre where the upper layers of society saw themselves portrayed on the stage in interesting situations.

The story of this shift is well-documented. Less understood is the way in which the new West End theatre asserted its hegemony over peripheral London and provincial theatres. Davis (Booth (1996) p.202) records the decline of East End theatre so that by 1902 only three survived and, of these, only one remained as a theatre through to the end of Edward VII's reign. One reason for this decline was that increasingly the East End theatres had come to depend on recycled

West End fare which displaced local material. The same seems to be true of provincial theatre though the transition is not well-documented. Trussler (Trussler p.231) notes that provincial theatre circuits, which in 1827 still numbered forty-one separate fixed management companies, mostly working circuits, plus some eight 'strolling' companies, increasingly seem to have fallen on hard times. Theatres in smaller centres were given up or were idle for years at a time though no single reason seems to be available for this trend. It was certainly economic, for these companies existed only for economic reasons, and in the second half of the nineteenth century the normal pattern of an industry under financial stress seems to have been followed; the various circuits combined and gradually fell under the control of the emerging West End management companies. What had developed by Edwardian times was effectively a London-based oligopoly based on a system of pre-West End try-outs, West End runs followed by post-West End tours which could continue for years spiralling down a careful hierarchy of venues. The ultimate endpoint of this was the passage of much theatre into the control of one, centralised group, a situation believed by many to have been reached in the period immediately after the second world war.

It would be wrong however to see, as Pick tends to, *simply* a plot by West End managers to increase their profits. Other factors also have to be included, one of which is just that class segregation followed the fact of class development in society at large with a growing middle-class who wanted to spend their leisure money on pastimes which reflected their habits and mores. And not just the classical middle classes in London suburbs. The East End included not just the murky Victorian nightmare of Whitechapel but also comparatively affluent Hackney with increasingly good transport links to the West End. A night out 'up West' was increasingly within the reach of at least the skilled working class in London. The traditional working class venues showed a dramatic decline in the period from 1860 to 1900 at least in London with. As already noted, a decline from a peak of just over 400 in 1860, of licensed premises for *'theatres, music halls and pleasure gardens'* dropped to about 120 by 1900 in the area of the London County Council whilst the numbers of licensed theatres rose slightly to about 50. A great tightening up of licences in the period accounts for the closure of many venues which were little more than rooms behind pubs but an overall trend is clear.

The music hall became separated from theatre as a form of entertainment for the working class with its own genres and styles whilst late-Victorian and Edwardian theatre itself underwent an aesthetic transformation which essentially involved the formation of two genres both under the same social banner of 'West End' but which were quite separate; the musical and the naturalistic spoken play. These two forms allowed the old style of melodrama to be dissolved into two, quite distinct categories which nevertheless both functioned under the same umbrella of respectability. In a sense, the existence of Gilbert and Sullivan's Savoy musicals or the 'naughty but nice' Gaiety Girls, discussed by Bailey, (Booth p.96) allowed room for the 'serious' plays of Shaw or Barker to emerge.

The rise of the great late-Victorian and Edwardian playwrights has been taken for granted as the ending of the great British theatrical 'coma' particularly when taken alongside the foreign writers, such as Ibsen and Chekhov, who were increasingly taken up by British theatre. It is no part of this study to comment on the merits of these but one thing is clear; this aesthetic transformation was the very reverse of popular theatre despite the often radical views of many of the main playwrights such as Shaw, Barker and Wilde. Theatrical reformers, notably Granville Barker who resolutely tried to present new plays in the Edwardian period, made little effort to alter the West End system. In the performances in 1913 of Shaw's *Androcles and the Lion*—a play with clear suffragette sympathies—at the St James, a sign was placed by the box-office that read *"We should like our patrons to feel that in no part of the house is evening dress indispensable"* (Booth (1996) p.145) but it probably made little difference to the audience who had presumably dressed already. It would never have occurred to Barker to put on his productions outside the West End nor to Shaw to have, for example, his play about the East End, *Candida*, put on at a Mile End theatre. (The play is actually set in a vicarage, albeit one in the East End). The audience, which Granville Barker and others associated with the Edwardian New Drama seemed to seek, was not really wider than the existing West End audience but was in fact focussed on an intellectual elite within that audience, an avant-garde whose number were small but whose tastes were 'discerning'. It is interesting to compare these ambitions with those of Yeats[18] and Synge who in this period had genuine, if muddled, visions of a new popular theatre based on Irish culture and who, at the Abbey Theatre in Dublin, had mixed success in this direction.

It seems likely that the reformers of the Edwardian theatre had no real vision of a popular theatre. Kennedy quotes Granville Barker *"I do believe my present loathing for the theatre is loathing for the*

---

[18] Though Yeats increasingly played in England to highly elitist audiences sometimes in the drawing rooms of patrons.

audience. I have never loved them" (Booth (1996) p. 146) and goes on to write

> *"More than any other characteristic, that loathing for the audience tied him to the early modernists, most of whom were convinced that high art could only be valued by a small coterie of the like-minded. The avant-garde suspicion of popular success eventually split twentieth-century art into two parts: the larger part got the audiences but little lasting attention, the smaller part, the critical and historical acclaim…Not until Bertolt Brecht, writing around 1930, did any major theatre thinker or practitioner seriously consider that it might not be the spectators who needed reformation, but rather the artists and their art."*

The high-Edwardian period of British drama was brought to an abrupt end by the First World War. Although Shaw, for example, continued writing plays, it is fair to say that theatre lost a great deal of its intellectual position of social commentary in the post-war period to the novel. It is tempting though, in the end, difficult to demonstrate in any direct way that this failure was linked to this disdain for the popular audience which marked such as Granville Barker.

The late-Victorian and Edwardian eras marked the end of the 'long coma' in English theatre as measured by the emergence of great writers and plays which have remained part of the general repertoire of theatre ever since. Viewed from this perspective, there is virtually nothing in the whole period from 1658 until the late 19th century which deserves much mention apart from a few comedies whose main virtue is an almost endless variety of sexual innuendo. If one adds to the solid virtues of such as Shaw, Pinero and Wilde, the set of foreign playwrights (notable Ibsen and

Chekhov) whose plays have almost been adopted by the English stage, then this period does indeed shine in comparison with the preceding three centuries.

However, as discussed above, the price paid for this was the effective closing down of theatre as a popular cultural form. There is little doubt that one strand of this was the deliberate commercial stratagem which derived from the final abandonment of the patent system in 1843. As Shepherd and Womack perceptively observe (Shepherd & Womack pp. 112-114) the London patent theatres and their provincial replicates retained a sense of old customs and practices well into the 19th century. The famous Old Price Riots in 1809 which followed Kean's attempt to alter the price structure of Covent Garden ended in victory for 'the pit' after sixty-seven nights of rioting. It took another fifty years before Bancroft was able to implement Kean's commercial ideas, a passage of time which had almost destroyed the aesthetic reputation of the theatre as well as allowing the legal dismantling of the patent system. It is illuminating to associate the changes in the theatre with other changes in society at large, such as the introduction of examinations into the Civil Service and promotion by merit in the army, which were justified in the name of modernisation. Late-Victorian theatre was a 'modern' theatre in the same sense that Kitchener's army was modern.

However, the shift in theatre practice and form was not simply a commercial manoeuvre by West End management. There is a very complex relationship between the aesthetics of Edwardian theatre and its class-based economics exemplified by the odd and, to modern perceptions, perverse relationship between the radical political ideas of Shaw and Granville Barker and their apparent alliance with the reactionary commercial practices of the London theatre managers. This perversity is heightened by the fact that the drama critics of the time who campaigned most vociferously against the closing of the cheap and voluble pit and its replacement with the silent and expensive stalls were often those who were most outraged at the new drama represented by, say, Ibsen's *Ghosts*.

> *...The genial conservatives who stuck up for the pit were also, in many cases, the opponents of any kind of intellectual daring in the new drama of the1890s and supporters of the Lord Chamberlain's censorship of plays in the most narrow and timid period of that institution's history. In short, it raises the possibility that in the closing decades of the nineteenth century, populism in the theatre was inescapably aligned with ideological reaction.*
>
> *(Shepherd & Womack p.116)*

It would take this work too far afield to discuss the difficult relationship in Britain between radical artists and mass politics in the 19th and early 20th centuries. One example would be Dickens' treatment of the French Revolution in *A Tale of Two Cities* which is able to deal sympathetically with general social problems but recoils at mass mobilisation against social evil. The subject matter of many of the great Edwardian plays is very daring in both political and social terms and, up to 1914, there remained the possibility that drama could re-engage with popular culture perhaps through the new repertory theatres opening in cities outside London. However, writers such as Shaw and Wilde, whilst able to describe themselves as socialists, were never themselves able to engage effectively with the mass left politics of the time nor to explore any aesthetic which might arouse any popular interest. The only popular British movement of the time in which theatre seems to have engaged in any way is the suffragettes largely because this had a large middle-class component some of whose members were able to turn the new 'respectability' of the theatre to their advantage. One might add to this the role played by the theatre in the rise of a new form of Irish nationalism, exemplified by Yeats' *Cathleen ni Houlihan* which did play widely in England though this may also suggest that the Irish cultural tradition has always run differently to the British.

In this, the second great period of British dramatists, there is both a contextual similarity and an odd inversion. The similarity is that both the Jacobean and the Edwardian playwrights functioned in a time of rapid social change and political unrest. The Edwardians were clearly more overtly aware of this than the Jacobeans and they attempted to engage with the social movements of the time. Shaw's involvement with the Fabians is well-known and it was Wilde who wrote that "*No map of the world is complete unless it includes Utopia*" and prepared a guide to socialism. Yet whilst the Jacobeans functioned in a theatrical context which allowed them access to a mass, popular audience, the Edwardians almost ostentatiously avoided any connection with such. It was as though the aesthetic which they had adopted, that of naturalism, forbade any such contact for fear that they would be dragged back to the bad, old days of melodrama.

The short coma

The Great War effectively sealed any options for popular engagement by the theatre even if the will had existed. London commercial theatre had little appetite for such themes whilst, in the aftermath of the Russian Revolution, radical politics moved down channels which very few British artists cared to follow until the 1930s. It is easy enough to see what aroused the derision in the 1950s of such as John Osborne just by listing some of the themes of the most 'serious' plays of the period; drug problems of the upper classes (Coward), the difficulty of getting servants and keeping up appearances in the middle class (Maugham), goings-on in public schools (Rattigan). These are to a degree cheap shots in relation to the specific plays but there is little defence to the general charge that the theatre between 1920 and 1950 retreated into a ghetto of shallow West End runs followed by provincial tours just at the moment when the mass popular audience abandoned in the late 19th century found its alternative in the cinema.

The artistic problem within the theatre between the two wars was that increasingly the 'new' Edwardian drama had become a ghetto within a ghetto, that is to say that plays regarded as 'serious' as opposed to light comedy or musicals, the staple fare of the West End, had become a genre in their own right. A production of one of the classics—Chekhov, Ibsen, a Restoration comedy, above all Shakespeare—could be found a place in the West End for a limited season. More rarely, a new 'serious' play by one of the limited number of writers awarded this accolade would be presented provided it fell within the by now well-worn rules of naturalist drama. Such productions were designed to meet the intellectual needs of a certain sub-set of the middle-class audience to which theatre had become attuned, the teachers or other professionals who felt that one ought to 'do' Shakespeare or Chekhov every so often. It helped, of course, if the production contained one of the rising stars, Olivier or Gielgud or Ashcroft, doing 'their' Hamlet or Juliet. Outside London, a handful of repertory theatres, supported by private sponsors, attempted to do much the same kind of thing in Manchester, Bristol, Birmingham and Liverpool, but their originality was tightly constrained. The period was not entirely barren, however, and two distinct lines of theatrical development can be seen. Neither has been particularly well researched and the considerable amount of individual memory which has gone into such work as has been done may well over-estimate their importance. But the lines exist and they act as the major points of continuity with the second part of this book.

The first strand of development was that directly associated with left-wing politics.[19] Starting, roughly, at the end of the 1920s, a number of groups dedicated to exploring ways in which live performance could be used to support socialist causes were set up. The progress of these groups was marked by considerable political factionalism which often seems to have led to an almost total estrangement between them despite their small size and apparent sympathy of aims. Thus, Ewan MacColl and Joan Littlewood were expelled from the Communist Party in 1936, allegedly in a dispute over artistic style[20], and were then largely isolated from the various Unity Theatres set up at around the same time which were politically dominated by the Communist Party. Echoes of these

---

[19] The best sources for the left theatre movement are Chambers (1989), Goorney (1981) and Samuel (1985).
[20] Personal reminiscence suggests that MacColl and Littlewood would always have been uneasy belonging any political body that did not want to expel them.

disputes can be found down to present day research; for example in Samuel's criticism of the workings of Unity Theatre (Samuel *et al*) rebutted by Chambers. (Chambers (1989))

Although relatively submerged at the time, almost all the dramatic techniques explored by these left theatre groups were to be taken up in the 1960s both by the explicitly left-wing touring companies and by less obviously political productions, particularly in regional theatres, looking for new ways to gain a local audience. The initial work by groups such as the Red Megaphones in Manchester was quite crude, something which they themselves realised when they saw the work of the German and Russian groups on which they had modelled themselves.[21] One of the most extraordinary features of what became Theatre Workshop was the degree to which the group members studied dramatic techniques and developed training programmes for movement and voice. Goorney records how they adopted the lighting methods of Appia, a Swiss theatre designer, after reading about them in a Manchester public library. (Goorney p.5) The innovative use of lights became one of the hallmarks of Theatre Workshop in its arduous post-war touring programme whilst the introduction of dance and music into prose drama was also developed. (And remained so. In the text of the Theatre Workshop production of *Taste of Honey*, a landmark play in the late 1950s, stage directions often read "Enter Dancing" and in the original production there was a jazz group on stage even though the play was critically seen as part of the new working-class realism.)

---

[21] Ernst Toller, one of group of influential German playwrights, spent some time in Manchester in this period when the city was, theatrically, more creative than London.

The Unity Theatres in London, Liverpool and Manchester, also developed styles of production— 'living newspapers', political pantomimes as well as stylised 'agitprop'—which were widely used thirty years later. In both Unity Theatre and Theatre Workshop there was a strong awareness of left-wing theatre on the continent particularly in Germany before the Nazi takeover. Perhaps the strongest characteristic of both groups was their willingness to explore just about any alternative to the naturalistic form which both saw as attached to a superficial and class-based view of the world in which action and the role of broad social currents was subordinated to verbal interplay between representatives of the dominant class. In effect, they were trying to find ways of combating Shaw's explanation as to why he had so few working-class characters in plays devoted to radical themes. He asserted that ideas could only be represented on the stage by verbal interplay and that this required educated, that is middle-class, characters. Lawrence had attempted to subvert this by presenting articulate working-class characters; the left groups in the 1930s followed a different path—they replaced individual articulate dialogue by other dramatic devices.

The second strand of development was the small-scale, sometimes partly amateur, productions of experimental arts theatres, often run as clubs to avoid a Lord Chamberlain's censorship which was applied as rigorously in this period as at any time before.[22] One well-known example of this is the Group Theatre, documented by Sidnell, which was unusual in that it tried to set up a permanent company of highly-trained actors. Interestingly, some of the techniques explored

---

[22] MacColl and Littlewood were both fined in 1938 for breaking the law in this respect.

by the Group Theatre are close to those of Theatre Workshop though on themes very distant from theirs. For example, in 1933, T.S.Eliot was asked to write for a religious drama entitled *The Rock* in which *"the main action is the construction of a church by a crew of Cockney labourers. ..Eliot's assignment was to write prose dialogue for 'scenes of the usual pageant pattern' and verse choruses."* (Sidnell p.93) The play itself was based on a *"Cochrane-type revue"*. There was a certain amount of overlap between the this kind of experimental theatre and the left-wing theatres— one Group Theatre production was actually performed at London Unity[23]—and many of its associates and writers (including Auden, Spender, Swingler, Britten, and McNeice) saw themselves as socialists or even communists. But, broadly, there was a greater affinity with 'respectable' West End theatre in the sense that successful 'small theatre' productions aimed for a West End showing. In the provinces there may have been a closer relationship between the left groups and semi-amateur experimental theatres, particularly in Manchester.

The Group Theatre, which also placed a strong emphasis on actor-training and the use of dancing and music, led on, indirectly, to the Old Vic theatre centre set up in 1945 by George Devine and Michel St Denis and this in turn, indirectly, led to Devine's setting up the English Stage Company at the Royal Court in 1956.

In this sense, both the major theatrical enterprises which were to dominate the New Wave of 1956 had developed out of an experiment with theatrical technique which had begun in the early-1930s[24]

[23] *Trials of a Judge* by Stephen Spender in March, 1938
[24] Both too were concerned with training actors. Much of present-day drama training comes from these two sources.

though this was something which might more easily recognised in Stratford than in Sloane Square. But the central fact was that theatre in Britain was dying in the 1930s, a process which if anything accelerated after the war as will be seen in some detail in the following chapters.

Modern British Theatre

1945-2005

The Fifties: Resolving the Crisis

In 1950, British theatre was in a bad way. It was caught in a spiral of decline which seemed, at best, likely to result in live performance being confined to a small middle-class ghetto supported by discreet state subsidy and controlled by a London-based cartel. Just how many theatres actually functioned around this time is not entirely clear. Over the previous twenty years, there had been a big shift in the use of buildings from theatre to cinema, a process of change which was still going on after the war though at a reduced pace. Most of the conversions had been one-way and irreversible but a number of venues still functioned as dual-purpose operations retaining wings and dressing rooms and a movable screen.[25] Even so, the number of live venues lost to cinema had been huge. The rise of the cinema seemed inexorable and the replacement of live theatre by the screen almost inevitable. In fact national attendances in cinemas peaked shortly after the war in 1946 at an astonishing 1,635 million admissions, some 54 per year per person. They then entered a period of long-term decline, though this could hardly have been envisaged at the time; by 1963, numbers had dropped to 357 million annually.[26]

The most accurate picture of the number of operating theatres at the time is that provided by the careful study of theatre ownership published by the Federation of Theatre Unions in 1953 and based upon data for 1950. This used as its marker for a theatre the existence of technical capacity for live performance

---

[25] Very few venues still exist with this format. One example is the unusual municipally-owned cinema in Hebden Bridge.

[26] A decline which has continued since though at a slower pace; in 2003, annual UK cinema attendance was 167 million almost exactly one-tenth of the peak level.

plus some management intention to do so. It notes that official government statistics *"for January, 1949 gave the number of theatres in Great Britain and Northern Ireland specifically excluding pier pavilions and concert party halls as 402. The lists embodied in this report total 520. The number has no particular significance—it could easily have been 600."* In addition to this number there were a variety of halls used on occasion for live performance. Probably the most important of these from a theatrical point of view were the Miners' Welfare Halls, most numerous in South Wales and the North East of England which had formed the main base for a number of touring shows after the war when these still received a degree of state subsidy. However, in round terms, it would be reasonable to accept that in 1950, there were about 500 venues showing some form of live theatre.

The drop in numbers from the heyday of live entertainment is hard to estimate accurately but its extent can be seen from the much longer list of venues provided in *Dobson's Theatre Year-Book* as characterised by their then-current use. In the Greater Manchester region[27], for example, this lists 56 venues used at some time in the past for live theatre and which in 1948 were split into 29 sole-use cinemas, 8 which had some degree of dual use as cinemas and theatres though with emphasis on the former, 6 used for twice-nightly variety, 6 amateur theatres, 5 repertory theatres (though one of these also showed some variety), 1 used for No. 1 tours and 1 which, obscurely, had had its licence refused. One of the repertory theatres, based at the Central Library, was supported by Manchester Corporation as was one of the amateur theatres. The rest were entirely

---

[27] That is Manchester plus Salford, Stockport, Bolton, Wigan, Bury and Rochdale

commercial ventures. In other words, two-thirds of the places recently used for live entertainment had by 1948 shifted to showing films.

Nationally, the theatre unions' survey concluded that:

> *It is estimated that at the time of writing 162 theatres are used for repertory. Of these, seventy-three were permanent and eighty-nine seasonal. As the seasonal repertories are roughly equally divided between winter and summer seasons the average number of theatres playing repertory may be taken to be about 120.* **The Stage** *in November [1950] showed about fifty shows of a general character (musical and non-musical, No. 1s and No. 2s) to be on tour, and seventy touring "revues" ("Nude, Neat and Naughty", "Figleaves and Apple Sauce", "Strip, Strip Hooray" etc.), the latter naturally at No. 2 and 3 theatres.*

To this must be added the 40-45 theatres classed as the West End giving a total of around 320 which accounts for almost two-thirds of the 520 venues which they listed in the report. The function of the remaining one-third is obscure though probably some were used by the amateur companies which played a significant part in drama provision at the time. The point is that even within the much reduced number of 520 theatres, it seems some had an existence even more precarious than presenting *Strip, Strip, Hooray.*

During the war the theatre, at least in London, had had a period of both boom and bust. At the outbreak of war, all venues in central London had been closed. This had enabled a few places outside these limits to reap some windfall benefits among them the left-wing Unity Theatre whose packed houses enabled them to set themselves up for a later and not particularly successful shift to a semi-professional basis. These strict closures were relaxed later on, though with the times of performances brought forward to six-thirty so that audiences could catch the reduced public transport after the performance. Central London was crowded with soldiers on leave and with all the additions of wartime exiles, mostly men, who flocked to the theatre when it was available and whose concerns about quality may not have been too rigorous, the theatre boomed. This wartime boom continued after 1945 but it seems to have collapsed in 1947 during a particularly hard winter when fuel shortages precipitated power cuts and a general sense of austerity and when the capital was no longer thronged with soldiers on leave.

The war-time situation outside London is less clear but may well have been similar with a large number of transient soldiers and workers searching out available entertainment. One war-time development which was to be a seed for very significant postwar change was the formation of the Council for Encouragement of Arts and Music (CEMA) which was almost entirely focussed on providing cultural performances outside London. *"During the war period the main work of the drama department [of CEMA] was devoted to assisting or creating companies to tour in villages, small towns and war-workers' hostels, wherever audiences could be collected and the regular commercial theatre was not available"* (Dobson's) The London Old Vic theatre company, already regarded as a quasi-national theatre left its London base and moved to Burnley, apparently with some success in terms of audiences though it moved back rather quickly after the armistice.

It is clear with hindsight that theatre in Britain was in a state of complex crisis at the half-century, a crisis that was apparent to some at the time though contemporary perceptions were very mixed. It might, loosely, be described as 'strip, strip, hooray' on a national scale. The basis of theatre was being stripped away both in terms of scale and of cultural meaning whilst, at the same time, the glamour and glitz of its central symbol, the West End, was being maintained at least to a degree. Although a number of venues had suffered bomb-damage, some permanently, the number of West End theatres had stayed fairly constant for some years. In 1936, there were about sixty venues compared with forty-five or so in 1950.[28] This was much the same number as were licensed in the late nineteenth century. In the intervening period, of eighteen theatres closed down, seven had been bombed and never rebuilt whilst the remainder had been turned to other uses. In terms of theatres actually in use, the numbers seem likely to have remained almost constant at around forty. (Arts Council (1959) Vol.1 p.12) In terms of scale, West End theatre had apparently escaped the provincial contraction associated with conversion to cinemas. In 1948, the first of the great Broadway musicals, *Oklahoma!*, arrived, beginning a period when the arrival of one of these showcases was the highlight of the West End season concealing the impoverished state of British musical theatre. Yet it was clear that the theatre faced serious problems. These can be separated into distinct economic, cultural and aesthetic crises. Naturally, these were linked together and with common roots in the 'modernising' transformation of the British theatre some eighty years before. However, although in the end these crises cannot be wholly distinguished it is convenient to describe them separately.

---

[28] The precise definition of the 'West End' has always been somewhat unclear, whether, for example, it included the Royal Court or the Lyric, Hammersmith, Covent Garden or the Arts.

The economic crisis was based upon two quite clear factors, the sharp decrease in the number of theatres nationally and the apparently inexorable rise in costs together with an inability to increase revenue to any comparable degree. In the words of the only general review of the time *"During the past seventy years, theatre rents have increased, sometimes up to one thousand per cent, production costs by 600 per cent, and prices of admission by only 50%...The margin between profit and production cost has steadily decreased since the heyday of the Edwardian actor-manager, and it is still diminishing, for costs are still rising, apparently beyond control."* (Findlater p.35)These estimates are rather difficult to corroborate in any detail but the overall conclusion is undoubtedly true. Ironically, the underlying reason for the pincer in which theatrical finances found themselves derives from the very success of the Edwardian theatre which had finally established itself as respectable and theatre workers as professionals. Actors, although suffering the usual high level of unemployment, had managed to establish the widespread adoption of standard contracts with minimum pay-scales and most theatres had their Equity[29] representative whilst backstage staff had become highly organised and were paid increasingly well. It is likely that a major contributory factor in this was the advances in technical standards of sound, lighting and stage machinery which meant that the theatre electrician, sound engineer and carpenter, led by competent unions, were highly skilled and drawn from a relatively limited pool. Directors (then usually called producers) and to a degree designers had also been able to lay claims on contracts which gave them a portion of the box-office whilst playwrights were also more highly rewarded

---

[29] Equity is the live performer's trade union.

compared with the hack writers contracted to Victorian theatres at £10 the play and no subsequent royalties. Findlater quotes R.F.Delderfield, a reasonably successful writer of the time:

> *...having determined to become a professional writer at the age of seventeen I rapidly arrived the conclusion (since proved) that one makes far more money out of an unsuccessful play than a successful novel. I now write plays for a living and novels for my own satisfaction. (Findlater p.117)*

and goes on to comment:

> *Today an established playwright may make as much as £50 000 from a single play...and is reasonably assured of a regular income in repertory and amateur royalties even from a play which has failed in the West End*

Of course, established playwrights were small in number compared with aspirants but the point is that in a contracting overall market, it became more and more necessary to use established writers to minimise the risk of failure and these did not come cheap.

The increase in costs over the whole of the century had continued though the war and afterwards. In 1954, he asserted that running costs for theatres had risen by nearly 90% since 1939.

Findlater blames the inability of theatres to meet rising costs by raising prices on the Bancroft's as when introducing:

> *...the ten shilling stall at the Prince of Wales in 1874, they set theatre prices at a new and dangerously high level. The increase was necessary to pay for higher salaries and royalties, greater comfort and efficiency, better plays and productions: it helped to*

raise the prestige of Playgoing and to make the theatre safe for the middle classes. Yet not only did the introduction of the expensive stall help banish the working class from the theatre and set the middle class in authority, but it put a price on admission which left no room for advance.

(Findlater p.35)

Certainly, the level of good seat prices in central London set in the late-Victorian period introduced a theatre which was inaccessible to a large part of the population. A stalls seat in the West End in 1950 would have cost about 16 shillings (80p) at a time when £4 was a decent weekly wage. Upper circle and gallery seats would, of course, have cost much less but with a corresponding drop in comfort and view. Although it is unlikely that a significant price rise would have caused riots as they did at the beginning of the nineteenth century, Findlater may well have been correct in his view that audiences would have reacted badly to price rises. The cost of cinema entrance, often to a new building a good deal more comfortable than an old theatre, was a fraction of theatre prices.

The profitability of theatres has always been hard to discover hidden behind a maze of operating companies, usually private, with little legal requirement to disclose their profits. It is clear that from an early date, minimisation of tax payments was a preoccupation not confined to Archie Rice in Osborne's *The Entertainer*, a factor which encouraged complex and opaque accountancy. One public company, which had been a favourite with small investors at the beginning of the century, Moss' Empires Ltd, published profits and these had shown a slide from the late-20s onwards. The net profit of Moss' Empires Ltd which was £103, 681 in 1929, shrank to £64,537 in 1930 and turned into a loss of £24,653 in 1931. By 1932 the position had become even worse and the group was facing disaster. In the same year it was announced that twelve of the theatres would be converted to cinemas beginning a process whereby theatre companies first attempted to stay in business by moving into cinema later to either close its remaining theatres or sell them off. Ironically, some of these companies did poorly when they attempted to enter film production and recouped their losses by rationalising the 'bricks-and-mortar' end of the business.

The process of rationalisation went on during the war when a number of deals were done which avoided close public scrutiny by the temporary suspension of a number of laws relating to disclosure of accounts. The result was that in the immediate post-war period, British theatre had come under the domination of a unique corporate empire known in general parlance as The Group.

The Group
The extent of the Group's activities is known reasonably precisely because of the detailed study of theatre ownership in 1950 carried out by the Federation of Theatre Unions. This work is as comprehensive as could be undertaken and is very detailed though it acknowledges that the central issue, that of the ultimate profitability of the theatre, remained elusive, hidden behind a maze of private companies and shared control. As the report notes

> *"Some degree of concentration in theatre ownership is no new development. In the years between 1890 and 1910 a number of provincial and suburban groupings arose, chiefly, though not entirely, in the variety field...No real attempt at the rationalisation*

of the West End theatre was made until 1925, with the formation of Associated Theatre Properties—a venture that met with indifferent success. The present concentration of theatre ownership...differs from the earlier attempts not only in degree but in kind. For the first time in history an important, and indeed the most important, part of the theatre industry has been put on a proper industrial footing, employing all the devices of horizontal and vertical combination that this involves. The group that dominates the West End theatre and the main touring theatres today began to assume its present shape in the spring of 1942.

(Federation of Theatre Unions, p.7)

The Group was created by the Littler family; Prince Littler, the financial partner, Emile, more an impresario, and a sister, Blanche, whose role was more shadowy and who seems to have faded from the scene. This family group, whose original roots were theatrical, were supported by two other men, Harry Cruickshank and Tom Arnold, whose names appeared as co-directors on the multitude of companies which made up the Group. They were, apparently, backed by some financial interests in the City who appear to have provided the money for the crucial acquisitions in the war but whose identity was not clear. The essential business heart of the Group was to grasp the fact that in a period of market decline it was necessary to control all the various aspects of theatrical production from ownership of the building through production of the plays to outside ticket agencies and down to supply of beer to the bar and to take profits at each stage. (The Group owned a brewery and a mineral water producer).

The structure of theatre in the pre-war period was that building owners tended, particularly in London, to lease out their theatres to lessees on a seasonal or longer basis. These lessees themselves might sub-let to producing companies either for a single show or for a season. The main exceptions to this pattern were the provincial repertory theatres, mostly fully commercial but with a small number of flagship theatres supported by private sponsors. The process of closure and conversion which went on in the 30s and 40s had thoroughly undermined this system. Even the flagship repertories had suffered, sustaining losses which even the munificence of such as Sir Barry Jackson in Birmingham were unwilling to bankroll. The Group commenced a process in 1942 of buying up theatres and of developing production companies to use them. They also bought up enterprises covering all facets of theatrical life including catering (bar profits were a large part of overall profitability), technical supply of scenery and costumes, even casting agencies. The FTU report discovered dozens of companies with Group directors whose activities were, presumably, correlated with those of other Group companies even when no formal relationship existed. The result of this process were that by 1950

> *In the West End, the Group directly controls eighteen out of the forty-two functioning theatres and has an interest of some kind in two more. These eighteen theatres…contain over 50% of the seats; of the theatres seating over 1000 fifteen are controlled by the Group and only nine by other interests. In the provinces the situation is similar. Out of the list of provincial No. 1 touring houses close on 70% are connected with the Group. What is more, should the list be pruned to weed out those theatres whose status as No.*

1s is open to serious doubts, the proportion would increase.

(Federation of Theatre Unions p.27)

The status of a 'No 1 touring house' was essentially based upon size—above 1000 seats was the usual criterion—and the lack of any permanent company. The Group focussed its attention on those large venues remaining after cinema conversion. A large venue has considerable economies of scale compared with a smaller. A 1000-seat theatre has much less than double the fixed running costs of a 500-seat house. The drawback of the larger venue is that it needs to draw consistently a larger audience; if average audiences are only 500 then the small house will be profitable and the large one not. However, to breakeven, the large venue may need only 60% houses whilst the smaller may need 80% or more. In other words, big houses make big profits provided they can be filled. The Group aimed to fill its large venues by setting up a set of production companies to provide a steady stream of plays which could progress through a standard pre-West End, West End and touring cycle. It was by no means totally exclusive. Non-Group production companies could book their West End theatres and Group productions occasionally appeared at non-Group theatres. However, the scale of Group activities combined with the existence of informal agreements meant that the Group played a major part in setting the cultural agenda for British theatre.

The musical shows and spectaculars in the Group were handled by Emile Littler and Tom Arnold whilst its straight drama was largely handled by a production company, H.M.Tennent Ltd, headed by the redoubtable Hugh 'Binkie' Beaumont, a major cultural figure in British theatre throughout the 1950s. Beaumont had made a good deal of money producing musicals in the war and was, in effect, put in charge of West End theatre by the Littlers at its end. He has been described by his biographer as the *eminence grise* of West End theatre but this is rather unfair to a man who was very visible; perhaps gatekeeper would be a better word. He had a very important role in deciding what would and would not be produced and he subsequently played an intrusive role in many productions. He was known to favour glamorous sets and star names though he was also notoriously parsimonious in paying for less well-known actors. Possibly his most important single act was to obtain tax relief for the productions of Tennent Productions Ltd, a production company affiliated to H.M.Tennent Ltd. Entertainment Tax, charged at this time at 8% on box-office revenue, was a major financial drag on live entertainment. The Inland Revenue was persuaded not to charge this tax as well as other forms of corporate tax on non-profit-distributing productions, a dispensation granted *en bloc* to Tennent Productions largely it seems because the Arts Council, which had been formed out of CEMA in 1946, allowed itself to be 'associated' with the company. This association required no money but apparently provided the Inland Revenue with evidence of non-profit-distributing intentions.

The tax dispensation for Tennent Productions was bitterly disputed by other theatre managers and does seem at this distance a curious and discriminatory practice, particularly given that some Tennent productions were transferred lock-stock-and-barrel to fully fledged profit-making once they had shown themselves to be popular. As the F.T.U. report asserts *"It might seem from the point of view of the holding companies [the Group] there was little difference between the joint subsidiary [H.M.Tennent Ltd] and its non-profit-distributing affiliate [Tennent Productions Ltd], except that the former was able to pay the managing director's [Hugh 'Binkie' Beaumont] wages." (p.79)* Certainly, a scrupulous tax investigation would surely have recognised that payments in rent and for other services such as catering must have generated profits for other Group companies, profits which were certainly distributed. The tax advantages given to Tennent's diminished after a particularly blatant transfer between the two and corporate income tax was re-imposed. However, the fact that such a measure was allowed for a time probably reflects a widespread view that Tennent's, whether H.M. or not, were providing a service to the theatre which was in the public interest. Thus Findlater, whose contemporary commentary was scathing about most aspects of the theatre and who was suspicious of the overall Group says:

> *During the last ten years H.M.Tennents has done a great deal to raise the standards and advance the prestige of the English theatre, in co-operation with the Arts Council and with leading actors and producers, by its non-profit-making subsidiary...The parent firm of H.M.Tennents has shown far-sighted generosity and wisdom in its affairs...Much of the credit for this record must go to Mr Hugh Beaumont, the managing director, and the past ten years have shown that under intelligent direction the resources of the trade may be made to promote the art of the theatre as a whole.*

> *(Findlater p.44)*

Dispensation from tax was allowed to most of the productions at the small art houses which existed around the periphery of the West End and formed the bulk of indirect state funding for drama in the early years of the Arts Council. The best known of these was the Arts Theatre where Peter Brook did some of his early work. Other included the Boltons and Mercury theatres. In all about fifteen London theatres of various sorts, mainly small, had tax-free status as did most of the dozen or so provincial repertories which attempted to retain some semblance of artistic standards by having two or even three week runs and venturing outside the normal pattern of West End standards.

There was surprisingly little hostility to the Group despite their well-known grip on both London and provincial theatre. Most people seemed relieved that at least the Group was controlled by 'theatre folk' and not by business-men interested mainly in switching into other more profitable channels. In fact, it was not long before members of the Group began dabbling in the 1950s equivalent of the cinema, television, and turned away from the theatre. Outside of the Group, British theatre continued its downward plunge throughout the 1950s. The repertory companies so luridly described by John Osborne had only a few years of life left in them. Osborne's comments are worth sampling ranging as they do from a repertory theatre in a medium-sized Midlands town through a bottom-of-the-pile repertory in a dilapidated seaside resort to a theatre in a London working class suburb which still played Victorian Gothic melodrama such as *Frankenstein*. It was semi-destitute world peopled by failure and resentment. Osborne's dip into theatre management, a period when he played a peroxide-haired Hamlet at Hayling Island, ended in front of magistrates' court charged with fiddling the excise tax so neatly avoided by Binkie Beaumont.

Osborne's general ferocious anger at the world may exaggerate the condition of such theatres but they are a useful antidote to the usual theatrical memoir which tends to gloss over the impoverished conditions in favour of a rose-tint. However one fact which does emerge is that in the early-50s, a young man, good-looking but with absolutely no professional training, could scrape a living as an actor simply by responding to advertisements in *The Stage*. Michael Caine, for example, became an actor by this route passing through the Royal Court at one point. There was very little training available apart from the elite schools at RADA and the Central School which functioned almost as finishing schools for upper-class young men and women with artistic inclinations.

Overall, the Group acted after the war to stabilise the decline of the theatre and to preserve a functioning West End and touring circuit. The holdings of the Group with some small additions from other companies in the West End effectively defined the extent of wholly commercial theatre in Britain. Outside their control, the precipitate decline in theatre numbers continued throughout the 50s until municipal support of local theatre rescued such as the Derby Playhouse where Osborne started his rather inauspicious acting career. The Group's influence failed to outlive the Littlers, particularly as the brothers seem to have fallen out at some point, something that was probably inevitable given the somewhat mysterious patterns of control which they exerted. Serious financial pressure on their West End heartland was delayed by just fifteen or so years after which a new generation of integrated theatrical entrepreneurs was needed to revive it. Elsom's summary is all the more telling for its sympathetic tone:

> One of the most telling criticisms of The Group was that it was over-extended. The Group could not afford to renovate the properties it had acquired, and the burden of post-war theatre reconstruction fell on its

> *shoulders. In the mid-1950s, The Group faced the challenge of television and tried to sell off its assets, diverting the capital raised into record companies and television. Unprofitable touring theatres on valuable property sites were sold; others were run as dance halls and (later) bingo parlours. The touring circuits shrank from 150 theatres to 30 within fifteen years. In Leicester, there were three theatres during the early 1950s, two of them belonging to The Group; by 1956, all had closed.*
>
> *(Elsom p.13)*

The cultural crisis

The economic and financial malaise of the theatre in 1950 was paralleled by a equally acute cultural crisis. As described above, some eighty years before, British theatre had been redefined as a cultural pyramid with a relatively small number of venues, mainly in London, presenting a rather strictly defined dramatic form in a context of social decorum, sitting on top of a mass of other venues, some taking their cultural message from the top tier, others coming from rather different cultural traditions and mixing together a variety of dramatic forms. The cultural relationships between these are unclear, less clear even than the financial links. The 'high culture' of refined Edwardian theatre in London relied financially upon a large provincial touring circuit to sustain it and, as this crumbled, the finances of the West End were equally, though indirectly, stressed. The repertory movement in the provinces required substantial private subsidy to maintain standards and as the long period of the Depression progressed this became less and less available. What is much more difficult to appreciate is the extent to which the rapid decay of theatres as they were converted to cinemas also sapped the cultural position of the theatre. In the 1920s, cinema still possessed a rather rackety, curiosity-show image. However, very quickly, cinemas backed by the fast-growing marketing machines of the studios adopted many of the techniques of theatres to develop a hierarchy of venues designed to move the medium up-market. The advent of sound and colour rounded out the technical aspects and allowed new custom-built cinemas which went beyond theatres in the lavishness of their style and segregation of the audience according to seat price. Central London cinemas had the first showing of new films followed by carefully chosen distribution to major city-centre and London suburban sites. Second and third-run cinemas allowed for cheaper showings down to the local 'flea-pits' shunned by respectable filmgoers and beloved of local youth. Most of the last together with a good proportion of the second-run venues were converted theatres.

The development of a hierarchy of venues was accompanied by a similar hierarchy of types of film; lavish musicals, large-scale epics, romances, cheap thrillers and westerns, now-vanished genres such as the 'wrestler movie' which forms the backdrop to the Coen brothers' fantasy *Barton Fink*. A further refinement was the invention of the art or experimental film, usually French or Russian, and the art-house venue which allowed intellectuals to feel good about the cinema without blocking major venues. Some of this was the product of conscious marketing and product development, some the natural processes of a new cultural medium with different creative talents. The point is that the overall result of the growth of cinema was to isolate theatre as a cultural form, to eliminate entire sectors of the overall form and to reduce others to a plainly derisory level. (No one after all ever considered *Neat, Nude and Naughty* to be other than the bottom of the cultural pile—even its clientele).

The West End and, to a very limited degree, some provincial theatres retained their pre-war status; West End openings attracted considerable publicity and its stars remained high-profile celebrities. Even so it is clear that by 1950, the major theatre stars were beginning to age; Olivier was forty-three, Gielgud forty-six, Coward fifty-one and Ashcroft, also forty-three, whilst Hulbert and Courtneidge, probably the biggest stars of musical theatre pre-war were in their fifties and had effectively given up theatre in the war. There were rather few young actors achieving any comparable stature in the theatre. **Dobson's Year-Book** mentions three young actors in its survey of London theatre in 1948, Richard Burton, Dirk Bogarde and Jack Hawkins, all of whom switched quickly and almost totally into films. Cinema was not simply the largest and most lucrative job market, it was the cutting edge of artistic innovation, if not particularly in Britain then certainly on the Continent. Beginning with the new realism of the Italian cinema, in France, Sweden, Japan and, later, Germany, film was beginning one of its most fertile periods. Elstree comedies shone rather wanly in comparison, however much they are now praised as niche 'gems', and it is plausible that successive collapses and premature rebirths of the British film industry were, indirectly, an important saving grace for British theatre in that they provided very little outlet for genuinely creative talent. Even so, Peter Brook, twenty-five in 1950, and one of the two or three innovative theatrical presences of the time, began his artistic career dabbling in experimental film and remained actively interested in film in the early 1950s. It was perhaps only the lack of a decent job offer that preserved him for the theatre. The young Kenneth Tynan did in fact start his career in films working as a script editor at Ealing Films. He failed to convince the head of the studio, Michael Balcon, of the benefits of producing some New Wave scripts alongside the comfortable Ealing comedies and resigned in some disgust. Again, even a modest venture upmarket by the conservative British film industry might have re-routed the career of the most dynamic theatrical critic of the 1950s.

The effective collapse of creative theatre into London and the lack of much new talent coming into the profession served to heighten a further factor in the increasing cultural isolation of the theatre, what Rebellato has called *"a widespread queering of the theatre in the forties and early fifties"*. (Rebellato p.223) It is only relatively recently that this has been explicitly referred to as a factor in the cultural context of British theatre of the time. Obviously until 1966 when criminal sanctions against homosexuality were significantly, though by no means entirely, removed, the whole topic was effectively off-limits except when used, as Rebellato demonstrates, as a crude homophobic attack on gay men in general and the theatre in particular. Even after this legal relaxation, it has taken a long time for the situation to be openly reviewed if only because many of the men involved maintained a stout resistance to publicly acknowledging their sexuality until they died then removing any potential problems with the lethal British libel laws. The extent and reason for this "queering" can be interpreted in a variety of ways particularly given the necessarily ambiguous and shielded life which gay men led in the theatre. Whilst there is little doubt that the theatre did offer various protected havens in which they could openly share their sexuality, it was also true that outside these, transgression against the repressive laws of the period could bring public humiliation at the very least. This was demonstrated by Gielgud's conviction for "persistent importuning" in 1953. One general consequence seems clear however.

The secretiveness and ambiguity of the situation produced a theatre which was itself full of signs and secrets, some quite open, some deeply buried. The fact that Rattigan's *Deep Blue Sea* was originally written about homosexual love and then changed to a heterosexual focus because of the impossibility of obtaining a public performance licence for the original would only have been known to a small number of people and does not alter the play's emotional intensity. On the other hand, Noel Coward flirted very close to the edge with his verbal ambiguities and probably only got away with it as he had moved from being a serious theatrical figure to a version of that English icon, a 'card', a kind of gay Max Miller. Ivor Novello's sexual preference was a very badly kept secret and he was brought close to ruin in the war by a tax scandal said to have been stimulated by a desire of some in authority to bring him down. But he survived and wrote some of the most popular musical shows in the immediate postwar period. He died suddenly during the run of his last show, *Gay's the Word* (1950).

In a sense one might illustrate the ambiguity by a well-known popular song of the 1950s, *Green Door* by Frankie Vaughan. The chorus of this mundane pre-rock-and-roll swinger runs "*Green door, what's that secret you're keeping*" and goes on to describe how behind the green door there is "*an old piano*" but also something else, unstated and desirable, but clearly rather more adventurous than a pub singalong. The Green Door was at the time a very private and highly-protected gay club in Chelsea, a fact that Frankie Vaughan, a gay man playing the sexy heterosexual for his fans, would have known quite well. The song about a secret is itself a secret, a joke about Vaughan's public and private personae which would probably have been shared within the small circle privy to Vaughan's private life. At the same time, the deliberate ambiguity of the song clearly contributes to its appeal. What Rebellato describes as *"The proliferation of meanings, the apparently secret coding, the hidden audiences, the self-conscious fictionality of the stage discourse"* (Rebellato p.223) is capable of producing a similar kind of tension in a play.

The perception that London theatre was dominated by some kind of gay 'mafia', whether totally true or not, contributed to the sense that theatre was an elite and metropolitan cultural form, largely dying out except in a few specialised forms. It is difficult to speculate on the personal motivations of individuals but it is reasonable to assume that a consequence of leading a persecuted but, within the select group, privileged life is a degree of contempt for the 'straight' world, the world of mass popular culture, the non-metropolitan life. Clearly this was not a homogeneous perception. Rattigan's firm left-wing views[30] and his acute social perception is a long way away from Coward's open condescension. But placing secret codes in one's work whether as writer, director, designer or actor inevitably produces an inbuilt inclination towards contempt for one's audience.

The case of Rattigan is the key example of this problem. In some of his work, the disguised messages and subtext may assist dramatic tension, for example *The Deep Blue Sea* (1952) and *Separate Tables* (1954) particularly the latter where the fact that the crime of which the protagonist is accused is unspoken and

---

[30] On moving to the Bahamas, Rattigan took out a postal subscription to the *Daily Worker*.

shameful is the point of the drama. However against this must be set plays like *Adventure Story* (1949) and *Ross* (1960) based on the lives of Alexander the Great and T.E.Lawrence respectively, whose dramatic impact seems flawed by the 'coding' that they are about two apparently bisexual men. Rattigan's status as a playwright has been revalued several times probably because his work is sufficiently variable to allow of many judgements. One interesting comment is that due to Peter Hall, a director who came of age in the decade after Rattigan's 'Aunt Edna' had been swept from the stage. Darlow, Rattigan's biographer quotes him as saying " *I think that the problem with Rattigan was that, even if had had the opportunity for frankness, his whole repressed class background, the stiff upper lip of Harrow, would have made it impossible for him. Deception and restraint are at the heart of that kind of Englishman*" (Darlow p.20) One might generalise this: that the secret codings and ambiguity of many plays of this time were secure only within a wider class coding of repression and unspoken emotion.

It is hard to give precise consequences to the retreat of theatre into a metropolitan base centred around southern, middle-class audiences, to the stripping away of wider audiences and to the loss or degeneration of several forms of theatre alternative to the naturalism of the 'new' Edwardian theatre. It is clear that the revolutionary naturalism of Chekhov, Ibsen and Shaw *et al* was already being enervated through the 1920s and 30s perhaps because of its inability to cope with the horror of the First World War and the subsequent economic depression and rise of fascism. In the immediate aftermath of the Second World War, the financial strictures placed upon the theatre industry and its effective reorganisation upon almost industrial lines placed a premium upon playing safe, something which amounted to filling a set of West End theatres and laying a publicity basis for the provincial tours in what remained of the theatres outside London. Even so, it would be wrong, as several recent authors have noted, to write off the decade after the war as a theatrical desert. The tyranny of the naturalistic form was clear to several writers. Priestley is perhaps an odd figure to use as an example given his deserved reputation as a writer of solid, middle-class plays, albeit from a non-London perspective, but in 1948 he wrote:

> *Although various breakaway experiments have been made—and I have made some myself—the theatrical tradition of our time is a naturalistic tradition, and so I have in the main come to terms with it...Actually I have fretted and conspired against downright naturalism. I have spent many of my working hours devising means to conjure audiences away from the prevailing tradition.*
>
> *(Shepherd & Womack p.250)*

A play such as Priestley's *Johnston over Jordan* (1939), which was high-profile enough to star Gielgud at the West End's New Theatre and which had a score by Britten, was as non-naturalistic as could be desired even down to the use of masks. It closed in a month and was not revived for sixty years.

After the war, two broad and quite different attempts to break out of the clamp of naturalism can be seen. The first was the brief flowering of poetic drama, the second an influx of foreign plays in particular from France.

Poetic drama
The Poetic Drama movement, which is now particularly associated with Christopher Fry, T.S.Eliot

and Ronald Duncan, effectively sprang into life in 1945-46 under the auspices of E. Martin Browne who presented a season of poetry plays at the Mercury Theatre, a small venue just outside the West End which had a reputation for presenting experimental plays which might have a chance of West End transfer. As noted above, Eliot had been associated before the war with at least one production of the Group Theatre, a production called *The Rock*, for which he had written both prose and verse contributions to what was described as a 'Cochrane-style revue' though without, one may surmise, much in the way of scantily-clad women. The season at the Mercury produced one, brief, West End transfer for Duncan's *This Way to the Tomb* and led on to the better-known work by Eliot (*The Cocktail Party* (1949), *The Confidential Clerk* (1953)) and Fry (*A Phoenix Too Frequent* (1946), *The Lady's Not for Burning* (1948), *Venus Observed* (1950), *The Dark is Light Enough* (1954), *Curtmantle* (1956)). These plays were given quite high-profile productions, Eliot's *The Cocktail Party* being one of the first recipients of the part-subsidised productions of Beaumont at Tennent Productions whilst in 1953, Robert Donat, a pre-war stage star, was brought back from Hollywood to play in Eliot's pre-war *Murder in the Cathedral* at the Old Vic. During the eight years in which verse drama was at its height, it is fair to say that it represented the intellectual peak of British drama and almost the only challenge to the French plays which largely occupied that cultural niche. The virtual abandonment of the form after 1954 and the disdain shown for it subsequently by numerous critics has been followed by something of a critical rebound though without any great enthusiasm for revivals.

Whatever the aesthetic merit of individual plays, the existence if only for a relatively short time of group of writers working, self-consciously, within a form of drama thought long archaic does prompt the question: What was it trying to do? What was the point of it all? There are necessarily several answers to this but before looking at these the point should be emphasised that this was a writers' theatre, a literary theatre, started over ten years before the term was applied to the Royal Court and with somewhat greater justification. There are no significant actors, directors or designers who developed from poetic drama. It was also a writers' theatre which started from a relatively homogeneous ideological stance, that of a conservative Christianity opposed to both communism and, it should be said, fascism and also hostile to what was seen as the depredations of the modern popular culture exemplified in particular by the cinema. If one wanted to find a political continental equivalent it would be the Christian Democrat parties of Italy and Germany though these were Catholic whilst the poet dramatists were definitely Anglican though, at least in Eliot's case, Anglo-Catholics.

In the 1930s, often seen as a decade when British intellectuals and artists turned to the left, there had been efforts to rally Christian writers, something which in the theatre focussed on the Canterbury Festival. Christianity had had a fairly good war, particularly Protestant Christianity. Its key spokesman, Archbishop Temple, had not gone along the route taken in previous conflicts of directly blessing British guns but had adopted a more general view of soberly assessing the war as one of regrettable necessity, of a stand against barbarism. As Weight points out, (Weight p.29) saving St Paul's Cathedral in the Blitz became a symbol of national survival whilst Eliot's famous poem *Little Giddings* placed the church at the very heart of the war effort:

> *So, while the light fails*
> *On a winter's afternoon, in a secluded*
> *chapel*
> *History is now and England*

During the war, the Pilgrim Players, sometimes in two companies, one based in Canterbury, one in Oxford, had diligently toured England with a mixed bag of mostly Christian plays including *Murder in the Cathedral* under the auspices of CEMA, the precursor to the Arts Council.

In aftermath of the war, Britain was a confused and repressed society ideologically. The British people had decisively rejected its Conservative war-leader and elected a left-wing government committed to sweeping reforms in education, health, social welfare and the nationalisation of basic industry which, between 1945 and 1950, were mostly carried through. At the same time, the war-leader opened up the next phase in what has been called the long world-war in his notorious 'iron-curtain' speech at Fulton, when still Prime Minister, and ushered in a policy of anti-communism and pro-Americanism which was taken over in its entirety by the Labour government. Whilst throughout continental Europe, intellectuals and cultural workers were absorbed in huge moral and political debates about fascism, communism, occupation, war-guilt and collaboration, in Britain it seemed enough that the war had been won and the peace had to be built. The 'blood-price' had been paid and that seemed enough even though the level of military casualties and of bomb damage was actually rather small compared with the devastation in Germany, Italy and most of eastern Europe.[31] Like

---

[31] A famous night-raid on Coventry which destroyed its cathedral killed about six hundred people. A single raid on Hamburg later in the war killed more than ten times this number.

Christianity, Britain had had a pretty good war and no one seemed too inclined to raise any fundamental moral issues. (The only theatrical exception to this was, of course, MacColl and Littlewood's indefatigable Theatre Workshop touring with a play called *Uranium 235*).

The Poetic Drama movement was not, in this context, particularly concerned to revitalise theatre as such. Rather they saw drama as a way to bring key moral issues before the public, not of course any old public, but the very specific audiences of the West End theatre; educated, doubtful of the socialism of the Attlee government and appreciative of high culture. Uniquely, the central figure of the group and the author of some of its most successful work, Eliot, also wrote a book expounding his ideas of culture, *Notes Towards the Definition of Culture*.

Verse drama came and after 1954 it disappeared. Subsequently there was a deal of bitterness about this, that in some sense they had been excluded in particular by Devine at the Royal Court. Yet in practice, judgement had already been passed by the very audiences to whom Eliot had hoped to appeal. Fry wrote:

> *I think one writes best when you feel that someone is waiting to receive it, that you have ears attending as it were. One had rather ceased to feel that...*

(*Rebellato p.227*)

The Poetic Drama group had had, ironically in view of Eliot's passionate opposition to state funding, more access to subsidised productions than any previous group, probably more in some respects than the English Stage Company was to receive. Yet ultimately it failed to make any headway despite a series of top-flight showcases at the Old Vic and the Arts theatres. The idea that it was crushed by hostility from a few critics really makes little sense; their ultimate failure was that they failed to make any significant breakout from the theatrical form of the time just by alteration of the rhythms of the language spoken. The archaic feel of verse drama, used quite deliberately to develop a conservative ideology, proved in the end to be a failure. One strange little wave did however continue. In the early 1980s, the radical Conservative prime-minister, Margaret Thatcher, produced her most famous sound-bite in a speech ghost-written by a playwright, Ronald Harwood, who carried his own resentments about exclusion from a theatre that was by then largely left-wing. *"The lady's not for turning"* she exulted, pausing for applause from her audience presuming, one must suppose, that her largely middle-aged and certainly conservative audience would pick up on the resonance from the one occasion, thirty-five years before, in which a conservative ideology had had its run on the British stage, a resonance which for most people then under fifty would have been totally baffling. And, oddly, they did, suggesting that even in this context, theatre could create its own echoes.

Paris in London: the dominance of French theatre

Poetic drama overlapped with the second unusual feature of the London stage up to the mid-fifties, the profusion of French drama which was presented. The two most prominent writers in this influx were Anouilh (1910-1987) and Giraudoux (1882-1944), both having had at least eight plays in a London production by 1955. The number of productions arose to an extent from both having a large unperformed back-list to choose from; Giraudoux wrote his plays mainly in the 1930s (the last, *The Madwoman of Chaillot* in 1945 was produced posthumously) whilst

Anouilh began writing in 1935 and turned out virtually a play a year after that. Although Anouilh moves across a wider range of genres than Giraudoux, they are linked by working at what can perhaps be best described as light-hearted tragedy. Both are adept at producing the kind of aphorisms about life, love and death which seem profound at the time though rather lose their flavour on closer examination. They are amusing, clever and allow an audience to leave feeling that they have an entertaining evening but not a hollow one. Perhaps the most similar recent writer is Stoppard though there is no reason to suppose that he was directly influenced by them. And both in various ways break out of a rigid naturalism; Giraudoux commonly wrote versions of Greek mythology lightly-updated whilst Anouilh always operated on the edge of fantasy often using music and dance as integral parts of the drama. There is a connection between these two dramatists and some of the Poetic Drama playwrights, notably Fry who translated and adapted both Anouilh and Giraudoux.

These two were the main figures but there was also a profusion of other French dramatists. Sartre's quite heavy-duty pieces range from his version of the Oresteian myth, *The Flies*, written under German occupation in 1943 through to *The Condemned of Altona* in 1959. All received London productions though usually at the smaller art-houses. His *Nekrassov* was produced in the second season of the English Stage Company at the Royal Court along with Giraudoux' *The Apollo de Bellac*. Rebellato lists a further seventeen French dramatists, including Genet and Cocteau, who had some form of London staging by the end of the 1950s. (Rebellato p.128) If one adds in the work of Beckett, who wrote in French, and Ionesco who was culturally very close to France then it is no exaggeration to suggest that the dominant intellectual current in London drama throughout most of the postwar period up to around 1957 was French. Then, almost as suddenly as they came, French plays disappeared leaving little apparent impact except, perhaps, for the fact that both Brook and Littlewood made their homes in France some years later.

There is one fairly obvious reason for this Gallic dominance. A sizeable number of the plays seen were boulevard comedies first produced in Paris and dealing, one way or another, with a topic which the English found impossible to deal with themselves yet found irresistible—sex. In the immediate postwar period, sex was beginning to appear on the radar of the notoriously repressed British middle-class. After all in 1945, one-third of registered births were illegitimate, a record that still stood at the end of the century. However on the stage it remained largely submerged thanks to the quite astonishingly stringent censorship of the Lord Chamberlain and the general obscenity laws. Yet, as noted above, the basic staple of the touring theatre had been reduced to the simplest of sex shows; tableaux of naked women in tawdry poses forbidden to move a muscle or say a word.[32] The French farce or light comedy provided a form of entertainment, which English writers seemed unable to provide, in which innuendo and *double entendre* plus an occasional glimpse of women in underwear provided ample room for titillation without incurring the displeasure of the censor. Brian Rix' later Whitehall farces were a rough equivalent but lacked the Gallic touch of intellect. In fact it may be suspected that French plays got away with just that

---

[32] This was a consequence of the interpretation of general obscenity laws then prevalent as the Lord Chamberlain presided only over the spoken word. Physical display was the responsibility of the police.

little bit extra just because they were French and, therefore, by definition, naughty but not serious and certainly not gay. The assumed heterosexuality of the French defied even Genet' assaults on it though the censor was decidedly wary of the lesbian overtones of *The Maids* eventually given a club theatre performance.

There is a more to Anouilh, Giraudoux, Genet and Sartre than sex though it does form a fairly central theme to at least the first three. One other thing they carried was a certain moral cachet from having experienced German occupation and of being to some degree preoccupied with moral issues derived from that experience. Anouilh's *Antigone* and Sartre's *The Flies* were both written and first performed under German occupation and dealt in a coded fashion with the moral dilemmas of that experience. The British attitude to France was curiously ambiguous; on the one hand it was the defeated nation, the one which surrendered without much of a fight, a nation devoted to pleasure, knowledgeable about sex and in which adultery was the national pastime. On the other, it was the country of the resistance in which the conflicts of the war remained unresolved and in which communism, nationalism and capitalism were still active political issues. The French had a cachet of being both intellectual and sexy.

This perception was not confined to drama. Sinfield notes that Stephen Spender, a notable literary figure, travelled to Paris soon after the war and writes:

> *Spender was deeply stirred by the desolation of much of Europe. But still he found Paris 'the market place of the human spirit, the central world exchange of civilised values' (European Witness, p 109)...In postwar Paris Spender found a particular challenge to 'the*

*fusion of sensuous with spiritual experience'
which he considered the distinctive French
contribution to the modern worl.*

(Sinfield p.97)

It is difficult now to credit Anouilh and Giraudoux
with much intellectual weight given the muscle carried
by a succession of British writers from the 1960s
onwards whilst Sartre seems doggedly undramatic in
his pursuit of the illustration of existential dilemma. It
is something of a cheap shot to note that Giraudoux'
last play, *The Madwoman of Chaillot*, had the dubious
distinction of being adapted to become a Broadway
musical, *Dear World* (1969), which folded rather
quickly despite gaining a Tony award for its
celebrated lead, Angela Landsbury. It does, however,
form a tenuous link to the third dramatic innovation of
the immediate post-war period, one which lasted
longer and had a far greater impact than either of the
other two; the Broadway musical.

Conquering the world: the Broadway musical

The crisis of American theatre under the impact of the
cinema began even earlier and went even deeper than
in Britain. The last vaudeville act in central New York
closed in 1932 and at the time the future of Broadway,
an even more defining national centre for American
theatre than the West End was for Britain, seemed in
doubt. The major national theatre chain was put into
bankruptcy and the general expectation was that it
would sell off its prime city centre sites for
development or for conversion to cinemas. In fact, its
major shareholders, Lee and Jacob Schubert, bought
the company in its entirety out of their own money and
proceeded to set up a theatrical quasi-monopoly which
possibly served as the model for the Littler's activities
ten years or so later. Their lock on the national theatre
was partially broken in the 1950s after prosecution

under anti-trust laws brought about, so the legend has it, when even top politicians were obliged to buy $8 tickets to *South Pacific* (1949) for ten times the face value through ticket agencies owned by the Schubert's when they were unavailable at the box-office.

Even under tight control, Broadway struggled throughout the 1930s during the prolonged US economic depression. Musical comedy and revue dominated the scene but in terms of dramatic theatre they were at best mediocre. The decade is notable for a long list of some of the most popular songs ever written by the Gershwin's, Cole Porter, Irving Berlin, Jerome Kern and so on but it takes a dedicated *aficionado* to name the productions in which they first appeared. Nor were the shows themselves particularly successful in financial terms. *Girl Crazy* (1930) written by the Gershwins, starring Ginger Rogers and Ethel Merman and with '*I Got Rhythm*' as a showstopper ran for 191 performances, whilst at the other end of the decade, Rodgers and Hart's *Babes in Arms* (1937) with the classics '*My Funny Valentine*', '*Johnny One-Note*' and '*The Lady and the Tramp*' ran 289 times. The one show of the decade still constantly revived, the Gershwin's *Porgy and Bess* (1935) which sits squarely on the unwritten divide between musical theatre and opera[33] managed only 124. Broadly speaking, revues, that is unconnected songs, dancing and comic sketches were cheaper and more popular though these seldom ran for more than a few months. One of the few shows of the decade to top a 1000 performances was *Pins and Needles*, (1937) put on by the International Ladies Garment Workers' Union, a semi-amateur show which featured '*Sing Me a Song of Social Significance*' and '*It's Better with a Union*

---

[33] It was included in New York's Metropolitan Opera's repertory in 1985.

Man' by Harold Rome. In 1940, a Cole Porter musical starring Ethel Merman, *'Panama Hattie'* ran 501 times, the first Broadway musical to top 500 performances in twelve years. (Kenrick) The wheels may not have been finally falling off but this kind of success with high-cost shows did not provide much in the way of financial return and almost none made the journey to London. The decisive shift came in 1943 with *Oklahoma!* by Rodgers and Hammerstein, the show which may have saved both US and British theatre and which was certainly the originator of the dominant cultural force in both theatres for two decades.

The key artistic point about *Oklahoma!*, as Steyn has pointed out, (Steyn p.87)was that it was dramatic theatre, that is a play about real people. In 1927, with *Showboat*, Kern and Hammerstein had done much same thing but *Oklahoma!* was the show that lit the fuse. As Steyn puts it, with Lorenz Hart and Cole Porter, you hear the lyricist—with Hammerstein you hear the character. The reaction of the audience is not to applaud Ethel Merman, Noel Coward, Danny Kaye or Gertrude Lawrence as they strut their stuff in their showcase pieces but to cheer Curly and Laurie when they finally make it; to encourage Eliza Doolittle to overcome Professor Higgins' challenge; to weep at Maria's death; and to shudder at the MC in *Cabaret*. The difference is not always decisive. In *Hello Dolly*, (1964) a succession of *grande dames* stopped the show with the title song but this was at a point where the line of Broadway musicals was faltering.

The key financial point about *Oklahoma!* is that it ran for 2,212 performances on its Broadway opening, for three years in London when it opened in 1948, toured the USA for seven years and gave a return of 2500% on its original investment as well as providing a still flowing set of royalties to the Rodgers and Hammerstein Corporation. As a further financial bonus, Decca Records came up with the immediately successful idea of packaging the full cast performance as a set of 78s packaged in a book-like 'album', the origin of the term which stuck to single long-playing records. In a single stroke, *Oklahoma!* invented the 'blockbuster', the show whose production costs could be spread over years rather than months and over several venues and which could thus provide a financial return sufficient to justify several comparative failures. It could make men rich rather than just comfortable. It was, however, more than just a financial bonanza for, as Knapp (Knapp p.122) shows, it also played an important part in the process of creating a new American national identity at the end of a troubled period for the USA. The justly celebrated prose dramas of the period by Miller and, earlier, O'Neill, told deeply problematic stories about the USA. *Oklahoma!* and the subsequent Broadway musicals were often also based upon apparently problematic aspects of US life but, always, whatever the individual heartbreak, they ultimately found a way out. As Richard Eyre, a major British director who, unlike many critics, sees the dramatic value of the Broadway musical, puts it:

> *They have a socially conscious dimension, and are politically progressive and didactic: 'You've got to be carefully taught' is their instruction. Yet for all their genius, it hard to avoid a sense of frustration even with their very best work. It is as if we are invited to feel for the characters—even the unsympathetic ones—to see their unhappiness and grant our compassion, and just as we are holding out our hand to them, it's brushed aside: don't*

> *bother we'll sing and dance and everything will be fine.*

(Eyre p.171)

This is not just a dramatic point it is also a key point about the story that is being told. *Oklahoma!* illustrates this. It elided two facts of the American and specifically the Oklahoman past, the destruction of native Americans—the betrayal of treaties by illegal land-grabbing which delayed Oklahoman statehood for some decades—and the dustbowl of 1934 which had created the basis for Steinbeck's saga of the 'Okies', *The Grapes of Wrath,* and substituted a domestic and resolvable conflict between cattle ranching and farmers, both groups inside the required national image. The twenty or so years in which the musicals which followed *Oklahoma!* were the theatrical sustenance of Britain were also the years in which this new cultural image of America as a society of success became internationally dominant, a process in which they played no little part.

Oklahoma! hit London in 1948 at the end of miserable winter of shortages and power-cuts. There was a substantial backlog of the new musicals stacked up in New York (*Carousel* (1945), *Annie Get Your Gun* (1946), *Kiss Me Kate* (1948), *Brigadoon* (1947) to name only the best-known) so there was a steady stream of tested shows ready to sit in The Group's biggest London venues and fill their No. 1 touring houses after a decent interval.

There were several consequences of the coming of the big, new American musicals. An obvious one was the financial buttressing of commercial theatre at a time when its future was in considerable doubt. However, the price paid for this was that London became essentially a staging post on a line of financial and cultural calculation carried out in the USA. Try-outs in provincial US theatres followed by Broadway followed by American tours and a London opening. It meant that Britain received a product that had been extensively road-tested and passed through a demanding sieve of popularity. The financial risks involved in accepting such a piece were relatively small. (Contracts for a receiving house involved a share of the box-office so poor houses hit everyone). The other side of the coin was that the production values of the American shows were such that the financial stakes were raised for anyone who wanted to produce a British alternative. In fact very few did.

In 1952, Ivor Novello died aged 58. The streets were lined at his funeral which was broadcast live. Novello had been the outstanding star of British musicals since writing his first show, *Glamorous Nights*, in 1935. He starred in his own shows despite his lack of any singing talent which meant that an essential part of most of them was Novello accompanying the singing star on the piano. He had matinee idol good-looks and managed to survive a short term of imprisonment for a fuel-tax fraud at the end of the war brought about, it was widely believed, as a punishment for his almost, though of course not quite, overt homosexuality. Novello was the epitome of the 1930s style and his work ran into the 1950s with three reasonably successful post-war hits. In his last show, *Gay's the Word*, there is a song with the lyrics:

Vitality!
It matters more than personality,
Originality, or topicality!
For it's vitality!
That made all those top-liners tops!

It worked for Novello, whose postwar productions were even more successful than pre-war in terms of their runs but for few others. Even, dare it be remembered, The Master himself, Noel Coward, flopped in his musical *Pacific 1860* despite the presence of an immensely vital Broadway star, Mary Martin. The fact was that 'vitality', the pull of a celebrity star did not anymore provide success; perhaps the even bigger magnetism of Hollywood stars on the screen surpassed that of the live hoofer. What *Oklahoma!* demonstrated, however, that a specifically theatrical form could bring the audiences back.

Novello had no successors. Virtually the only attempts at British musicals in the 1950s, Sandy Wilson's *The Boy Friend* (1953) and even more so *Valmouth* (1958) were regarded, affectionately or derisively depending on taste, as throwbacks to a previous age. British musical theatre effectively died. The only partial exception to this, *My Fair Lady* (1956), which starred British actors and had a British designer was written and directed by Americans for an American audience.

In this sense, the American musicals were culturally destructive. However, in the end the forest fire which they lit in British theatre can also be seen as rejuvenating. They laid down a marker for popular theatre which took a long time to bear fruit but which made a massive contribution to destroying the elitism which lay at the heart of theatre of the time. It may be historically interesting to uncover the gay *double entendres* which Wilson managed to slip past the Lord Chamberlain in *Valmouth* (Rebellato p.176) but it is also a commentary on the state of British theatre that this, eight years after *South Pacific* and *Guys and Dolls*, is still what was being written. Albeit seen through a distorting lens of an American cultural machine, these were shows about real people written, mostly, with wit and intelligence and without a trace of condescension. That is the key word. Faced with a complex of apparently crushing problems, British theatre withdrew into a self-contained and self-justifying world which simply refused to believe there was a problem at all or, if there was, then it was a problem of a general fall in 'standards'.

Amateur theatre

At this point, mention should be made of one area of theatre almost invariably ignored by critics except to be ridiculed—amateur theatre. However, there is a case for suggesting that in the 1940s and 50s, amateur theatre played a significant part in preserving serious drama at a time when professional, that is commercial, theatre was collapsing.

The gap between professional and amateur theatre in Britain is now probably wider than in most other art forms. Novelists make the transition to being full-time writers by steps which are often almost imperceptible whilst poets seldom make the transition at all. A similar situation exists in painting. In music, there exist all kinds of intermediary stages between making music for a living and simply playing an instrument in the front room whilst some kinds of performance, for example, large-scale choral works, would scarcely exist without professional and amateur working together. In all of these, there is ample room for the semi-professional, sometimes a teacher of the subject, sometimes a worker in a related area such as journalism who makes some money getting material published or playing for a fee outside normal working hours. The theatre stands almost alone as an art form where the amateur is not only rigorously separated from the professional but is also the subject of routine denigration as being a kind of caricature of the 'real thing', a mess of personal vanities or just having fun in front of an indulgent audience of friends and relations.

There is a long history of this kind of appraisal reaching back to Shakespeare's motley band of mechanicals in *A Midsummer Night's Dream*. Shakespeare worked at a specific moment when the profession of actor was just beginning to emerge, as was the whole concept of commercial entertainment, and he probably had good reason to mock the amateur in order to emphasise the need for the professional. Even so, he must have been aware that theatre had been largely an amateur venture only a few decades before either in the mystery plays or in the performances of classical drama by students. Such activity seems to have largely ceased by the end of the sixteenth century but after the Restoration, perhaps because of a combination of Court favour for the theatre but one professionally limited in scope by the patent system, there developed a fashion for amateur theatre in country houses. In 1776, the London Post commented:

> *The rage for dramatic entertainments in private facilities has increased astonishingly; scarce a man of rank but has or pretends to have his petit theatre, in the decoration of which the utmost taste and expense are lavished.*

The bulk of the actual performances in these settings, many of which were probably much more like the informal staging described in *Mansfield Park* rather than permanent small theatres, were probably amateur though one might speculate that there was a degree of at least semi-professional involvement in the more elaborate ones. Enthusiasm for private amateur theatre seems to have waned in the early nineteenth century. Professional theatre was becoming both more spectacular and more widely available and less appealing to 'men of rank' and private theatricals became less popular. It was only in the second half of the nineteenth century that interest in amateur theatre revived in a much more serious vein as part of an effort to 'rescue' drama from the excesses of melodrama. The first recorded amateur dramatic society was the Manchester Athenaeum formed in 1847, initially to read plays and later to perform them. Dickens, whose reaction against what he saw as the vulgarisation of the theatre has been noted above, was involved in The Amateurs whose aim was to present work increasingly focussed on the new realist drama.

These groups were quite different to the private theatrical ventures in country houses. They were based on a locality with a membership drawn on some more or less open basis from those in the area interested in presenting drama. Their growth was linked closely with the development of the new form of realist drama and their ambience was decidedly middle-class with, one might assume, a more serious bent than the frivolity of the country house. One commentator suggests that:

> *It was the plays produced from Ibsen onwards that gave the amateur his opportunity of coping with characters he can recognise. In playing them there are many problems but they are problems that can be related in some way to personal experience and do not call upon the imagination of the actor.*

(Rendle p.8)

The growth of these amateur dramatic societies is relatively undocumented but there seems to have been an acceleration in their formation in the Edwardian period with the formation of such as the Stockport Garrick (1906), Letchworth D.S. (1906) and the Peoples Theatre (1911) in Newcastle. This last is particularly well-known for its performances of Shaw plays some of which, such as *The Shewing Up of Blanco Posnet*, had been banned by the censor. Shaw is known to have been sympathetic to their work though, ever one to watch the pennies, he straightened them out on touchy issues about payment of appropriate fees to authors. There was an explosion of new groups in the 1920s, including the formation in 1921 of the famous Maddermarket and the Norwich Players by Nugent Monck. One observer in 1930, admittedly biased, described this growth as *"A dramatic renaissance unequalled since Elizabethan times"*. (Bishop) This source lists 1500 societies, a number dwarfed by the estimate that in the 1930s, there were reckoned to be around 10,000 amateur groups in the north of England alone with a membership of half a million.

The 1920s and 30s was the period when professional and amateur moved more closely together than at any other time. British theatre, in particular the West End, moved into what we called the Short Coma and much new or experimental work was undertaken by semi- or wholly amateur groups. The Unity theatres in London, Manchester and Liverpool and the Group Theatre have already been mentioned. Other small theatres existed around the periphery of the West End which attempted to put on a mix of professional and amateur productions. The Tower in Islington was one such, the Intimate in Palmers Green another. Only one of these survives in anything like the form it had then, the Quaestors in Ealing, an amateur group which describes itself now on its web-site as the *"largest community theatre in Europe"* and continues to put on productions of professional standard. The People's

Theatre in Newcastle should also be mentioned in this respect. Bernard Shaw is said to have made his last public speech here in 1936 when he saw a production of *Candida* and it was the subject of a BBC documentary in 1939 to which Sybil Thorndike contributed. The People's had an overtly political base (it was founded by a branch of the British Socialist Party) and it was able to draw on support from left-wing writers. In 1940, it presented the world premieres of three O'Casey plays[34] and an early Peter Ustinov.[35] The Maddermarket in Norwich also pursued its own, slightly idiosyncratic way originally intended to present Shakespeare in a setting similar to that of the original productions.

The result of this boom in serious amateur theatre can be seen in the way in which a number of these started to provide themselves with permanent bases, a move which led to the formation of the Little Theatre Guild in 1946. This body which now has a membership of around one hundred requires that its affiliates operate their own fully-equipped theatre rather than working from hired premises. Such venues range from original theatres through conversions from other premises, often chapels or mills, to purpose-built theatres.

The first group includes the third oldest provincial theatre in England, the Grand in Lancaster, and the oldest working theatre in Scotland, the Theatre Royal in Dumfries. Less historically illustrious venues would include such as the Empire in Todmorden. The Grand and the Theatre Royal have followed rather similar trajectories. The Grand was built in 1782, the Theatre Royal in 1792 as part of boom in provincial theatre. Each closed their doors in the mid-twentieth century as commercial theatre entered into its long decline; the

---

[34] Cock a Doodle Dandy, Purple Dust and Red Roses for Me
[35] The Banbury Nose

Grand actually functioned as a cinema after 1931 until this too closed in 1950. Each was saved from demolition by a local amateur drama group, the Guild of Players in Dumfries and the Footlights Club in Lancaster, and each now functions as a kind of amateur receiving house adding to productions by the local group with a mix of amateur and professional performances. One striking feature of each, something held in common by most of the other members of the Little Theatre Guild, is that the initial purchase and subsequent refurbishment has been undertaken almost wholly with funds raised by the groups themselves rather than with any state assistance. In its original form as CEMA, amateur theatre groups received state funding almost as readily as professional (that is to say not very) but this rapidly shifted after the formation of the Arts Council under the initial domination of Lord Keynes. Any form of funding for amateur work was rigorously cast out with only some funding from regional arts associations moving into community theatre projects. The arrival of Lottery funding for capital projects has to a degree altered this and there is some pressure to extend Arts Council funding.

The histories of the main amateur theatres in Britain tend to be idiosyncratic and specific. The most common theme is that of a group in a small town, either without a theatre or in which the theatre had closed, forming an amateur company to provide some theatrical presence. The Nonenities in Kidderminster are a striking example of this, an amateur group who rescued the old Opera House, which had declined to use as a sugar warehouse, in 1948 and then ran it as a mixed amateur/professional house for twenty years. In 1967, they fought a compulsory purchase order for demolition to build a road and used the resulting compensation money to convert a church-hall to a theatre. This has since continued the original tradition of mixing professional and amateur productions.

Another group working in an area bereft of any professional theatre is the Lindsey Rural Players who operate out of a small village in Lincolnshire and were originally founded by a group of conscientious objectors in WWII who met in the evenings for music, singing and play reading. In 1948, they converted an abandoned Nissan hut into a theatre and performed plays there until 1960 when it burnt down. A replacement in the form of a disused Methodist chapel was purchased and has functioned since as a 100-seat theatre with a mix of professional touring companies and local amateur productions.

It is very difficult to estimate just how many people take part in amateur dramatics today or how many production take place each year. In 1979, a sample survey of five counties (Amateur Theatre) suggested that there might be about 8500 groups in the whole country with some half million participants and a total box-office attendance of about fourteen million. The average audience size was estimated at 146 biased heavily towards musicals with an average audience of over 300. Straight plays were seen by an average of only 97. Roughly 30% of all amateur production were put on in 'conventional' venues such as arts centres or theatres, the remainder used various *ad hoc* halls. This proportion is surprisingly high given the low opinion often held of amateur theatre but in practice a large number of venues mix amateur with various professional performances on a regular basis. Comprehensive figures are difficult to obtain for recent years but examples can be taken from Arts Council surveys of theatre use in the mid-1980s.[36] In

---

[36] Arts Council archives, ACGB/43/41

1985/6, the Derby Playhouse had 12 in-house professional productions and 5 amateur shows though the later only ran for a week each as against the professional average of 3-4 weeks. In their studio, amateur productions actually outnumbered professional though again the performance period for the amateur shows was less. In the same year, the Nottingham Playhouse had 2 amateur performances, the Oldham Coliseum had 4 and the Haymarket, Leicester, 2.

The best recent participation figures, and these very rough, are those given in the annual Household Survey which show that in 2002, about 2% of the adult population were "performing in a play" at some time in the 4 weeks before the interview for the survey. As most amateurs perform only two or three times a year and then for only a few days, it would be reasonable to multiply this percentage by two or three times for annual participation but even the 2% level would give participation rates close to the million mark.

One area of amateur work which became prominent particularly in the 1970s and 80s is the large-scale community theatre pioneered by Ann Jellicoe in Dorset and Somerset and taken up by other groups throughout the country such as Foundry Theatre. The basis of this work was to mobilise an entire community in the presentation of a play usually based around some aspect of local history and often presented in some kind of promenade pattern over several venues, some outdoors. These productions, some of which have been documented by Jellicoe, (Jellicoe) may involve some kind of professional involvement in direction and writing; Jellicoe, for example, hired David Edgar to write a play for Dorchester and Howard Barker for Bridport. Requiring several months to develop, such plays were often only done a handful of times and required some degree of support from such as local arts associations. As financial times grew harder in the 1980s, such support was less easy to come by and community productions on this scale have now almost disappeared. Perhaps the only regular reminder of the force of such work is the production of the York Mystery Play performed largely by an amateur cast prepared over some months by a professional core of actors and directors.

The York Mystery Play can be regarded as the oldest community play extant in Britain. It was revived in 1951 as part of the Festival of Britain and has been performed roughly once every three years since. It was first produced outside in one location, the ruins of St Mary's Abbey, then inside in the Theatre Royal and in a Millennium production inside York Minster when 28,000 people are reported to have bought tickets. There have also been performances of 'wagon plays' at various points round the city, a style closer to that of the original productions when each guild in the city sponsored a play. The play requires a cast or around two hundred, mostly amateur though the part of Jesus is usually played by a professional as are major supporting roles.

The growth in the number of people who have some kind of drama training at university but who pursue careers outside the theatre means that there is a growing pool of those with a basic grounding in theatre skills but no professional outlet. This, together with the fact that amateur groups maintain a number of venues round the country which support professional as well as amateur shows, suggests that in the future there may be a greater overlap between professional and amateur than there was in the twentieth century.

A Mission to civilise the nation

It was normal during the 1950s to regard popular culture somewhere along a line between condescension that it was good thing that the masses had enough cinemas to occupy their leisure hours on a Saturday night to horror that the Vandals were at the gates. Lord Reith, the man who required that news readers on radio should wear dinner jackets, referred to the possible introduction of commercial television as introducing *"Smallpox, Bubonic Plague and the Black Death"* into British cultural life. (Weight p.245) Reith was pretty much a dinosaur in the mid-1950s but consider the attitude of Richard Hoggart, a man of the centre-left, credited with inventing the study of popular culture in *The Uses of Literacy*, in his description of one of the new coffee bars:

> The young men waggle one shoulder or stare, as desperately as Humphrey Bogart, across the tubular chairs. Compared with even the pub round the corner, this is all a thin pallid form of dissipation, a sort of spiritual dry-rot amid the odour of boiled milk. Many of the customers—their clothes, their hairstyles, their facial expressions—are living...in a myth world...which they take to be real life.
>
> *(Hoggart p.204)*

His descriptions of mid-1950s youth have more than a whiff of the second-hand about them unlike his affectionate adolescent memories of 1930s working class culture. One might even describe them as typical *Daily Mail* were it not for the extreme hysterical and racist reaction to such as rock-and-roll then favoured by that paper. In 1956, it described rock 'n' roll as *"It is deplorable. It is tribal. And it is from America. It follows ragtime, blues, Dixie, jazz, hot cha-cha and the boogie-woogie, which surely originated in the jungle. We sometimes wonder whether this is the Negro's revenge*" (Weight p.304) Revenge possibly for the racism towards Caribbean immigrants which was at the time raising 'No Coloureds' notices on lodging advertisements across the country and which was to culminate in the Notting Hill Riots in 1957. The *Daily Mail* was and is, of course, the unchanging bastion of little-England racism. But Hoggart was a leftist academic and whatever the source of his description there is no mistaking the alarm coloured by condescension which fills it.

In general, there was a feeling that the state needed to do *something* to arrest this decline in cultural standards though there was precious little agreement as to just what. Some form of decent youth organisation was always a favourite, usually headed up by Lord Hunt, the man who had been the leader of the first expedition to climb Everest in 1953, wiling away the time whilst Tensing and Hilary were off climbing by reading Greek verse. Support for the arts was usually favoured in subsidiary paragraphs and the Arts Council of Great Britain was regarded as the main implementing body.

The Arts Council had had its origins in wartime in the Centre for the Encouragement of Arts and Music (CEMA). This body had been set up in 1940 to provide wider cultural activities than those provided by ENSA and to include the civilian population of the U.K. In the war, Britain was a country in movement as well as one which was far from homogeneous in its attitudes to the war. Although the war as such was generally accepted by most people as just and necessary, there was considerable distrust of the country's leaders and of their specific war aims. The level of strikes was actually higher than in pre-war years as skilled workers, sometimes resenting the use of less-skilled workers, even women, pressed for pay-differentials to be maintained and even increased. Hundreds of thousands of people were moved around the country on a semi-voluntary basis as industries and offices were moved out of vulnerable cities (the Prudential, for example, was relocated to Bournemouth) with their workers housed in empty hotels and temporary lodgings. The major parties exercised a moratorium on contesting parliamentary vacancies as they occurred but minor parties did not and both the Commonwealth and Scottish Nationalist parties had surprise wins reflecting a popular unease with the government's leadership.

When Churchill toured the blitzed East End of London in 1940, his rallying-call of "*We can make it*" was widely publicised. Less publicised but remembered was the response of at least one Cockney, "*What do you mean, we, you fat bastard*" Thirty or so years later, this incident would become part of Brenton and Hare's iconoclastic piece, *The Churchill Play* (1974), described by the theatre critic of the *Financial Times* as the one of the most disgusting plays he had ever seen. Some divisions never heal.

CEMA was set up as a deliberate exercise in raising morale (which was how local discontent was seen) by providing edifying entertainment in all spheres of the arts. It assisted touring shows in the visual arts and music as well as drama. In the latter, although it promoted various professional shows, (the Old Vic Company was persuaded to move to Burnley where it was apparently rather popular) it had a strong emphasis on promoting amateur groups and had helped found a number of these. As is noted elsewhere, amateur theatre at the time was rather less divided from professional than it is today. CEMA seems to have been quite successful in its drama work given its minute budget though there is little record left of it compared to the much higher-profile war-artists work.

The deputy-head of CEMA's art division was W.E.Williams and there is no doubt that he had considerable enthusiasm for continuing the work of CEMA after the war in the form of decentralised arts centres. In 1943, he wrote in *Picture Post* (and the choice of journal itself is interesting, most cultural discussion of the time taking place in *The Times* or magazines such as *The Listener*):

> *We must no longer be content with the Calvinist notion that any old upper room will do for cultural purposes—an attic over the Co-op, or an Infant's School classroom... Let us unify our popular culture that in every town we have a centre where people may listen to good music, look at paintings, study any subject under the sun, join in a debate, enjoy a game of badminton and get a mug of beer or cocoa before they go home.*
>
> *(Weight p.94)*

This seems a rather quaint phrasing now but at the time, its vision of bringing together the arts with sport supplemented by the occasional pint of beer was decidedly unusual, even revolutionary. The idea of local arts centres in small towns unable to support a theatre was put forward in 1945 in the form of a well-produced pamphlet *"Plans for an Arts Centre"* (Arts Council 1945) with the assistance of the Ministry of Town and Country Planning.

In 1945, on the back of CEMA's work, the Arts Council of Great Britain (ACGB) was created, with Maynard Keynes, who had been head of CEMA since 1943, as its first Director. Lord Keynes, as he was by then, was an unusual figure, a genuine English intellectual, a Cambridge academic, a gay man married to a Russian ballet dancer, he was a frequenter of the Bloomsbury set and the most eminent economist in the country. He was also a totally committed to the idea of high culture and his view of the role of the Arts Council was one of support for artistic citadels in the face of assault by the barbarians. In 1945, when engaged in setting up the international monetary system and obtaining American support for the British economy, he caught wind of the scheme for arts centres. *"Who foisted this rubbish on us"* he wired to London (Weight p.95) and thereafter the emphasis of the new body was firmly on funding what would now be termed 'centres of excellence', in particular support for Keynes' own icon, the Royal Opera House (ROH), which had been closed in the war. Uniquely, support for the ROH was specified in the original Treasury grant and the House has hung round the neck of the Arts Council ever since, a massive baroque pendant.[37] Keynes died in 1946 but he stamped his view of state support for the arts firmly on it. It was a view that chimed with his own view of the state's role in support of the economy, that it should be discreet, that it should *"comfort and support for the arts"* providing backstop funds for centres of high art but not attempting to compete with commercial art in its own sphere. The Arts Council's original charter when it was approved in 1946 stated that it was to *"develop a greater knowledge of the fine arts exclusively"* and by 1952, the Arts Council had withdrawn completely from supporting arts centres or clubs.

A second possible branch of state funding for the arts was opened up in 1948 by the Local Government Act

---

[37] The close relationship between the ROH and the Arts Council is detailed in Hutchinson, Ch. 2

which allowed local authorities for the first time to levy a rate for this purpose, set at 6d in the pound of rateable value,[38] and also to build performing arts venues. Up to this time, every such building had to be approved by a parliamentary Private Bill. The rate could have raised as much as £50 million annually had it been taken up fully by all councils. The minister responsible was the left-wing Aneurin Bevan and he harboured the same hopes for local arts centres as his fellow-Welshman, W.E.Williams. The Ministry of Town and Country Planning set up an exhibition on arts centres which travelled round town-halls throughout the country following the 1945 pamphlet. But at a conference organised by the Arts Council in 1952, its new Secretary-General, Williams, discovered that less than half the councils had used the new resource and, of those who had, the amounts involved were far below that possible. Only two arts centres were in fact built under this initiative.

In 1950, the British economy hit the buffers and, introducing a theme which would become only too common in subsequent years, serious financial stringencies were imposed. A big factor in this was the huge level of defence spending required to support overseas commitments, finance British participation in the Korean War and fund an independent nuclear weapons programme. Defence spending reached 10% of GNP at this time and many other programmes were squeezed. Arts funding was not excluded from this and the more ambitions plans of the Arts Council were shelved. In drama, the prime candidate for this was the proposed National Theatre whose foundation stone had been planted on the South Bank in 1950 by the

---

[38] At that time and until the late-1980s, local authorities in Great Britain were largely funded by a tax based on property value called the rates.

then Queen. (It was later shifted to less obvious sites and she is believed to have commented that they should have laid it on castors). In addition to this, most other areas of support were trimmed or frozen.

Even within this tiny budget, in the whole of the 1950s, drama came low on the list of priorities for the Arts Council. In 1957, £302,000 was spent by the Arts Council on the ROH compared to £69,000 on *all* drama, this last being about 7% of its total grant-in-aid. Throughout the decade almost the only beneficiaries of aid were a small group of prestigious venues, notably the Old Vic, the Shakespeare Memorial Theatre, the Bristol Old Vic and a small number of provincial repertories believed to be upholding appropriate standards. Devine's English Stage Company at the Royal Court joined the list in 1956 but it was far from generously funded. In its first five years it received a total of £30,000.[39] Overall, the biggest indirect contribution to financing theatre made by the Arts Council was the initiative described above whereby theatre companies were relieved of the burden of taxation by the Inland Revenue if they were accepted as non-profit distributing. This was mostly easily achieved initially by acquiring the appellation 'in association with the Arts Council' though this requirement seems to have been dropped after some years. Initially, Keynes' influence was undoubtedly important in gaining this privilege for H.M.Tennent Productions as well as for the principal repertories which it funded and it was also acquired by various other West End production companies though never as firmly as Tennent. There is a certain irony in this privilege of tax exemption. The Royal Shakespeare

---

[39] Inflation has made it difficult to visualise the value of these grants. For rough reference, £600-800 annually would have been thought a decent living wage throughout the decade.

Company has recently made a point of calculating the proportion of its central subsidy returned to the government by way of taxation; the figure in 2001/2002 was claimed to be 71%. In fact half of this comes from employee's taxation which is not really the issue. However, it is true that more than one-third was returned in the form of VAT and employer national insurance contributions.

In the immediate postwar period, there was considerable interest in state funding of the arts and it was debated at high levels. In the end, the radical elements, who favoured a much more widely spread form of support, lost out decisively in part because of the weight of the 'high culture' supporters such as Keynes and Kenneth Clark and in part because of the apathy of the local authorities who had been given a chance by Bevan to intervene massively in local arts funding. However, interest in state funding seeped away after the election of a Conservative government in 1951 and under the impact of successive financial crises. In 1957, Lord Clark, then Chairman of the Council, visited the new Prime Minister, Harold Macmillan. *"What's this trouble with your Arts Society"* Clark reports Macmillan as saying, suggesting that arts funding had moved down almost to invisibility in the minds of politicians. It took a new decade to inaugurate a new kind of thinking about state subsidy.

The Look-Back-in-Anger Moment

It is impossible to survey British theatre in the two decades after the war without running up against *Look Back in Anger*, hard. It has become a symbol of a time rather than a play to be judged against other plays. This process began quite early as did the ironic kick-back. As Elsom notes, in David Mercer's play *After Haggerty* (1970), the defeated lecturer, Link, begins every lecture in his course on Modern Drama with a regulation reference to *Look Back in Anger* whilst in real-life the critic, John Russell Taylor called his early survey of the period *Anger and After* as though this provided an obvious starting point. As Rebellato has pointed out, rather irritably, even through the 1990s, it was still used a marker of some kind, usually in a way which implies that things are not as vibrant or creative as they were back when John first blew Aunt Edna out of the stalls.

There are really three things mixed up here which need to be separated rather carefully even if one excludes any judgement about the play itself. These are the role it played within the English Stage Company and the subsequent impact of that company; the position it occupied in the cultural moment of the second half of the 1950s; and the problem of John Osborne himself. They will be looked at in reverse order.

This is not a book about celebrity. In fact one may note a distinct chilliness here to the idea of theatre as a succession of star personalities. But even so, it is difficult to avoid the star quality of Osborne as he strutted around from 1956 to his eclipse in the late 1960s in a haze of alcohol fumes and grumpy opinions. From angry to grumpy in under two decades might be used as his epitaph but, in his angry pomp, he was undoubtedly a force; not a force *for* anything in particular, certainly not a force for anything in the theatre which he seems to have largely disdained, just a force.

Osborne was born in 1929 and drifted into the theatre partly, so he explains it, to escape from a mistaken engagement to marry. He was not, it seems, a great success as an actor; no one who plays Hayling Island, even Hamlet in Hayling Island, could probably ever rise to that and in 1956 he answered an advertisement placed by George Devine in *The Stage* asking for unperformed plays. Osborne replied with *Look Back in Anger*, written so he says in fourteen days on a houseboat on the Thames. After a slow start, the fortunes of the play improved after a rapturous review by Tynan in *The Observer* and it quickly became a national byword especially after an excerpt was shown on television. He wrote some ten plays in the succeeding decade until after *Hotel in Amsterdam* (1968) he slowed down, writing less and less until his death in 1994.

Nothing he wrote after *Look Back in Anger* ever had quite the same reception though *The Entertainer* (1957) and *Inadmissible Evidence* (1964) are certainly better plays and could justifiably be placed amongst the best of the century. *Look Back in Anger* established him as an Angry Young Man, indeed he may have been responsible for the invention of the term, in the company of a group comprised almost entirely of novelists including John Braine, John Wain, Kingsley Amis and Colin Wilson. Whatever the angriness of their work (and it does seem rather mild set against the standards of even ten years later), Osborne stands out from this group by the sheer flashiness of his personality. He made a great deal of money very fast (proving Delderfield's point that a playwright at this time could earn a very comfortable living), spent it fast and became involved in a series of high-profile affairs and marital break-ups. When his marriage to Mary Ure was falling apart in the course of an affair with Penelope Goliath, the press camped outside his house waiting for a snap, a quote, anything for a glimpse of the man himself. He became a personality, a pop star, an icon of young, beautiful, fuck-off England and, as such, he made the theatre sexy. Perhaps, one might say, sexy again. In some ways, Osborne's successors were not dramatists but The Kinks and The Rolling Stones. His greatest influence on theatre in the years after *Look Back in Anger* might well have been that he made an image for dramatists that was irresistible. Who knows what David Hare and a succession of clever young men in the 1960s might have made of themselves if they had not had such a glittering role-model?[40]

This may seem rather dismissive of one of the major British dramatists of the century but the influence of Osborne's work remains unclear. The language, the sheer torrent of language, the at times incoherent rush to get things out remains his trademark. In *Luther*, he even uses Luther's constipation as a symbol for emotional and spiritual blockage and of the necessity of removing the block. Eventually it all has to come out, shit and all. The problem he has is finding a structure for the plays which can contain the verbosity. *Look Back in Anger* was a one-off, a young man sounding off to a series of dummies. In later work he flirted with other forms; *The World of Paul Slickey* and *Epitaph for George Dillon* before finding one almost completely successful structure in *The Entertainer* in which he almost invented the 'state of the nation' play a decade before a new wave of writers became almost fixated on it. By using the backdrop of the nude revue '*Nude Britannia*' as a totally realistic but also wholly symbolic backdrop he allowed Archie Rice to vent his rage and dismay in a context which gave it a breadth and meaning to which Jimmy Porter could never aspire. Again in *Inadmissible Evidence*, he used a dreamlike structure in which one is never quite sure what is real and what is inside Maitland's head as his world collapses to provide a context for what is

---

[40] Osborne's personal influence on Hare can be seen in Hare's funeral oration in 1994.

almost a stream-of-consciousness. Yet having probed these various dramatic forms, Osborne never really develops them further. They remain one-offs with the memory of the two huge individual performances they allowed, by Olivier and then Williamson, to some degree occluding the startling originality of the plays. Yet each time, Osborne retreats and, ultimately, is stuck in the stale realism of his last plays.

John Osborne's wider cultural importance is as ambiguous as his influence on theatre. He was in one sense, a swallow heralding spring, the break in the ice-jam. But in another, he was the last of the postwar old fogies, a role to which he swiftly relapsed along with nearly all the other angry young novelists. In 1972,he can be found grumbling about the negative impact entry into the Common Market will have on loveable, untidy old England. Jimmy Porter cries out that there are no good causes left just at the moment when in 1957, the Campaign for Nuclear Disarmament (CND) was beginning its Aldermaston marches and when the pressure for colonial independence was starting to gain a head of steam. Whatever its ultimate effect, CND was clearly a good cause, perhaps the best moral cause of the past half-century, something Osborne himself acknowledged by marching at least for a while under a Royal Court banner on the road from Aldermaston. Perhaps all that can be said is that for a time, maybe ten years, he was an icon, a living symbol of knee-jerk disobedience to normal deferential behaviour at just the moment when such deference was under attack. That may be his most lasting memorial.

The English Stage Company
The founding of the English Stage Company (ESC), set up in 1956 at the Royal Court Theatre, is often perceived as the key moment in postwar British theatre, though the moment tends to be confused and

sometimes regarded as identical to the *Look Back in Anger* moment discussed above. There is little that can be added to this perception; it is like all such accolades, largely self-fulfilling. If it was a key moment, however, then one thing is clear, it was key moment in the sense of focussing and heightening a shift that had gone on for some time before rather than representing any fundamental rupture with the past. The founding spirit of the ESC was George Devine, a man who laid his mark on British theatre in the 1950s though it is often unclear just how or why. In 1947, Devine had set up with Michel St Denis and Glyn Byam Shaw, the Old Vic Theatre Centre, at the original bomb-damaged home of the Old Vic in London's Waterloo Road.[41] Interestingly, Devine was in charge of the Children's Theatre there. The venture was not a success. It had acute financial problems and seems to have actually done very little. It was moved to an obscure location in the Dulwich High School for Girls in 1950 and closed in 1952 after the founding trio had resigned the previous year. After this, Devine worked as freelance director in opera at Sadlers Wells in London and drama with the Shakespeare Memorial Company. This work all had some state finance, albeit small, and one way of regarding Devine is as part of the small company of theatrical workers of the time who were largely disassociated from the commercial theatre and who were seeking to set up some alternative structure. It was in this spirit that in 1953 he wrote a memorandum with Tony Richardson, then working in television, on the need for a new theatre free of commercial constraints and able to develop the new kinds of drama to be seen on the Continent.

---

[41] The famous postwar Olivier/Richardson Shakespeare productions of the 'Old Vic' were actually put on at the New Theatre in the West End.

Such manifestoes calling for artistic change were not unusual. However this was different in that it contained detailed plans for a repertory, for budget, for a permanent company and for various kinds of training programmes. This last forms another component in Devine, the desire to raise the level of training in the theatre. As noted above, training for actors at the time was relatively rudimentary but in comparison with the absence of provision for designers and directors, it was almost abundant.

The two men set about putting these plans into concrete form, a process which took three years and had a number of false starts. Initially hoping to lease the Royal Court, they were set back by the very high annual rent demanded for the tenancy, some £70,000. The history of the Royal Court to that point was symbolic of the changes which had occurred in British theatre. It had become famous for the productions of Harley Granville Barker between 1904 and 1907, a highpoint of Edwardian new realism. However it was just outside the crucial golden circle of the West End on the edge of Chelsea, then a slightly seedy district with the reputation of being the haunt of artists and bohemians. It declined after the First World War and closed in 1932 for twenty years, failing even to survive in the usual transformation to a cinema. It was re-opened in 1952 by a former music-hall performer, Alfred Esdaille, who had some initial success there with revues and was convinced of its financial future.

The Devine/Richardson project was saved by its merging with another venture, initiated by Ronald Duncan, who had launched a literary festival in Devon in 1952 and who together with another group was trying to find a London base. The first key figure in this group was Neville Blond, a wealthy, rather left-wing, Manchester businessman, who became the chairman of the newly formed English Stage Company (ESC). The second key personality was Oscar Lewinstein, the General Manager of Alfred Esdaille, who would become one of a new line of West End producers, and who suggested that Devine be appointed Artistic Director of the ESC. Although the ESC at first tried to acquire the Kingsway Theatre, another of Esdaille's venues, it was bomb-damaged and too expensive to repair. Eventually, they returned to the Royal Court, this time with Esdaille on the Board of the ESC, and presumably at a more realistic rent. The first production, Angus Wilson's *The Mulberry Bush* (1955) opened in April, 1956.[42]

A number of features stand out from this saga. First, the venture was entirely private though philanthropic. The ESC did not receive any direct funding from the Arts Council until 1958/59 when it was awarded £5,500.[43] In this sense, the ESC was little different from the other pre-war repertory centres which had relied upon support from private donations. However, it did not rely wholly upon a single backer, instead Blond acted as the chief money-raiser and arm-twister. It needed such private backing. Early box-office was poor. The second production, Arthur Miller's *The Crucible*, played to only forty-five per cent box office. As the Royal Court was a small theatre—just four hundred seats after the gallery was closed—this meant that the weekly revenue would have barely paid the actors' wages.

---

[42] This brief summary is derived largely from Irving Wardle's key biography of Devine, *The Stages of George Devine*

[43] As a marker for this, Devine's initial salary was £1,500, the highest wage paid to the actors was £25/week and the rights to *Look Back in Anger* were purchased for £325. In other words, the Arts Council paid for about five or six of the company's actors out of an initial total of twenty-two.

In the years after it opening, the ESC opened new productions at a blistering pace—thirty-eight between 1957 and 1962, over six every year. These breakdown as follows:

Classics: 4 (inc. Wycherley, Ibsen, Chekhov and Shakespeare)

Foreign: 14 (inc. Ionesco (4), Beckett (4), Sartre (2), Genet, Faulkner, Albee, Williams and Brecht)

New British: 20 (inc. Wesker (5), Osborne (4), Jellicoe (2), Arden (2), Pinter (2), John, Hall, Coward, Simpson and Delaney)

One obvious feature of this list is the fascination with French Absurdism which had been a prominent feature of London small theatres in the first part of the decade. Outside this circle, in the first season, Devine had directed Brecht's *The Good Woman*[44] *of Setzuan*, the rights for which had been obtained after his visit to the Berliner Ensemble in 1955. Despite Devine's initial enthusiasm for Brecht, the production seems to have been decidedly shaky and the ESC returned to the better-known furrows of absurdism.

The second feature is the way in which Osborne and Wesker dominate the list of new British writers, the encouragement of which is so often said to have been the defining task of the early years of the ESC. They provide nearly half of the contributions from new writers while the remainder is a decidedly patchwork list. The two short Pinter pieces (*The Room* and *The Dumb Waiter*) shown as a double-bill in early 1960 are sandwiched between Pinter's debut with the *The Birthday Party* in 1958 and the *The Caretaker* in 1960.

---

[44] The correct translation is the *Good **Person**...* but Devine's mistranslation has largely stuck.

Both these were produced in West End theatres,[45] the first by Tennents, the second by Michael Codron whilst the double-bill itself was first seen in Bristol. Two years before the ESC production of her *The Lion in Winter* (1960), Shelagh Delaney had written *A Taste of Honey* for Theatre Workshop in 1958 from where it had transferred to the West End whilst Noel Coward was, of course, the most established West End writer of all.[46]

Thus Devine can fairly be described as discovering some seven playwrights in the first seven years of the ESC of whom only four (Osborne, Wesker, Arden and Jellicoe) can be said to have had any significant impact in the coming years. His support of Wesker was decidedly ambiguous, his first plays being banished to the newly-founded and local-authority supported repertory at Coventry. It was really the enthusiasm of his director, John Dexter, which supported Wesker in these years. To this record one should add the odd subsequent neglect of the Trinidadian writer, Errol John, whose *Moon on a Rainbow Shawl* (1958) won prizes for a first play and has since been recognised as a classic of Caribbean literature, but who wrote almost nothing for the theatre subsequently.[47]

The ESC at this time is really sitting uneasily between two worlds. Set up on the basis of private funding, it has a strong resemblance to many little theatre predecessors, putting on an eclectic mixture of foreign

---

[45] The venue for *The Birthday Party*—The Lyric, Hammersmith—was Tennents' try-out theatre and might be more accurately described as off-West End.

[46] Though the ESC production of his *Look After Lulu* (1959) was poorly received despite starring Vivien Leigh and Anthony Quayle.

[47] He wrote screenplays and acted in both Hollywood and for television.

plays, some classics and new work, hanging on the edge financially, occasionally getting in some star names prepared to work for low wages in an 'interesting' piece for a short run and, above all, hoping for a West End transfer to balance the books.

It also bears a strong resemblance to its illustrious predecessor—Granville Barker in the Edwardian era— in that it was appealing to a rather limited and very metropolitan audience, what we have described above as a grouping that *"was not really wider than the existing audience but was in fact focussed on an intellectual elite within that audience, an avant-garde whose number were small but whose tastes were 'discerning'."* Tynan's much-quoted comment on *Look Back in Anger* that it *"is likely to remain a minority taste. What matters is the size of the minority. I estimate it at roughly 6,733,000, which is the number of people in this country between the ages of twenty and thirty...I doubt if I could love anyone who did not wish to see 'Look Back in Anger'"*[48] is a fine and brave statement, a challenge. However it is also a touch credulous in its assumption that Tynan, who was himself pushing thirty at the time, was able to speak for these six or seven million people. What is apparent is that after this fanfare, Devine made no real effort to retain whatever impact had been made on the young of the time. Beckett in French, Faulkner, Ionesco and Sartre, plus Wycherley's *The Country Wife*, the bill for 1957, hardly amounts a bid for what was just becoming the first rock n' roll generation. Osborne's *The Entertainer* may have been more likely to attract a new audience with its inter-generational mix and its offbeat setting but the overall impression is essentially that of a small art-house.

---

[48] K.Tynan, *The Observer* 13 May 1956

This is not to suggest that Devine and his collaborators were doing no more than carry forward an old elitist view of the theatre. Like Osborne, the ESC was hung on a cusp, wanting to move forward into a new era but not really knowing how and certainly not having any real idea of how to generate any kind of popular audience. The Royal Court banner, much-photographed as it was carried on the Aldermaston marches[49], was not a publicity gag but a genuine involvement by people who identified with the left politics of the time. Osborne's superficial and soon-discarded left links should not obscure this. However only two of the Court's writers really tried to break out of the mould of past writing. Both would in their later activity try to reach out to new audiences though in different ways.

Ann Jellicoe wrote two, rather strange, plays for the ESC, *The Sport of My Mad Mother* (1958) and *The Knack* (1962), strange because in their unstructured almost formless mode they seem to be trying to find another form of dramatic expression. She then effectively decamped from mainstream London theatre and devoted herself to large-scale community theatre, a form which has pre-occupied her ever since.

The second was John Arden, whose play *Sergeant Musgrave's Dance* (1959) was the beginning, alongside *The Entertainer*, of a long line of work by many groups and writers on the condition of Britain. Using the symbol of the skeleton of a British soldier, killed in a colonial fracas and brought back to a strike-bound Lancashire town by a group of his comrades, it breaks out of its preceding structure in its final scenes as Musgrave swings his Gatling gun round to face the

---

[49] These were marches organised by the Campaign for Nuclear Disarmament for four days over Easter from the nuclear weapons plant at Aldermaston to London

audience and drags the audience into the play with his denunciation of colonialism and the audience's collective guilt in it. This scene together with Archie Rice's musical-hall patter in *The Entertainer* are the closest that the ESC comes in the period under consideration to break out of the naturalist theatrical forms that bind them outside second-hand French absurdism. Significantly, it they did not follow this absurdist path which so preoccupied the ESC but a kind of British Brechtian playwriting. Arden, together with his long-term collaborator Margaretta D'Arcy, having started in the conventional theatre then began a long process of withdrawal which led through the Royal Shakespeare Company and work with left-wing touring groups to virtual exile in Ireland. His last work, the extraordinary but almost unperformable (lasting as it does for twenty-four hours) *The Non-Stop Connolly Show* (1975) has had only one, largely amateur, full performance at Liberty Hall Dublin, the headquarters of the Irish Transport and General Workers Union.

The ESC then had produced not so much a breakthrough as a bridgehead, a focussing of an intent to change without a great appreciation of just what change was needed. This was becoming clear to some contemporary observers quite soon after the initial excitement of the new Royal Court. Even such an insider to the revolution as Tynan could only say in 1963 of London theatre that *"Apart from Wesker's **Chips with Everything**, the plays being presented [in 1961] were much the same as they had been in 1951. And that was more or less true a few months ago"* (Marowitz p.274). Tynan's pessimism was fairly general. Thus John Whiting in 1959: " *The struggle at the Royal Court and elsewhere, it would seem, was for the theatre to take on a greater social and political responsibility. Crying 'Forward', it is dwindling from* *our sight. Plays are being produced which rely for their effect on a false naivety. The problems they present are being simplified to appoint of non-existence...Socially, the whole way of thinking is out of date. And, I say this without malice, out of touch."* (Marowitz p.110) And in 1961 from Stuart Hall perhaps the foremost of the British New Left intellectuals, *"No* [British] *Brecht: no Arthur Miller: no Sartre. It is worthwhile beginning there. Things have been accomplished on the British stage which were never dreamt of in the philosophy of H.M.Tennent and Co, but it is necessary to say what has not happened...In spite of the windy reaches of Logue's **Antigone**, Bolt's rather flat intellectualism and Nigel Dennis's perverse academic card-trumping, British hostility to ideas has carried the day."* (Marowitz p.212) The focus of these comments is on the plays but lying behind them is the rather deeper question of just what is the point of having a revolution in a small theatre in Sloane Square when so little seems to be happening anywhere else. A few miles to the east at this time, another small theatre was collapsing under a set of problems which were in some ways similar to those of the Royal Court though a good deal more intense.

The premature dream

We last saw Theatre Workshop touring round small venues across Britain, touring being perhaps a rather too precise a word for their haphazard and often unpredictable progress round, to take a period of six months in 1946, a set of venues ranging from the Empire Dewsbury, the YMCA, Stockton-on-Tees, a number of amateur 'little' theatres, various miners' halls and the Butlin's Camp at Filey where they spent a week in May. The company had been reformed from its pre-war constituents in 1945 and had originally intended to base itself at Kendal under the auspices of a friendly Director of Education in the Borough Council. This fell through and for the next seven years the group followed this peripatetic life living off box-office returns, private patronage and a spirit of communal poverty. Their repertoire at this time included an adaptations of a Lorca (*Don Perlimplin*) and a Molière play (*The Flying Doctor*); a "ballad-opera" about a merchant seaman in the 1930s (*Johnny Noble*); and, perhaps the most extraordinary, *Uranium 235*, a play by Ewan MacColl about the atomic bomb with fifty-seven characters including a comic duo—Max Planck and Neils Bohr, two key scientists, digressing on quantum theory—sundry Atoms and a thuggish Energy. In 1947, they went on what became a series of tours in Continental Europe

Uranium 235 was very didactic, hectic and, possibly, vastly entertaining. Possibly, because there is almost no record, outside their chronicler, Howard Goorney, of just what these extended tours were actually like and what reception they received. It is an illustration of how lost theatre becomes at this time when one moves outside the critical circles of the West End. What is certainly true is that the work being done was aesthetically some decades in advance of anything else being produced in Britain at the time. This is demonstrated by the fact that in a time when the West End depended on foreign imports Theatre Workshop's main critical recognition in this period was abroad. Their production of *Richard II* in 1955 was received rapturously in Paris at an international festival despite the fact that, having no money to pay freight, they had taken the entire production as personal luggage on to the cross-Channel ferry. Harold Hobson, the revered critic of the *Sunday Times*, was able to write in 1956 that "*It is a pleasure to welcome Theatre Workshop into the West End...[it] has done more to raise the international reputation of Britain on the Continent than any of our most famous or chauvinistic actors or companies*"[50] whilst omitting to mention that, whilst he may have been pleased to see them in Paris or, possibly, Stockholm, he had steadily ignored their domestic performances for over a dozen years whilst, in the words of one chronicler of the period, they were having " *a wandering on-and-off sort of life in Wales, the industrial north and elsewhere*" (Taylor p.119) in between their foreign triumphs.

They received some domestic credit. In 1946 they were "offered the use of the east wing of Ormesby Hall by Lieutenant Colonel and Mrs Pennyman, after they had seen our performance of **Don Perlimplin** in the St. John's Hall, Middlesbrough" (Goorney p.54) It has to be supposed that their combination of humour, music, politics and simple but striking performance effects[51], struck some chords in the disparate audiences which they encountered. At various times, schemes to find a permanent home were explored. One of these was to take over the Library Theatre in Manchester, one of the few with any degree of local authority support, but these came to nothing until 1953.

Theatre Workshop is now renowned for having in 1953 finally been anchored to the decaying Theatre Royal in Stratford East, a part of London which still defies much in the way of urban regeneration. If the Royal Court, as it was when taken over by the ESC, was symbolic of the decay of 'intellectual theatre', the Theatre Royal, Stratford was symbolic of the virtual death of popular theatre. It had participated in the great days of melodrama when the East End of

---

[50] Harold Hobson, *Sunday Times*, 18 March, 1956
[51] An example of this was the use of a swaying light on a pole in a darkened stage to suggest a ship in a storm, claimed to have induced sea-sickness in some audiences.

London had possessed many such theatres, but, by 1953, was almost a wreck, requiring the personal efforts of the company to renovate though its space provided some of them with convenient lodgings. The decision to take up a lease on the Theatre Royal had not been taken without strife. One of their founders, Ewan MacColl, regarded it as abandoning their political commitment and had left, thus largely severing his direct relationship with the theatre. It was undertaken partly in the hope that the local council would assist with funding, a hope soon dashed.

The pace of Theatre Workshop in its early years verged on the mad. Thirty-six plays were put on in its first two years. In effect it almost adopted the practices of the much despised fortnightly repertory in its efforts to stay afloat financially. The company seems to have accepted this partly because it offered some relief from the gruelling round of one-night stands, perhaps partly because, as they literally lived in the theatre, leisure and work merged together. They were sustained by the weekly ration of seven and half free Abdullah cigarettes, provided in return for a programme note and carefully doled out by the company manager, an early example of business support for the arts. The repertoire of the company leaned heavily on classics with various plays by MacColl being almost the only new writing.

In terms of critical reception, their presence in London produced an early impact. The main papers began covering them and by 1955, Harold Hobson was comparing their production of *Richard II* with that running concurrently at the Old Vic. In 1956, *The Good Soldier Schweik* transferred to the West End and, although this particular transfer was a commercial failure, a pattern was set which persisted for the next few years of regular and financially life-saving commercial transfer. The next in the line was Behan's *The Quare Fellow* (1956) with its successor, *The Hostage* (1958) together with Delaney's *A Taste of Honey* (1958). This trio is often regarded as Theatre Workshop's defining achievement and as major contributions to the wave of new writers appearing at the end of the 1950s. Certainly *A Taste of Honey*, and to a lesser extent Behan's two works, have become classics in terms of their enduring popularity. Delaney's play can lay claim to being the most popular British play of the half-century in terms of revivals and playbook sales. It is, far more than *Look Back in Anger,* a play about youth and about the real hopes and fears of the time. However, regarding these plays as contributions to written drama is largely to miss the point with regard to the impact of Theatre Workshop on the development of British drama.

There remains some degree of vagueness, not to mention controversy, about the degree to which both Behan and Delaney actually 'wrote' the plays for which they are credited. Certainly they were developed in a collaborative way both with Littlewood and with the general company. Both authors were involved in the production process and there were more-or-less extensive rewrites undertaken. There were also elements introduced by way of music and movement in the course of this that were not present in the originals. Songs and jokes come and go in Behan's plays, both of which are essentially comedies, whilst in the original production of *A Taste of Honey* there was a jazz group onstage. None of the plays were 'musicals' in the normal sense of the term but neither were they straight naturalistic drama. All proved hard work for the censor to control as whilst they clearly contained unsavoury, possibly subversive, material (homosexuality, illegitimacy, religion, hanging, the IRA, royalty) much of the problem lay in innuendo, joke, song and a general irreverence rather straight-up script lines. It is also likely that the initial productions of Behan's work contained a degree of improvisation over and above the script.

The output of Theatre Workshop throughout the 1950s was enormously varied. Despite its reputation for new work, Littlewood had great respect for classic drama and a successful West End transfer was very likely to be followed by a Jacobean tragedy unperformed for three hundred years and possibly destined for a further period of scant recognition.[52] At the end of the decade, however, there was a sharp swing to musical productions possibly under the awareness that, if the desired local audience was to be persuaded to come, then some form of musical theatre had to be performed at least in tandem with the classic revivals. The first of these was Mankowitz' *Make Me an Offer* (1958) followed by Stephen Lewis' *Fings Ain't What They Used to Be* (1959) and the Norman/Bart musical *Sparrer's Can't Sing* (1960) all set in the East End and all destined for the West End. These were the first genuinely home-grown versions of the great American musicals and were the direct precursors to the one huge hit to rival them, *Oliver!* (though the Lionel Bart wagon was to lose its wheels with the unfortunate *Twang*). It is very relevant to note here that although Theatre Workshop is sometimes remembered for the actors it produced perhaps its greatest lasting impact in terms of people was its two designers, Sean Kenny and John Bury. Kenny's later use of stage machinery and John Bury's design for the Royal Shakespeare's *Wars of the Roses* were turning points not just for design as such but for the whole way in which theatre was subsequently, and quite literally, visualised. This

---

[52] In 1959, *Fings Ain't Wot They Used To Be* was followed by Marston's *The Dutch Courtesan*.

was a rather unexpected, though with hindsight quite natural, development of the devotion to lighting and visual atmosphere which could be seen in its peripatetic beginnings. At the Royal Court, the influence of Jocelyn Herbert had been to strip away naturalistic sets and move towards rather bare box-like enclosures focussing on actors and text. Theatre Workshop also moved decisively away from naturalism but, so it turned out, more in the direction of effect and visual impact. These two, oddly complementary, trends were key elements in the later shifts in British theatre.

Despite all this apparent success, by 1960 Theatre Workshop was sinking. It received a public grant of little more than an eighth of the £16,000 it was said to need in annual operating costs, a sum which itself illustrates its desperate poverty. The small size of the house meant that it could never hope to run solely on box-office receipts so the West End transfer was its only route to financial survival though this was precarious. Goorney states (Goorney p.116) that if two West End transfers ran for a year then Stratford would get £9,000 in extra revenue. It says something for the shifts which were taking place in commercial theatre that by the end of the 1950s, there were a number of producers willing to take chances with its productions, notably Oscar Lewenstein, but at the same time, the need to adapt to their standards had to mean a change in the underlying basis of the company's work. The policy of paying actors the same meagre basic wage when in the West End was soon abandoned and, reasonably enough, few of these returned. There was also a shift in its underlying values. *Fings Ain't Wot They Used to Be* was a clever and genuine effort to portray the Cockney community around the theatre but it also contained a good deal of the mock Cockney which delighted West End audiences. (*They've turned our local palais/Into a bowling alley/Fings ain't wot they used to be*) It was funny and catchy and hit the right buttons but, as Littlewood probably knew, was not the whole story of East End life.

In 1961, Littlewood walked out, ostensibly to travel to Nigeria, but essentially because she could no longer cope with the erosion of her ideal. She had developed plans for a bold multi-arts centre in the community, a "university of the streets" which would allow participation in all forms of artistic activity. The fact that this concept was reduced to being Littlewood's 'Fun Palace' suggests that little had shifted in the eyes of the great and the good since Lord Keynes decisive rejection of W.E.Williams' ideas for arts centres, and the project foundered on delays both over planning permission and funding. Littlewood returned, once, to the British stage[53] in 1963 and that was to produce the climactic show of our period. She was not only the best director of the time, she was also the best organiser of a theatre (in conjunction of course with Gerry Raffles) with an extraordinary ability to encourage talent. She had a vision of theatre which transcended its simple artistic intent and engaged with a much wider cultural role. There are a few 'might-have-beens' in postwar British theatre and she is without question the greatest. Inside a decade, community arts centres were being funded all over the country and community theatre was an accepted objective. What might have happened if Littlewood had been allowed to engage with that change is impossible to say. She was, so it was said, a 'difficult woman' and was allowed to drift away while a great number of 'difficult men' were given every chance.

---

[53] It is best to ignore her ill-judged return to Stratford East in the 1970s when she believed that her precious theatre was under threat.

Oh! What a Lovely War seems to have happened almost by chance. During a temporary return to Stratford, Littlewood was taken with a recording of Bud Flanagan singing songs of the First War and set about developing a show based on them. The result was a collaborative process between Littlewood, Charles Chilton (who is normally given formal credit for the show), Raffles and the resident company. Its form is that of a pastiche musical, a show given by pierrots on a seaside pier who become, variously, soldiers and generals and the soldier's families. It has no plot save that of the war itself whose casualties were spelt out on a signboard as the show progressed. It is, however, perfectly cohesive with a beginning, a middle and an end; the end being Victor Spinetti speaking about the ever-continuing fact of war and saying "Goodnight" to the audience.

In its confusion as to exactly in what genre of theatre it belonged[54] and its explicit politicisation, *Oh! What a Lovely War* points decisively to the future and marks rupture with the past the past in a way not really achieved by any production that went before. This, it needs to remembered, was a time when men still doffed their hats they normally wore to the Cenotaph in Whitehall as they passed and when Earl Haig, the son of the British general mercilessly lampooned in the show, presided over the Remembrance Day parades when still able-bodied veterans of the First War displayed their medals. It also engaged the audience as a self-conscious exercise in its own form of remembrance. At one moment, the pierrots after singing a sweet, sentimental song as they are shipped off to Verdun come down to front-stage and baa at the audience as lambs to the slaughter. The entire skill of

---

[54] It is, of course, a musical but many surveys of the period regard it as a 'play'.

eighteen years of company work came together in one single, chilling piece of bravura theatre.

The influence of the show was both immediate and diffuse. It transferred to the West End and is still widely revived by both amateur groups and by such as the RSC. In a wider way, it is unlikely, for example, that Peter Brook could ever have produced *US* (1965), an RSC show about the war in Vietnam, without it. It was, after all, the only occasion in which Brook acknowledged the existence of an audience. Its style spread throughout British theatre at a moment when it was just beginning an explosive growth. In its wider effects, it showed that serious drama could be mixed with music and comedy to deadly effect and that popular theatre did not have to lack intellectual bite. It is the best moment to leave this uneasy time.

Conclusion

At the beginning of this section, three separate crises of the British theatre were identified; financial, cultural and aesthetic. By 1963, only one of these had been in any sense resolved. Aesthetically, the rigid hold of Edwardian naturalism had been broken though not yet decisively. This is an achievement which can be laid largely at the doors of the two companies working in small, redundant London theatres and it was a major advance. Both in terms of content and form, the range of dramatic presentation had been enlarged enormously though this may not have been readily apparent at the time. There had not been any one dominant breakthrough; instead there had been a series of piecemeal movements which added up to major change. It is hard, except for the one show mentioned above, to point to any one production which was a real breakthrough either in form or content though several nibbled at the various edges of conformity. With hindsight, one can see that some of the prominent writers of the period, notably Osborne, Wesker and Pinter had reached almost as far as they were ever going to go in terms of dramatic form though others, notably Arden and Jellicoe, had scarcely begun to scratch the surface of their future work. The major breakthrough in drama remained the American musical, something which had begun as early as 1948 with *Oklahoma!* and had scarcely begun to have its full affect. 'Epic' theatre remained as little more than a phrase from a theorist's notebook whilst a full integration of dramatic effect, visual, aural and verbal, was rarely even attempted. It is characteristic of the period, that Peter Brook, soon to be seen as the most experimental mainstream director of the 1960s, had spent the 1950s doing rather conventional work[55] in the West End and at Warwickshire Stratford. As noted above, in the early 1960s, there was a tangible sense of disappointment with what had been achieved. Even so, it can be seen now that the seeds of much that was to come over the next decade was sown though yet to come into focus.

The major unresolved problems lay in the other spheres, financial and cultural which had shown very little change since the war. In particular, the financial crisis which was engulfing the theatre in the late-1940s was, if anything, intensifying. The closure rate of theatres had slowed in terms of numbers but in proportionate terms may have got even larger. In Leicester, for example, which had had three theatres in 1945, there were none at all in 1963. It has been noted that the formation during the war of what was in effect a cartel, the Group, had to a degree stabilised the

---

[55] Rebellato's survey of 1950s theatre has five references to Peter Brook. Two of these comment on how well-known he was while the other three quote from his writing. Anouilh's *Ring Around the Moon*, Olivier in *Titus Andronicus* and Gielgud in *The Tempest* are his most-referenced pieces in the decade.

national structure and had certainly sustained the West End. However, the Group had over the years decayed, both because of internal splits and from objective external factors notably the larger profits to be found in television. The gravy-train of the big musicals had continued but was showing signs of the decline which was to occur rapidly after 1965 and no replacement had been found. Competition from the cinema had, rather surprisingly, levelled off but only because it too had come under pressure from another entertainment medium, television. In some ways, television may have initially rather aided the theatre in that it was common in the fifties for television drama to consist of theatre plays shown from the venue itself, an obvious second-best which may have enticed some people to actually see the real thing. It is often noted that it was the publicity given to *Look Back in Anger* by a television broadcast which turned the tide of its box-office returns. But by the beginning of the sixties, television was developing its own drama, sometimes tackling topics ahead of the theatre and certainly attracting new writing talent.

Financially, the efforts to sustain both the English Stage Company and Theatre Workshop by private sponsorship and West End transfers was failing, both in strict financial terms and also aesthetically. The attrition on Stratford East proved fatal but even at the better resourced ESC it is possible to see the strains. Its output became notably more benign as the need to attract star actors and use material orientated to the West End became more obvious. It was noted above that the seeds of aesthetically new forms of theatre were sown in the 1950s but that these failed to make any clear breakthrough. It is tempting to equate this with the nature of funding in the period though of course any direct linkage is impossible. Yet it is difficult to believe that the Peter Brook who spent the

1950s directing star-vehicle Shakespeare and West End boulevard plays suddenly acquired new artistic vision when he joined the new Royal Shakespeare Company in 1963. The *Marat/Sade* (1964), *US* (1965) and *A Midsummer's Night Dream* (1968) are all remembered to this day as landmark *productions* whilst his *Titus Andronicus* is remembered mainly for Olivier's bravura performance.

The difficulty in making any clear connection between new drama and state support is shown by the fact that the subsidy given in this period went mainly to the Old Vic, the Shakespeare Memorial Theatre in Stratford and one or two provincial repertory companies. None of these showed any inclination towards new forms of drama with the partial exception of the Bristol Old Vic which put on some of the shows later showcased at the Royal Court. The one new theatre of the period, the Belgrade in Coventry built by the local authority who continued to support it, did put on several innovative productions including the first plays of Wesker but hardly to the extent that it broke any mould.

The broad cultural position of the theatre had improved during the fifties in that it was no longer seen as such an enclosed coterie revolving around the whims of Binkie Beaumont. The publicity given to the 'angry young men' of the Royal Court was in itself some guarantee of that. However this did not go very far. It should be remembered that although Osborne may have been the most flamboyant member of this exclusive set, the remainder of the club were all novelists including, for example, Braine, Amis, Waine and Wilson. In 1958, Kenneth Allsop wrote a book on what he termed, rather prematurely, the 'angry decade'. This mentions one other playwright apart from Osborne—Nigel Dennis whose 'anger' barely registered even then. In a concluding chapter, Allsop lists about a dozen young writers who he presumes are likely to carry forward the mood of the decade; none is a playwright. This illustrates the fact that throughout the 1950s, the dominant progressive culture was essentially literary. Novelists and to some extent poets were seen as the main forces in cultural change with film and even television as the media of the future. The revolution which is now sometimes claimed for theatre in the second half of the decade seemed at the time something of a minor shift in a relatively unimportant art-form.

This attitude continued into the following decade. In 1964, Stuart Hall and Paddy Whannel wrote the first book on what would shortly become a new academic genre of cultural studies. It now seems a rather dated work but at the time it was path-breaking in its attempt to classify and analyse cultural forms across their full spectra without making any initial assumptions about relative merits. Its success in this is arguable but its main interest here is that theatre is virtually ignored. A couple of plays are mentioned in a list of popular literature suggested by Hall and Whannel as good examples of literary work suitable for secondary school study but their role as pieces of theatre is ignored.

In short, in the early 1960s, British theatre still hung in the wind, an isolated cultural form whose future was in doubt and whose wider impact was still minimal.

The Sixties and Seventies

Introduction

The previous chapter had a rather simple, linear form; a story of the continuing decline of regional theatre, of a London West End hanging grimly on to the fortunate gold-mine of American musicals in the midst of general decay and of two, small and hard-pressed metropolitan theatres which provided almost all that was theatrically new, at least in the British theatre, in the eighteen years covered. In the final year of the period, 1963, one of those theatres effectively folded under its long drawn-out financial crisis whilst the last of the great US musicals, *Cabaret* (1966), would arrive shortly afterwards. It is interesting to juxtapose *Cabaret* with *Oklahoma!*, the first of the long line, and to see in it the arrival of new era in cultural expression, abandoning the hopeful American vitality of the latter with an enervated, European cynicism summed up in one of its central song, *Money, money, money. Oklahoma!* has been aptly characterised by Knapp as forming a key part in a cultural reinvention of story of the USA after several tough decades. In particular it elides those parts of American history which are unresolved, specifically the destruction of native Americans and the 1930s dustbowl and focuses on conflicts which end in harmony. *Cabaret* deals with another part of the American heritage, its relationship with Europe. An American man and an English woman[56] meet in a Berlin night-club and work through

---

[56] In the film version, these roles are swapped to allow Liza Minelli to play Sally Bowles. Several other crucial changes are also made including the inclusion of a redemptory scenario of the secretly Jewish Fritz admitting this to win Natalia. In the stage version, the Aryan woman Schneider rejects marriage to the

a tangled relationship with a background of the rise of Nazism. Devised with explicit consciousness of the then current civil-rights movement in the USA (Knapp p.240) it finishes with its conflicts not only unresolved but with the American virtually stranded in an increasingly hostile world. Just how conscious Kander and Ebb, the show's creators, were of the way in which this could be seen as symbolising American global isolation during the Vietnam war is uncertain. But Cabaret was certainly the least successful of the big Broadway musicals of the early sixties.[57] The popular American musical had moved into difficult territory and, both artistically and financially, it was suffering. The mother-lode of the gold-mine had been almost worked out.

Theatre had survived, just, the impact of the cinema at the cost of shedding a great deal of its central popular appeal, its music, its fun, its variety. It was with hindsight about to face up to a challenge which might have damaged it mortally in its remaining heart—the realist drama—that of television. In the decades after 1963, television was to have a complex relationship with the theatre, particularly with writers. Some, like Dennis Potter, committed themselves wholly to the new medium whilst others such as Alan Plater, devoted most of their best efforts to it. A few, such as David Mercer and, to a degree, Trevor Griffiths, moved back and forth with equal facility. One of the most interesting and influential was John McGrath, who made a reputation as a theatre writer with *Events*

Jewish man, Herr Schultz. Sally Bowles' abortion is also obscured in the film. Overall, the stage version is much darker and more unresolved than the film.

[57] It ran for 1,165 performances compared with *Hello Dolly!* (1964) at 2,844, *Funny Girl* (1964) with 1,348, *Fiddler on the Roof* (1964) 3,242, *Man of La Mancha* (1965) 2,328 and *Mame* (1966) 1,508. (Kenrick)

While Guarding a Bofors Gun (1966), had worked in television writing with *Z-Cars* in 1962 and also wrote film scripts before making a decisive and influential shift to theatre.

The fact that the theatre not only survived the challenge of television but actually, in cultural terms, achieved its own golden age to an extent which rather overshadowed the achievement of television drama is a mark of the shifts which took place within it and which are the subject of this chapter.

The shifts are not simple. There will no longer be any single linearity in theatrical change of the kind which seemed to exist in the 1950s. In itself, this apparent simplicity can now be seen as a signal of the paucity of drama in the period. The 1960s heralded a return to a much more varied theatrical tradition. The chapter is broken into sections which run alongside each other and overlap in complex ways. People cross-over, there are multiple influences back and forth; there is a sense in which theatre remains an indivisible whole and dividing it into sections is misleading yet at the same time new theatrical genres did separate out. (One such important development, the role of drama in education is discussed in the next chapter to preserve its own chronology). One fundamental reason for the complexity is that throughout this period the decline in the actual number of theatres was halted and then reversed. Some thirty new theatres were built up to 1975 following the opening of the Belgrade in Coventry in 1958, the first new theatre in the U.K. since the war, and a number of old commercial venues were reconstituted as subsidised repertory houses. At the top, so to speak, of the pyramid, the National Theatre would finally open its three theatres on the South Bank in 1977 whilst the RSC moved into the Barbican in 1982. As significant as these headline events was a vast proliferation of venues not regarded as theatres but as places where theatre was performed. By 1978, there were 140 arts centres throughout Britain whilst there were estimated (Itzin (1979)) to be around 200 other venues where touring theatre companies performed plus uncounted streets and impromptu sites for theatrical events. In a very important way, theatre reverted to something like its position two hundred years before with a number of big, fixed, performance sites and a much larger number of places where various kinds of drama could, on occasion, be seen. As a consequence, any appraisal of the period cannot be confined to simply a handful of theatres.

A second reason is that during this period, the definition of what constitutes theatre shifts in ways which remain confusing and ambiguous. Roland Muldoon, one of the founders of CAST (Cartoon Archetypical Slogan Theatre) in 1965, is reported (Itzin (1980) p.14)[58] as saying that, when Peter Brook came to see them, he used to ask for the origins of their style as though seeking some theatrical reference. Muldoon claims that rather than theatre, their influences were Chuck Berry and Little Richard, that they were the first pop culture theatre group. Muldoon also came out of Unity Theatre and the long tradition of militant socialist theatre but at this moment in the mid-1960s it is certainly arguable that art schools and rock-and-roll were the major cultural influences in Britain and it shows in the way that almost without warning the boundaries of conventional theatre suddenly expanded. It is as though the cultural straightjacket which had been placed on theatre for several decades broke and its practitioners were

---

[58] This is an indispensable guide to the period discussed here and is used here sometimes without full referencing.

allowed to acknowledge that all around them there existed parallel forms in music and visual art which, until that moment, might as well have been on another planet.

And as ever the great influence of the period was money and, in particular, the new channels through which it began to flow.

Money

In the previous section, the issue of money was dominated by the steady decline of commercial theatre, the dominant force in British theatre. As we have described, although there was a brief flurry of *interest* in public funding for the theatre in the immediate aftermath of the war, this led to virtually nothing. The Arts Council of Great Britain was set up in 1946 and given a minute Treasury grant but even within this small budget, interest in supporting the theatre was negligible. In 1957, the Arts Council grant stood at just under £900,000 of which £69,692 0s 7d went to drama compared with £650,318 spent on music, opera and ballet including £302,000 to the Royal Opera House (Elsom p.137) whose grant was, uniquely, hypothecated by the famously music-loving Treasury. The tiny amount for drama was parcelled out in thirty-six projects, the largest being £12,000 to the Old Vic. Other recipients included Birmingham Repertory (£5,000), Bristol Old Vic, (£2,000), the Belgrade Coventry (£5,686) and Theatre Workshop (£1,000). One can visualise the scale of such funding by placing it against what would then have been a working wage; it would have funded the employment of less than a hundred people.

Throughout the whole of the 1950s, the Arts Council was little more than a well-meaning pressure group for the artier wing of commercial theatre. Its biggest achievements were, first, in the postwar period, the support it gave to some managements in getting tax-breaks and then, in 1957, being a successful lobby to get Entertainment Tax abolished. However, towards the end of the 1950s, its role began to shift. The most obvious sign of this was the report it published in two parts in 1959 and 1961 *"Housing the Arts in Great Britain"* This essentially surveyed the lamentable situation of the theatre[59] in Britain outside London and concluded, essentially, that theatre was in some danger of ceasing to exist unless some major effort was undertaken to reverse the trend. Shortly afterwards funding for drama began to increase rather sharply to climb resolutely upwards for over a decade. In addition to this increasing level of central funding, local authorities at last began to use the financial leeway granted them in the 1948 Act and to support local theatres. In the decade of the 1960s and into the 1970s, local authorities financed along with the Arts Council the construction of several dozen theatres (the exact number really depends upon when a theatre becomes an arts centre. together with renovation of a number of existing theatres which had been effectively abandoned by the commercial theatre which had originally built them. At the end of the 1960s, the major commercial operations, Howard & Wyndham and Moss' Empires, had effectively given up on theatre outside London and had an open policy of selling off their remaining provincial houses to local councils.

There were a wide variety of strategies adopted to finance all this. Nottingham council used a pot of money which had been acquired in the nationalisation of Nottingham's municipal gasworks back in 1948 whilst Hammersmith used the planning laws to require

---

[59] Provision for music and the visual arts was also surveyed but theatre dominated the report.

that a renovated Lyric be maintained within a large office development which shrouded the theatre. But, however achieved, the result was that by the 1970s, the centrepiece of live performance in most towns and cities including London had become a subsidised venue which could not survive without such state support. Outside the West End, commercial theatre became almost wholly subsidiary not to say vestigial compared to these venues. In 1967, a report commissioned by the Arts Council and conducted by a wide-ranging panel concluded *"Outside London the theatre of private enterprise is on its last legs, physically run-down and morally disheartened"* (Arts Council (1970) p.11)

This shift is fairly easy to describe. What is less easy is to explain just *why* it happened at *that* moment, particularly as at a previous moment when public funding had seemed to be about to take off in the late-1940s it had so signally failed. Inevitably, any analysis has to be partly speculative and certainly complex given that several factors were involved. However, five underlying factors can be isolated.

First, one must give some credit to the 'buzz' given to drama by the Royal Court and Theatre Workshop. The importance of the new wave of theatre from these two companies may have been exaggerated by the more excitable of its adherents, who after all had a very strong personal stake in talking it up, but it in the small world of the 'chattering classes' (an even smaller group in 1960 than now), drama had acquired a rather higher cultural profile at least in London.

Second and in rather constructive contradiction to this was the collapse of the theatre outside London. The quantitative basis of this was spelled out in *Housing the Arts*. (Arts Council (1959)) At the end of the 1940s, a count of theatrical venues in Great Britain amounted to 520 houses, a number admitted to have been a rough estimate given the uncertainty which then prevailed as to the actual use of some places. In 1960, the officials of the Arts Council counted a total of 224 venues in England outside London of which 50 were mainly in use as cinemas and a further 85 were only used for summer shows. The English seaside resort was still in full flower and, for example, Great Yarmouth could sustain seven summer shows and Scarborough six. London contributed a further 45 houses and Scotland about eight though no one seems to have been too bothered about an exact count there. Wales was almost entirely bereft of professional theatre outside of its seaside resorts with their summer variety shows. Thus on the broadest count, the number of theatres seems to have almost halved in one decade. Of those remaining, about 18% already received some kind of public subsidy. The growth of the overseas package holiday would shortly take a scythe to British resorts so that by the end of a further decade, there seem to have been more commercial theatres in London than in the rest of the country, something not seen for at least two hundred years. The Arts Council survey made for its 1970 report on the state of theatre (Arts Council 1970)) was not as detailed as that made in 1960 and there seems to have been some confusion as to what exactly constituted a 'commercial' theatre. Hugh Beaumont supplied a list of 23 provincial houses but Derek Salberg of Birmingham's Alexandra Theatre, one of handful of independent houses, discusses 31 venues in some detail.[60] The differences may just be a matter of timing as in 1968, when this work was being done, the remaining commercial houses were either being sold to local councils or

---

[60] Archives of the Arts Council, Victoria and Albert Museum, ACGB/38/36(1)

turned over to bingo. In a sense, the rise of public funding was a last-ditch response to commercial collapse. A comparison between the new-found excitement about the 'new' drama around Sloane Square and the effective collapse of provincial theatre suggested to the highly centralised cultural mandarins of England that 'something had to be done'.

To these two factors specific to the theatre, can be added a rather more general belief at the end of the 1950s that the general level of 'culture' in Britain was under serious threat. This was not, of course, a new complaint. T.S.Eliot had prophesied the end of culture as he knew it a decade before and, as noted in the previous chapter, the basic theme had been taken up by Hoggart in the mid-1950s in his hugely influential *The Uses of Literacy* though from a quite different direction, the decline of a specifically working-class culture. The mixing of these two, really quite different, strands produced by the end of the decade an almost universal disdain for mass popular culture which extended, politically, from left to right. Arnold Wesker, a staunch man of the left, put a coruscating critique into the mouth of Beattie in *Roots*:

> *So you know who came along? The slop singers and the pop writes and women's magazines and the Sunday papers and the picture strip love stories...*
>
> *The whole stinkin' commercial world insults us and we don't care a damm. Well Ronnie's right—it's our own bloody fault. We want the third-rate—we got it*
>
> *(Wesker p.148)*

In *The Trilogy*, Ronnie is often identified as Wesker himself and there is no doubt that, based on his subsequent actions, Beattie's diatribe is Wesker's own view of the his contemporary culture. In the theatre, as

Lacey puts it, *"The solution to the problem is one that gained ground as the fifties moved into the sixties, the classically welfarist one of a 'middle-brow' culture based on government sponsored theatres."* (Lacey p.84)

However, these three factors of themselves do not add up to a complete explanation of why at this point in time, a decision seems to have been taken to rescue the theatre. The two other, more general, issues need to be added in.

The first of these was the beginnings of the uneasy feeling that pervaded British economic policy in this period that Britain was falling behind Europe and Japan in economic growth. Continental Europe had emerged from the war almost on its knees economically. However from the late-1950s onwards it became increasingly clear that the economic situation in countries such as France, Germany, the Netherlands, Sweden and Italy as well as Japan had moved beyond reconstruction and into a phase of economic dynamism which greatly surpassed that of the United Kingdom. This sense of economic malaise intensified through the 1960s and became focussed in the following decade on a series of major industrial struggles. However at the earlier period, there was a good deal more interest in remedial measures and in particular the adoption of the various kinds of state planning which, it was believed, had been responsible for the economic transformation of continental Europe and, increasingly, Japan. There was a big shift in the economics profession in the 1950s towards quantitative methods such as input-output analysis and large-scale econometric models of the national economy given that Keynesian theory seemed to have provided theoretical tools for guiding economic growth. There was great interest in state institutions such as IRI in Italy and the Ministry for Trade and Industry in Japan and in the use made of so-called indicative planning particularly in France and the Netherlands. In their various ways, such state intervention appeared to offer a 'third-way' between the rigid central planning of the Communist countries, which although at that time had the appearance of economic success also had unacceptable political dimensions, and the uncontrolled free-market capitalism of the USA and Britain which seemed to offer relative economic stagnation. The irony is that both Britain and the USA achieved economic growth rates in the 1950s which now seem like a golden age. However, continental Europe and Japan achieved notably higher growth and this came to matter politically.

Various kinds of planning and state intervention in failing economic sectors were widely discussed and culminated in the National Plan prepared by the Wilson government after its election in 1964 along with a wide range of initiatives developed by such as the new Ministry of Technology and various state/business agencies. Nationalisation of major sectors such as steel came back on to the agenda whilst it became commonplace for the state to provide various kinds of cash injection to support pilot projects and start-ups and general research and development in what were seen as the new technological industries.

It all ended in disaster. Whatever the merits of the continental systems, Britain possessed neither the political will nor the social structures to emulate them. The cash handouts passed through industry without discernable result, the National Plan collapsed under the weight of its own grandiloquence and Treasury hostility whilst the trade unions refused to accept any kind of limitations on their role. Although the Labour governments of the decade were the most dynamic in social terms of the entire century[61], their economic policies went uniformly awry. However, in one small corner its efforts proved notable successful.

The sums of money were, of course, derisory even by the standards of the day. However seen as an exercise in indicative state planning, in the provision of cash injections to support new initiatives in a failing industry and in the formation of new enterprises based on central government/municipal/private sector partnerships of a new kind, the expansion of funding by the Arts Council was a notable success. The turning point can be seen in *Housing the Arts in Great Britain* published in 1959 and 1961. Up to this date, Arts Council funding, such as it was, was essentially confined to limited support for a few houses which, almost by tradition, were regarded as the core of classic British theatre. The number of these had gradually increased through the 1950s but the level of public subsidy never seems to have become a dominant source of funding. In terms of their output, one would almost certainly find that Shakespeare occupied the pole position in terms of authorship and it would be no surprise if Chekhov came in at number two. They were, in other words, seen as the guardians of a small and very particular slice of culture, one which ranked with the performance of Beethoven symphonies and Verdi operas though at a markedly lower financial cost.

---

[61] Legalising to a degree abortion and homosexuality; abolishing the death penalty and theatre censorship; pushing for comprehensive secondary education and expansion of universities; easing divorce laws; introducing laws against racial and gender discrimination—all contributed to pulling Britain into the twentieth century.

The shift marked by *Housing the Arts* was that theatre was seen as a national industry in need of state intervention to secure its future in the face of increasing competition. It was marked by the kind of confident quantitative assertions about industrial development which were the hallmark of indicative planning, in this case that all towns over 70,000 population could support a properly managed repertory theatre and laid out a blueprint for theatre construction over the succeeding fifteen years. (The belief that this was the cut-off size for support of a repertory theatre seems to have come from a somewhat back-of-the-envelope calculation by Charles Landstone in 1950 published by the Arts Council as *Notes on Civic Theatres*. It rested on the assumption that only 3% of a town's population could be persuaded to go to the theatre regularly though this might rise to 6% in decent places like *"Salisbury, Colchester and Guildford"*.)[62] The core of its proposals was that the Arts Council should be able to provide funds for theatre construction matched by local authority grants of an equal size together with some level of operational support thereafter. The option of full state support, essentially nationalisation, was never on the cards except for the perpetually uncertain status of the National Theatre but there was a clear shift from status as a patron to that of a planner. The shift was decisive but required support from other quarters to succeed. As in other parts of the efforts to introduce this form of state intervention, the private sector failed rather dismally to enter into the bargain. Apart from a few isolated examples—Pilkington's in St Helens and I.C.I. on Teesside—business sponsorship

---

[62] Jumping ahead of the story: recent audience surveys suggest that the figure is now closer to 20%.

was extremely limited.[63] However, a third element in the package did provide much of the required funds— local councils.

Economic development in the sixties was marked nationally by the failed efforts at national planning and, locally, by the last great period of civic expansion in British history and this forms the fifth element in the reasons for the decisive shift in funding from 1960 onwards. The example had been set by Coventry which in 1958 had opened the Belgrade Theatre, the first new theatre in the country since the war. Coventry, whose town centre had been almost obliterated in a night's bombing, had embarked upon an ambitious programme of redevelopment which included a new cathedral, the first pedestrian shopping precinct in the country as well as the large new theatre. The Belgrade took its name from a donation of fine wood from the Yugoslav government and used to panel the walls. It was notable not so much for its stage but for the large foyer, restaurant and bar areas intended for use in the day as a civic amenity as well as for the flats, some intended for theatre workers, also included in the development In later years, Coventry Council may have been less generous in its operational support of the theatre its had founded (in 1968, it paid out £12,750 in subsidy but charged the theatre £14,484 in rent) (Arts Council (1970) p.76) but its initial foundation was on a grand scale.

By 1961 when the Arts Council made its survey, this kind of civic redevelopment incorporating a new theatre was well underway with towns as diverse as Birmingham, Torquay, Croydon, Leicester and

---

[63] In 1958/59, the biggest private supporter of theatre was TV with £5500 nationally. Other commercial sources amounted to less than £2000 apart from £6429 from Whitbreads for the Old Vic (Archives ACGB/38/2)

Nottingham having advanced plans for new theatres built as part of city-centre development, often as part of a new Civic Centre. (Arts Council (1959) vol.2 p.93) Even in Chichester where a new Festival Theatre was, uniquely, being funded on the basis of local private patronage, the local authority played a crucial role in providing a site at a peppercorn rent.

City centre developments of the 1960s with their tendency towards 'new brutalism' in architectural style and an often cavalier treatment of old quarters have not received much in the way of lasting acclamation, often being lumped in with municipal tower blocks as planning disasters. However for the theatre, the sudden civic enthusiasm for incorporating a new theatre into their development plans along with a sports centre, a pedestrian precinct and a new town hall was a lasting and possibly saving boon. Theatres became a symbol of civic virtue in much the same way as art galleries were in the late nineteenth century. In 1960, civic theatres were not entirely new. Outside London, there were about fifty-five regular repertory theatres in Great Britain. In England, eight of these were owned by local councils together with one in Scotland.[64] However, civic expenditure on theatre was very low. Liverpool, for example, gave nothing to theatre in its entertainment budget of over £47,000, all of which went to subsidising music even though the 6d rate allowed for this purpose under the 1948 Act

---

[64] Canterbury, Cheltenham, Chesterfield, Colchester, Coventry, Hornchurch, Manchester and Northampton in England and the Citizens in Glasgow. The English focus is on small southern towns beginning with 'C'. It is interesting that there was a bias towards municipal funding in Conservative rather than Labour towns.

would have raised £242,718.[65] (Arts Council (1959) vol.2 p.49) Manchester Corporation actually made an operating profit out of its Library Theatre, built underneath the central library, whilst providing nearly £25,000 aid to local music. In general, large cities supported their orchestras but ignored theatres. The shift towards providing funds for drama during the 1960s is all the more marked because of this previous total neglect.

After 1965, civic funds for new or reconstructed theatres were assisted by Arts Council funds under the Housing the Arts programme, an initiative which provided over £2 million between 1965 and 1971 to over fifty new or reconstructed theatres plus another £328,000 to a further forty arts centres most of which would have had some provision for performance. However, given that between 1957 and 1971, the Arts Council counted 82 *"major new buildings, conversions or reconstructions"* devoted largely to the theatre plus a further 22 under construction or at an advanced planning stage (Arts Council (1970) p.56), it is clear that civic funding plus local appeals provided most of the capital for this expansion. The cost of these projects would have varied very widely with a large new theatre climbing up to the half million pound level. However most of the 82 major projects would have been in six figures and only three Housing the Arts grants ever exceeded £100,000.[66] To this list of civic theatres one could add the National Theatre

---

[65] The Arts Council made a point of calculating the exact amount which councils could spend on subsidising the arts as a way of emphasising just how little they actually did.

[66] Bromley's Library Theatre received £118,000, Bristol's Theatre Royal, £140,000 and the new Crucible Theatre in Sheffield, £300,000. The diversity of these large grants suggests that the scale of Arts Council involvement owed much to chance and, probably, astute lobbying.

itself which in 1961 appeared once again to have run into the buffers when the then Chancellor of the Exchequer, Selwyn Lloyd, announced that no state money would be allocated for the much-delayed project. It was saved by the London County Council which pledged more than half the necessary capital funds as well as providing the South Bank site rent-free. This expansion in theatre building was far in excess of Arts Council expectations in 1961 when it commented in its final conclusions *"Even with this extra stimulus* [of Treasury capital funding] *it is unlikely that in the next ten years more than six or seven major provincial repertory theatres will be built either as new theatres or as replacements of existing theatres."* (Arts Council (1959) p.25)

This excess over expectation is certainly true if one takes account of the huge expansion of a virtually new category of performance venue, the arts[67] centre. There is no one definition of exactly what constitutes an 'arts centre' and in reality it can range from a small, if quite sophisticated, performance venue to a centre for local adult education with a bias towards artistic activity. The original inspiration for such places came from the work of CEMA and immediately after the war there had been some moves to implement this vision. However, a combination of Keynesian elitism and local authority lethargy had quickly killed it off despite initial interest in the Arts Council's acquisition of a disused army barracks in Bridgewater to serve as the model for a small town arts centre. (It is still operating). The arts centre originally fitted into the Arts Council plan of things as a place of artistic activity suitable for towns below 70,000 population which could not support a full-scale theatre and by the

---

[67] Strictly perhaps the 'arts' centre' but the apostrophe has become redundant in normal usage.

early-1960s, perhaps a dozen such existed. No exact count is really possible but by 1980, somewhere between two and three hundred arts centres were operating, most capable of sustaining some kind of performance.

Financial support for arts centres was devolved heavily on to regional Arts Associations and local councils. According to Hutchinson, the amateur performance element present in many arts centres led the Arts Council to shy away from ever providing them with central support. (Hutchinson p.51) Consequently there is no way of estimating the degree of subsidy paid nor of its ultimate source which even with local councils came from a variety of different budgets. However, the provision of some hundreds of small, flexible performance venues throughout the country would prove crucial to the development of theatre thereafter.

The expansion of subsidy in the 1960s was such that whilst in 1959, 19 theatres were receiving some annual subvention from the Arts Council, this had increased to 48 by 1968. The scale of this funding relative to box-office receipts varied widely but, overall, box-office provided 56.8% of total income, the Arts Council, 34.5%, local authorities 7.4% and other sources only 1.3%. Thus although councils had borne the brunt of capital expenditure on new theatres, they provided very little support for the continuing operation of these. Only Middlesbrough funded the local Billingham Forum Theatre to an extent which exceeded the Arts Council grant whilst the relative generosity of Coventry and Nottingham's grant to their theatres was lessened by the fact that each clawed back in rent the equivalent of the grant.[68] Very few

---

[68] All figures in this paragraph taken from Arts Council (1970) p.74/75 and exclude Scotland

companies had a subsidy which exceeded their box-office. One of these was the National Theatre at the Old Vic but, notably, the Royal Shakespeare Company, much the largest of the subsidised theatres, annually playing to nearly 700,000 paying customers, was getting little more than a quarter of its total income as subsidy. The scale of the subsidy which developed in the 1960s set a pattern which has continued to this day; theatres could survive on it but only if seat prices were high enough and the houses large enough to ensure good box-office receipts. The theatre was destined to remain a relatively high-price option[69] compared with cinema whilst popular success was still needed to ensure financial survival.

Thus the financial crisis of the preceding chapter had, in part, been resolved by the end of the 1960s. Subsidy for public theatres had become accepted as the norm though its extent was a perpetual battleground. What remained at stake was the cultural role of the theatre in this new, subsidised form. The fact was that bums-on-seats were still required to provide most of the income of public theatres and these were far from guaranteed. Audience levels at those residual commercial theatres which offered what the Arts Council would regard as 'quality' product were poor and largely confined to an aging audience. There also seems to have been a real shortage of the kind of attraction which would appeal even to this declining audience. The survey of the theatre carried out for the Arts Council in the late-1960s quickly found a common complaint from theatres, both outside London and in the West End, of a lack of 'quality product'. Appendix 1 reproduces the

[69] The average seat price for most theatres was around 7 shillings (35p.). Only the Chichester Festival Theatre could charge an average above £1 and only a few in southern England more than 10 shillings. Cinema seats would normally be 2 or 3 shillings.

comments on the plays then showing in the West End from a theatre insider who ran one of the smaller producing companies. Even allowing for a certain level of acerbity, it is easy enough to see that the constant complaint of provincial theatres that they could not book any 'quality attractions' had a real basis given that it had been the West End which provided the flow of material out from London. The problem facing the new public theatres was how to crack the cultural problem of providing a theatre which had some relevance to their audience.

Here we can add in the final ingredient to the cultural revival of theatre, politics.

Politics
Item 1

A group of Americans are called up before the House Un-American Activities Committee to answer allegations that they are subversive elements. They appear dressed as Davy Crockett, Geronimo and assorted cowboys and cheerfully accept the charge.

Item 2

A young woman pushes a pram filled with bits of rubber and pieces of meat into a pedestrian shopping precinct in a small English town. Stopping, she pours paraffin over it and lights it. A reeking black smoke fills the air. "Now you know what it's like in Vietnam", she shouts through a loud-hailer.

Item 3

At 11 am, a group of a dozen young men appear in the centre of Bradford. They are dressed all in black with red armbands and, mounting the steps of Queen Victoria's monument, they begin to read aloud the thoughts of Chairman Mao. At the same time, a procession of more than a hundred, led by a band, swing out of the gates of a park about two miles away. They are also dressed in black but wear white armbands, the women carry wooden rifles. They are followed by four huge puppets made of cardboard and painted black. Outside a bread shop in the centre, a queue of about two dozen forms. Each one buys one tea-cake which they take to a derelict post-office in the middle of high-rise council flats. Placards are left in the window saying that anyone could take anything they liked from the shop for free and could leave behind anything but money.

All of these things happened around 1967. One was contrived by what may loosely be called a theatrical group.

It is commonplace to observe that from the early 1960s, British theatre became highly political. This is sometimes reduced to the idea that there were a number of socialist playwrights at the time[70] or that there were several touring groups formed with the objective of supporting left-wing causes. (Shellard pp149-153) However, anything other than superficial observation suggests that such reduction fails to address the situation. In 1972, Trevor Nunn, then Artistic Director of the Royal Shakespeare Company, was able rather casually to observe in a letter to *The Times* that *"basically, the RSC is a left-wing company."* Ironically, he made this comment when in the middle of an industrial dispute with two of the company's commissioned writers in order to defend his company's progressive credentials. This statement caused a mild sensation and the MP for Stratford resigned from the Board but no one seriously disputed the claim. Nunn's assertion—from a man who had no apparent personal political involvement—was seen as

---

[70] A useful reference here is Bull.

simply a statement of the obvious; that theatre was political and that its natural bias was to the left.

Certainly this is something which, looking backwards, one can see most clearly marked out in the roll-call of writers. There *were* playwrights at the time who did not write plays that were clearly marked out as socialist. Itzin provides a list of them (Itzin (1980) p.ix) headed, rather interestingly, by two *"pillars of the establishment"*, John Osborne and Harold Pinter[71] followed by Ayckbourn, Storey, Schaffer, Nichols, Whitehead and Gray, some of whom might be surprised at their exclusion. Certainly Storey's *The Contractor* directed by Lindsay Anderson, who would have been outraged at the idea that he was not a socialist, was regarded by many as an exemplary piece of social-realism. In its way, this kind of characterisation shows up the problem with trying to categorise this play as political and that as not without taking into account the general context of the times. Arden's *Sergeant Musgrave's Dance*, now seen as an evidently political anti-colonial masterpiece, was both little regarded when it opened[72] and subsequently chided for confusing the audience by not taking sides and having no moral position. (Taylor p.84) In the 1950s, broadly, plays were not seen as 'political' even when they were presented by companies, such as Theatre Workshop, with an overtly political base. Increasingly from the mid-1960s, plays were viewed and judged from a different perspective which was, broadly, political. In fact there is a case for saying that the only significant non-political playwright of this time in the sense of resolutely not being political was

---

[71] At the time, Pinter's plays were regarded as mainly concerned with sexual frisson rather than any political involvement although personally he was a socialist involved with the Committee of 100 and other left campaigns.

[72] *"Another dreadful ordeal"* – Harold Hobson

Tom Stoppard even when writing plays with political sub-texts.

In 1966, Stoppard wrote *Rosencrantz and Guildenstern are Dead*, a play in which the eponymous heroes are embedded in a political context which baffles and ultimately kills them. Ingenious, if overlong, *Rosencrantz and Guildenstern* was followed by a series of successful plays, notably *Jumpers*(1972) and *Travesties* (1974) in this period, all of which are fundamentally concerned with the bafflement of Stoppard, a clever, educated man, embedded, socially, in a politics which he simply does not get and which he both spurns but also wants to understand. Long after the impetus of this politics has died, in 2002, he was still trying to find its roots at even greater length in his trilogy about nineteenth century political radicals, *The Coast of Utopia*, as though his youthful bafflement still bothers him and can be resolved in such history. *Rock 'n Roll* (2006) really just continues what has become a rather repetitive saga.

It is easier to understand the shift in theatrical performance in the mid-1960s by appreciating not how politics came to the theatre rather than the other way round, how, if you like, politics became theatrical. After a decade which was to become a byword for its dull conformism, there appeared an escalating succession of political events whose images became, to use Debord's idea, a spectacle. The civil rights' campaign in the USA, the Vietnam War, the cultural revolution in China, a series of nasty guerrilla wars in Portugal's African colonies, Guevara's long drawn-out passage to iconic martyrdom, the May *evenements* in Paris in 1968, the Prague spring and its crushing in the same year; all put the images of a world-wide political upsurge as lead stories and photographs on the television news and daily papers. When in 1967,

Albert Hunt's students from the Bradford College of Art re-enacted the Russian Revolution on Bradford's streets they were bringing home images which had become the daily fare of the media. In a sense, what they were doing was similar to Black Jack Musgrave's theatrical journey, bringing home the skeletons of the past. Very shortly, Britain would have its own theatres of politics; first in Northern Ireland when, following the televised attacks on a civil rights' march at Burntollet in Northern Ireland, there would be civil disorder, riots, shooting and the first appearance of what would become a familiar image, that of black-balaclaved men with Armalites, then in Britain a series of increasingly tense industrial disputes and student disorders. The revival of theatre, as seen in the increasing funding from state-sources, coincided with the most dramatic political era of the second half of the twentieth century. Alongside the new municipal theatres and, increasingly overlapping with them, there grew up a generation of theatrical workers who saw the theatre as the natural place to present their politics in a multitude of forms.

When in 1973, The Pip Simmons Theatre Group produced *The George Jackson Black and White Minstrel Show*, it culminated in the George Jackson character being swung aloft in a red sack, struggling to be free until one black-gloved hand emerges before shots ring out and the sack is still. (Ansorge p.33) A stunning theatrical image but one that could hardly surpass the originals: Bobby Seale in 1969, shackled to a chair, physically gagged at his own trial following political demonstrations in Chicago, all at the order of a white judge, or George Jackson's later murder in Soledad prison.

Theatre tells stories the form and content of which derive from the world outside. In the late-Victorian period, the public play, the play which in Howard Brenton's distinction is set in the open-air rather than in a room, effectively disappeared from the British stage. In the late 1950s when Wesker wrote his trilogy of plays about socialist politics, the same convention is observed. The Battle of Cable Street in 1936[73] occurs offstage and is described from inside a room. Around 1963, this convention is abruptly broken and plays move outside. There was not necessarily any overt political reason for this. In its second season, the new National Theatre produced Schaffer's *Royal Hunt of the Sun* (1964), a play reportedly turned down by Binkie Beaumont when he heard that it contained the stage direction, "The soldiers then climb the Andes". (Lewis p.20) *Royal Hunt*, reviewed by Bernard Levin as *"The finest new play I have ever seen"*, (Shellard p.120) now seems pretty turgid stuff on the page but directed as lavish melodrama with exotic costumes, original music claimed to be inspired by Peruvian birds and mime sequences devised by a French mime artist, it was the first popular hit of the new institution and it was in the broad sense, political, that is it was about public affairs. Its revival in 2005 was greeted with far less rapture probably because after forty years, audiences had seen this all done better and failed to see its originality.

In the same way, though with greater conscious intent, when Peter Hall opened a new era for the Royal Shakespeare company, he effectively laid out his stall with *The Wars of the Roses*(1963), part Shakespeare, part John Barton,[74] a version of four original plays, in a production which took Shakespeare decisively outside. Hall's intent was to provide a 'relevant'

---

[73] A street confrontation in East London between fascists, socialists and the police.

[74] Barton wrote about 20% of the final script.

interpretation of Shakespeare and that meant in 1963, a social and political slant distanced from the personalised focus of previous decades. John Bury was at last freed from the miniscule budgets of Theatre Workshop and on his set of copper plates and steel floor, the audience could actually hear *"the inhuman tramp of authority"* (Hall p.177) as Hall later put it. (He designed *Wars of the Roses* at the same time as designing *Oh! What a Lovely War*, Hall having failed to persuade Joan Littlewood to direct *Henry VI* at Stratford). The text for the RSC over the coming decade would be Jan Kott's **Shakespeare Our Contemporary** which always comes back to the politics even at a strain to the text. Hall, one of the great showman of British theatre, was alert to the shifting cultural patterns of the 1960s before most others and knew the direction in which theatre had to go to achieve any popular purchase.

This perspective on Shakespeare as a political playwright carried through the RSC's work over the following decade until in 1972, Trevor Nunn attempted an entire season of the Roman plays in chronological order seeing them as coherent expression of the development of Roman society and of Roman politics. This unwieldy conception largely failed under the weight of its misconceived ideas about the dramatic coherence the plays actually possess, but it does illustrate the fact that the 'politicisation' of British theatre in this period extended much further than a few 'red' touring groups and some socialist playwrights. Ironically, it took the work of the most explicitly political of the RSC directors of the time[75] to drag the RSC back from what had become a slightly predictable pattern of public spectacle back to a more intimate and personalised

---

[75] Buzz Goodbody, an active Communist and feminist.

view of plays such as *Hamlet* even though Buzz Goodbody's *Hamlet* was still set in a precisely measured social and political context.

Hall's leap was a bold one particularly when measured against the 'great actor' versions of Shakespeare still being put out by the newly formed National Theatre. In 1964, for example, Olivier famously blacked-up as Othello, three hours to get on and two to get off, in a totally star-centred production. However, Hall's judgement was accurate insofar as *The Wars of the Roses* proved to be extremely popular, undoubtedly the criterion by which Peter Hall liked to be judged. The 'politicisation' of the RSC, as seen for example in Brook's *US*(1966), is all the more remarkable in that it was undertaken by a group of men with very limited political interests. Even so it was very influential. One historian of the RSC[76] goes as far as suggesting that it was the emergence of such 'public' versions of Shakespeare together with other RSC productions which provided the base on which a more obviously socialist generation of playwrights could flourish. Towards the end of the 1960s, a small group of mainly touring companies emerged which had the explicit purpose of supporting and enlarging socialist politics, groups such as 7:84 and Red Ladder. They operated, however, within a much wider theatrical milieu in which politics in its most general sense was a dominant theme.

The shift towards the public play lasted about twenty years. One can mark its end, roughly, by Edgar's *Maydays*(1983) and the Brenton/Hare collaboration *Pravda*(1985), the one elegiac, the other angry and rather bitter. They were performed by the two flagships of public theatre, the RSC and the National

---

[76] Colin Chambers, personal communication

Theatre, and they coincided with the protracted and bitter miners' strike of 1983/84 when the ambition of the British left finally collapsed. There is a sense in which politics in Britain ceased to be a matter of public spectacle when the men of Tower colliery, amongst others, marched back under their union banners, defeated, and in which, subsequently, British theatre also turned away from the public play. It is too easy to suggest that this was simply a matter of decreased public funding and political pressure from a right-wing government though these played a part. It jumps ahead of the story but plays after 1985 showed if anything a greater degree of rage about the existing social system than before. But it became more and more a matter of private pain and frustration in a society which seemed to be more and more based on various forms of privatisation, personal and public. The stories which the public plays of these two decades told varied very widely and not all, perhaps not even the majority, were particularly optimistic. Bond's *Lear* (1971), Brenton's *Weapons of Happiness* (1976), Barker's *The Hang of the Gaol* (1978) can be seen as notable examples of a view of change in Britain which was decidedly pessimistic. These were not agit-prop socialists but story-tellers trying to say something true to a damaged social system in the midst of a convulsion. A common theme was hypocrisy and corruption often on the left as well as the right. Barker's words in *Hang of the Gaol* could stand for the message of many plays of the time:

> *...we are in England, and in England you may think a man a liar but you had better not call him one. That is called maturity. The more mature you are, the less you use the word you want. The purpose of wrapping meanings up in cotton wool is to stop them*

> *hurting. This is a very sick and bandaged*
> *race. (Chambers (1987) p.88)*

If the shift in general political culture was an important force on the theatre of the time then one must also add an obvious but under-regarded factor, that at its very roots, British theatre became literally public rather than private. This will be considered in more detail later but, in summary, it is clear that as more and more theatre became publicly funded to some degree it also became more socially aware. The extent to which this was an influence varied widely. Some regional repertory carried on with a range of plays scarcely distinguishable from a good-quality repertory of the 1930s even though their funding base had shifted from private to partly-private. Others went to great lengths to place the new publicly-funded theatres within their local communities. Peter Cheeseman at the Victoria Theatre, Stoke-on-Trent is probably the extreme example. He produced a series of historical documentaries, one of the best-known being *The Fight for Shelton Bar* (1974) about the struggle to keep open a local steel-plant which played for most of a year and which often took the form of an update on the outside campaign. Naturally these plays and others like them did not try to take any neutral view about the events they portrayed. Usually based in union-towns, they took the union side as much as a form of civic pride as of militant politics. The link between public money and social responsibility is a vague one but it exists and in many cases amongst the new recipients of subsidy it was quite clear. However what happened to British theatre in the 1960s and 70s was more than just an acceptance of some form of public responsibility deriving from public finance. It also involved the theatre breaking out of the forms which had tightened round it since the late nineteenth century and becoming aware of the artistic world around it.

Alternative venues and alternative cultures

Shifts in British theatre in the 1950s were marked by a strong sense of continuity. Reformers, such as George Devine, emerged from the classier repertory companies whilst even someone who later became known for his commitment to radical experiment as Peter Brook had passed his early years in rather conventional London art theatre and the West End known as much for his stylish direction of Anouilh's *Ring Around the Moon* as for anything particularly radical. Even the one personality who had not had this kind of theatrical background, Joan Littlewood, had been initially trained at the Royal Academy of Dramatic Art and in her partnership with MacColl had maintained a strong link with continental and classical theatre.

One consequence of this was that in the early-1960s, theatre seemed to be a deeply conventional, indeed old-fashioned art-form with an audience to match. Tynan's claim that *Look Back in Anger* would appeal to anyone aged between twenty and thirty contained much more hope than reality. There is no real sign at all up to the early-1960s of any broad appeal of the theatre to the young. At the same time in music and in the visual arts, there was both popular interest and also huge cultural innovation. In music, the various fusions of black American blues and gospel, American country and British folk music together with smatterings of forms as diverse as music-hall songs has been well-documented and argued over. Its importance here is two-fold; first is the obvious impact of a genuine revolution in the way popular music was created with the emergence of performers and groups from clubs and pubs and the way in which bands like the Beatles and the Rolling Stones either wrote their own songs or picked up and adapted blues or soul standards. Both these groups owed a lot to skiffle, the self-consciously home-made music of the late-1950s. The second is the great emphasis on performance in this new music, an emphasis which grew as bands began to create touring shows with an ever more grandiose degree of what can only be described as 'theatricality' associated with them.

The visual arts did not operate on this plane of popular interest. However, under the impact of artists like Joseph Beuys in Germany, the shift towards the rather vague category of conceptual art began, a shift which moved visual art closer and closer towards the territory occupied by theatre though from new, usually non-verbal directions, a shift which quickly began to challenge fundamental definitions of what constituted art let alone visual art. Until the mid-1960s, the relationship between theatre and visual art was mediated by theatre 'designers'. Conceptual artists broke this indirect link by placing visual art at the very centre of performance itself. Emblematic of this was the work of Mark Boyle and Joan Hills who in 1965, just before starting on their Journey to the Surface of the World, led an invited group into the back entrance of a building signposted as "Theatre". After sitting down the curtains were drawn and the 'audience' found themselves in a shop window looking at the people in the street who were simultaneously the show and the audience looking in at the 'audience' who were also the performers.

This kind of performance art largely remained as an *avant garde* fringe to more conventional theatre though performance groups, such as The People Show, Hesitate and Demonstrate and John Bull Puncture Repair Kit, gained a significant and loyal audience around the art centre circuit and were amongst the best known British groups touring continental Europe. (Ashford, *The Jazz of Dreams* in (Craig)) Their influence went much wider than this however. Their audiences, particularly in London, always contained other theatre workers interested in picking up on the odd and tangential techniques on display which then filtered back in other work.

It is difficult to pick up the channels through which these swift and parallel developments in music and visual art impacted on British theatre. Certainly some people inside 'conventional' theatre understood the need to expand the theatrical form away from naturalist drama, not least the two major innovators of the 1950s. In an article in *Encore*, George Devine wrote "*My own thought is that the use of music, song and dance in the so-called straight theatre is the direction in which we must go*". (Devine pp.23-26) Devine's own productions showed little sign of implementation of this 'thought' but the same cannot be said of Joan Littlewood's Theatre Workshop where music and dance were important. However, what is clear is that from the mid-1960s onwards, there was a major influence from people whose background was scarcely, if at all, inside the theatre and whose ambitions for theatre were not in any way based on continuity with past performance. This is illustrated by a clutch of Americans who at one moment in the 1960s seemed to be creating a new British theatre almost by themselves.

The role played in the 1960s by the expatriate Americans Jim Haynes, Charles Marowitz and Ed Berman, essentially rested upon a kind of cultural entrepreneurship previously virtually unknown in Britain rather than any specific artistic innovation. The previous pattern for anyone interested in any kind of new or experimental theatre had been to insert themselves into one or other of the existing institutions and to develop inside it. Only Littlewood had broken with this and, as described above, even she had had to make compromises with the West End to survive. When in 1962 Jim Haynes opened the Traverse Theatre in a disused brothel in Edinburgh, he set a precedent for an abrupt departure from this pattern by simply setting up his own theatre, albeit one which could, originally, seat barely sixty people on either side of a traverse stage, and then staging on it virtually anything which wanted to move. In its opening year, the Traverse Theatre staged 22 plays financed, if at all, largely by the bookshop and café which also functioned in the same building. In 1966, Haynes moved on to London leaving the Traverse under the direction of first, Gordon MacDougall, then Max Stafford-Clark and opened the Arts Lab in Drury Lane. This venue lasted less than two years (January 1968-October 1969) and its activities in this period were summed up by a note in the London listings magazine, *Time Out "The Arts Lab programme appears to be a mixture of chaos and chance and details should be obtained by phone for any one evening"* (Craig p.155) It is fair to say that whatever else clouded the mind of anyone associated with the Arts Lab, the chances of a West End transfer was never one of them.

This deliberate flouting of all the supposed rules of professionalism (as well as commercial survival), a deliberate creation of apparent chaos, the lack of any boundaries between artistic forms and the absence of imposed judgement about any artistic standards was a product of the times and could not last. However in the midst of the haze, Haynes produced the first plays of David Storey, C.P.Taylor and Heathcote Williams along with the first British performances of plays by

Adamov and Arrabal; supported the initial work of groups like The People Show, Freehold, the Pip Simmons Group and Portable Theatre; and brought the La Mama group over from New York and Grotowski's 13-rows Theatre from Poland. (Elsom p.142) There is no particular stylistic similarity between these and Haynes never attempted to find any. His crucial influence was simply that if the idea came, whether writing or performing, then one should just *Do It!*, as the title of the book by Jerry Rubins, later turned into a performance piece by the Pip Simmons Group, puts it.

Charles Marowitz was closer to a conventional theatrical tradition than Haynes, working in the late-1950s directing actor-workshops and then in 1964, collaborating with Peter Brook in The Theatre of Cruelty season at the LAMDA theatre in London. In 1968 he opened the Open Space Theatre in Tottenham Court Road intended to provide a base for new interpretations of classic theatre notably his own collage versions of Shakespeare. Marowitz fought a long and ultimately losing battle to find enough subsidy to avoid reliance on commercial box-office and West End transfers and the Open Space closed in 1979. However, the Open Space was a consistent base for innovative theatre.

The third prominent American, Ed Berman, was the most removed from conventional views of theatre in that he worked essentially to include theatre as one branch of social activism within the community rather than as a separate cultural enterprise. Itzin summarises the work of Inter-Action, the charity which formed Berman's base as follows:

> *[He] shared the distinction with David Halliwell's Quipu of launching the first permanent lunchtime theatre in 1968 and by 1978 had created a veritable empire of*

> *community arts and professional theatre
> activities. Over the decade, having used
> dozens of different venues and squats, Inter-
> Action moved, in 1977, to a purpose-built
> building in Kentish Town—the nerve centre
> for far-flung activities as varied as horse-
> riding lessons, self-help gardening clubs,
> summer sports camp, skateboarding, a city
> farm, education work with video,
> architectural advice and of course theatre—
> from community (Dogg's Troupe) to
> international (The British American
> Repertory Company). Servicing all of this
> was the community resource centre,
> including printing, video, recording,
> photography, silk-screening, music,
> electrical and textile work, Xerox and
> community transport.(Itzin p.51)*

Inter-Action helped start groups such as the Black
Theatre of Brixton, Gay Sweatshop and the Women's
Theatre Group but its main influence on theatre was
the emphasis on the role of theatre as community
culture, as a way of bringing people together and
developing their latent talent.

The impact of these three Americans should not be
over-stated. Each in their own way was a specific
embodiment of what came to seen as the brief moment
of 1960s counter-culture. However, they do rather
neatly epitomise the three key features of what came
to be called the alternative or fringe theatre in Britain;
its extraordinary degree of initiative and self-
organisation, its difficult and shifting relationship to
state subsidy and its focus on various forms of
community.

The first of these three can be seen in the moment of
origin of alternative theatre in the decade, one which
can be dated rather precisely to the odd festival

organised in 1962 by John Arden and Margaretta D'Arcy in the north Yorkshire village of Kirbymoorside where they had gone to live. It was advertised in the theatre magazine *Encore* as

> *John Arden has conceived the idea of establishing a free Public Entertainment in his house...No specific form of entertainment is envisaged but it is hoped that in the course of it the forces of Anarchy, Excitement and Expressive Energy latent in the most apparently sad person shall be given release.*
>
> *(Kershaw p.107 & pp.118-120)*

The festival lasted for about a month and comprised a mixture of readings, performance, films, darts matches, singing and telling stories. As Kershaw notes, it has the distinction of premiering the only play ever performed by the Royal Shakespeare Company and the Company of the Kirbymoorside Girl Guides in the same year, *Ars Longa, Vita Brevis*. Arden later maintained that the version directed by Peter Brook was inferior and he may have been right.

It is helpful to contrast the slightly self-conscious anarchism of Arden and D'Arcy with the contemporary and much better organised efforts of Arnold Wesker, another Royal Court graduate, to break out of the traditional confines of British theatre. The Centre 42 project was based on a resolution passed in 1960 by the British Trade Union Congress[77] which rather vaguely committed the British trade union movement to support for the arts. Armed with this resolution, Wesker, a man born in the lap of traditional left-wing politics in London, set out to organise a new kind of theatre centred in some way

---

[77] The national body representing nearly all trade unions.

round the working class. The centre-piece of this project was to establish the Roundhouse, a derelict engine-shed in north London, as a working class radical theatre venue. Centre 42 raised a limited amount of money, organised a few festivals which appear to have been only partial successes and after a few years collapsed amidst much recrimination leaving the Roundhouse as a theatrical venue whose potential was seldom matched by the companies bold enough to take it on. It is interesting that one of the few total successes it has held was the French director, Mnouchkine's promenade production of *1789*, an enactment of the French revolution. Mnouchkine's company, based in old military buildings in Valenciennes in Paris, had been set up to provide a new and accessible theatre for the surrounding working-class community. A visit to it in 1967 by Michael Kustow is credited with sparking some of the efforts by the RSC to engage in community theatre.

The reasons for Centre 42's failure were mainly contingent but three points are worth making here. First, even though Wesker was an established playwright, the festivals and other events never seem to have performed any of his own work which continued to be done with varying success at orthodox venues. The driving force of much alternative theatre was to perform one's own work, however quirky, in any place which was at hand. There was, in other words, a genuine and personal creative drive present not just a desire to provide a place where an undefined and rather idealised 'working class culture' could be shown. Secondly, getting money seems to have very quickly come to dominate Centre 42's priorities whereas for most alternative theatre, at least in its early years, funding was not the priority given that most participants existed either on other jobs or by signing on for regular unemployment benefit[78] with box-office receipts being a welcome though irregular addition. A good deal of alternative theatre in London, particularly at lunchtime, was for a time actually dependent on unpaid actors who used the opportunities to showcase their talents for paid work.

Thirdly, Centre 42 picked up on the idea of theatre as a 'centre' but failed to answer the question: A centre for whom? At this period, the use of the word 'centre' crystallised out as the key word in various kinds of urban renewal but Centre 42 failed to find any specificity in its own use of the word apart from an idealised 'working class'. This relates back to the general hatred of mass popular culture in which Wesker was embedded. The strategic purpose of Centre 42 was to bring 'culture' to the masses.

> *The festivals that Centre 42 organised consisted mainly of the products of high art—theatre, small-scale opera and dance, poetry readings. The exceptions to this were jazz and folk concerts (and Charles Parker's ground-breaking folk documentaries) but both jazz and folk music were in some ways the acceptable and 'authentic' face of popular art. It was a constant criticism of these festivals that they promoted a culture that was essentially that of the organisers rather than that of the audiences; there was little room for the kind of working class entertainment that Hoggart describes let alone rock 'n' roll.*

---

[78] In the 1960s and 70s, British welfare benefits, in particular unemployment benefit in an era of historically low unemployment, had become to a degree a matter of personal choice. Those 'signing on' as actors or designers were, in principle, required to follow up job offers but only from their chosen craft which were seldom if ever registered.

Alternative theatre groups, 1971-1989

(Lacey p.90)

The casual financing situation of the 1960s shifted in the 1970s as the issue of funding the small touring groups which had proliferated very rapidly became a key controversy within the Arts Council. The scale of growth of these groups is extraordinary as can be seen in the graph. In 1968, there were perhaps a half-dozen small touring groups picking up work mainly at venues like the Arts Lab and the Traverse Theatre plus various almost impromptu and sometimes unlikely places. By the mid-1970s, there were well over a hundred companies playing to an increasingly organised circuit of arts centres, pub and club theatres and colleges as well as the studios and, occasionally, main houses of the new repertory theatres. The number of groups continued to increase until the mid-1980s, when they seem to have peaked at a little above three hundred. These were not all full-time and some had very transitory existences. Even so their scale is striking.

The work which this alternative theatre presented varied quite as widely as the orthodox theatres to which they were often seen as opposed. In fact by the mid-1970s, there was such an overlap between the two that it becomes rather hard to retain the distinction. At one extreme, the performance groups retained their feel of being an intellectual fringe even though they might work in the studio theatres of large repertory houses. At the other end of the spectrum, many touring groups simply presented relatively conventional drama in places which lacked conventional theatres. Increasingly in the 1970s, the 'fringe' touring companies performed in some conventional theatres as part of their overall circuit. Some, such as Joint Stock, played mainly in such venues whilst preserving their reputation for innovatory technique. In many ways it becomes more useful to consider the wider concerns of theatre at this time as being rather more homogeneous than labels like 'fringe' or 'mainstream' suggest, in particular to consider them in relationship to the idea of community which became one of the main social organising principles of the 1960s and 70s.

Imagined communities

One of the central perceptions of theatrical work from the late-1960s on was the sense of Britain being a society which was in a state of dissolution. In a way Osborne's *The Entertainer* was, in an earlier decade, the first of these plays though this theme was undercut by its ambiguous nostalgia for times past. Nostalgia was, however, a commodity singularly lacking in the playwrights of the late-1960s who launched what amounted to a full-scale onslaught on the major and minor icons of British imperial history as well as displaying an unnerving and possibly prescient pessimism about the future state of the country.

> *Funny. My dream of a criminal England, it's all come true in the 1980s. The casino towns, the brothel villages, the cities red with blood and pleasure. Public life, the turn of a card, the fall of a dice. The whole*

*country on the fiddle, the gamble, the open
snatch, the bit on the side. From Land's End
to John O'Groats, the whole of England's
one giant pinball table. The ball running
wild, Glasgow, Birmingham, Leeds,
Coventry, London, Brighton. Wonderful*

Howard Brenton *Revenge* (1969)

There is an odd contradiction about Britain in this
period, one which was expressed in the theatre as
keenly as in other areas of life. The mid-1960s can be
seen, with hindsight, as the high-water mark of the
long expansionary swing of post-war Britain.
Unemployment was at historic lows and fifteen years
of steady economic growth had produced levels of
prosperity which were transforming the lifestyles of
much of the population. A very relevant consequence
of this, already noted, was the willingness of city
councils to stump up for new theatres as part of a
general programme of urban social development.
Universal and almost free healthcare had transformed
attitudes to illness and the new Labour administration
had from 1964 set about opening an education system
which had mouldered since the 1944 Education Act.
All this seemed to have covered Britain in the middle
of the decade with the benign aura of 'swinging'
London, the cheeky irreverence of The Beatles,
Carnaby Street and the first issues of the *Sunday Times*
Colour Supplement. The rather sudden and
unexpectedly easy way in which Britain had shrugged
off most of its colonial possessions in the first half of
the decade put an end to the vicious little wars which
had gone on throughout the preceding decade. The
country was at peace; no British soldier was killed in
action in the mid-1960s, the first time in the post-war
years in a brief lull before civil war in northern Ireland
erupted in 1970. Loss of empire did not, however,
prevent England attaining its historic destiny when it

won football's World Cup in 1966, an achievement which was to become an increasingly nostalgic and slightly bitter cultural icon in succeeding decades but which, at the time, was seen as no more than the country's just reward.

There was a darker side to 'swinging' London, one which was pinned down by Antonioni in his film *Blow-Up* (1966), co-scripted by the young playwright, Edward Bond, whose central character was one of the newly discovered celebrity heroes, a fashion photographer. He becomes obsessed by finding in the prints of one of his outdoor shoots, peripheral traces of a body hidden in bushes. He later finds the body which then disappears leading the film off into a trail of the real and the unreal which is never explained. In the end, the photographer is left watching a strange game of mock-tennis in which the participants play out the actions but in the absence of a ball. Celebrity London, it suggests, was a social setting whose inhabitants play a game without realising that they have lost its central purpose whilst around them much darker and more dangerous games are being played out.

Blow-Up was not the only 'state-of-the-nation' film of the time. In *The Charge of the Light Brigade* (1968), one of the main participants in the Royal Court of the late-1950s, Tony Richardson as director together with Charles Wood as scriptwriter, attempted an oblique critique of an ossified social structure, secure in its position maintained by outward display but wholly unable to move forward and given to catastrophically bad leadership. They did this in a characteristically theatrical way by giving a reverse view of a British historic national treasure; the pointlessly heroic display of the Light Brigade in the middle of the inept Battle of Balaclava set into the long-forgotten Crimean War. However, despite these flashes, the British film industry effectively collapsed at the end of the 1960s leaving the theatre to carry forward what became an almost obsessive search for some new national identity.

Benedict Anderson coined the term 'imagined communities' for nations: *"an imagined political community — and imagined as both inherently limited and sovereign"* (Anderson p.15) The essential core of this idea is that nations are, in most cases, too large to be formed by any kind of physical community but are an act of social imagination, a result of some confluence of language, culture, external threat, religion, political governance and contingency in which no one factor is either sufficient or necessary except for collective imagination. The community which is so formed may seem both inevitable and immutable but is in fact neither. It may also seem perpetually unstable yet have deep strengths. It might have appeared that in the immediate post-war period, Great Britain had achieved its grandest apotheosis, the island nation which had withstood total isolation and won a great victory. In practice, the dissolution of Great Britain had begun almost immediately after this victory with its hasty withdrawal from the Indian sub-continent precipitating mass civil disorder, hundred of thousands of deaths and almost continuous strife between the countries which emerged from the chaos. Subsequent imperial withdrawal had followed much the same pattern of bellicose manoeuvre followed by hasty retreat leaving behind a new country ill-equipped to face the future and a slightly sour taste in the mouth of a British public uncertain whether it preferred imperial grandeur or freedom-loving liberation but, in practice, getting neither.

Gradually through the 1960s, there emerged both a political and a cultural search for the 'imagined community' which would have to replace the discarded imperial Britain. Victory in the World Cup despite its immediate euphoria[79] failed to provide this. Indeed it really put the finger on one of the key problems with imagining the British community. It was specifically England which won. Dennis Law, a famous Scottish footballer, played a well-publicised round of golf during the final. It was immediately after 1966 that Welsh and Scottish nationalists won their first seats in the national parliament whilst the remnants of England's Irish colony entered its long agony. It is difficult to understand the nature of British theatre after 1965 unless its role in this process of more general cultural imagination is understood.

At a symbolic level, one might begin with the month-long journey undertaken in September, 1972, by the Welfare State company from Glastonbury in Dorset to Cornwall.[80] The 25-strong group would at points on the route erect a circus tent to enact various events related to local history or legend. The central character in these was one Lancelot Quaile described as 'a working class hermaphrodite strong man' who, on arrival at (possibly) St Michael's Mount, set sail in a small boat in search of Morvenna, an 'Ethereal Mermaid'. The following year, the search for Morvenna was renewed within a maze built in a large council rubbish-tip outside Burnley in Lancashire though it seems that she was never found. Welfare State International as they became in 1979 existed[81] on the edges of what is conventionally called theatre. In

---

[79] Harold Wilson, British Prime Minister at the time, is credited with the belief that the failure of his Labour Party to repeat its 1966 election victory in 1970 was due to the English team's failure to win again in Mexico in that year.

[80] The precise final destination differs slightly in different accounts which is, perhaps, just as it should be.

[81] Their dissolution was announced in 2006. R.I.P.

the words of their earliest manifesto they claimed that *"We make images, invent ritual, devise ceremonies, objectify the unpredictable and enhance atmospheres for particular places, times, situations and people. We are artists concerned with the survival and character of the imagination and the individual within a technologically advanced society."* (Fox p.3) Once settled into a permanent home at Ulverston on the Furness peninsula, their search has always been to find for themselves and for others, some form of community celebration which resists the homogenisation of a global, technocratic culture. In their own rather particular way they represent a key concern of the British theatre since the mid-1960s which, on a larger scale can be seen in the formation of the first national theatres.

National Theatres

Reference has already been made to the landmark productions of *The Royal Hunt of the Sun* by the National Theatre in 1963 and *The Wars of the Roses* by the Royal Shakespeare Company in 1964 as being a new kind of 'public' play performed by a new kind of public theatre. The formation of both of these belongs in part to the era discussed in the previous chapter but needs some recapitulation here to appreciate its significance.[82]

The idea of specific institutionalised national theatre had been first floated in 1848 by a Manchester bookseller, Effingham Wilson, who proposed a publicly-funded body which would perform the plays of Shakespeare. It received little support at the time but re-surfaced in 1907 when the influential critic, William Archer, and the director and playwright, Granville Barker published a pamphlet on the subject.

---

[82] The following draws heavily on Chambers (2004)

This proposal received rather more support; it was in effect the final step in the shift in perception of the theatre to being a morally sound cultural form, and the Shakespeare Memorial National Theatre Committee (SMNTC) was set up in 1908 followed by the passage of a parliamentary bill, albeit sponsored by a private member and not the government, in 1913. A site in London in Bloomsbury was actually purchased but the Great War eroded interest and in post-war Britain, private patronage of the theatre waned and government support was non-existent. The SMNTC continued, however, and in 1944 it effectively merged with the Old Vic Theatre trust and what some saw as a *de facto* National Theatre was set up there. A further parliamentary bill was passed in 1949, this time proposed by the government and buttressed by a promise of one million pounds funding. As noted above, although the foundation stone of a new theatre was laid in 1951, the project again foundered when state financial support was withdrawn.

Throughout the 1950s, arguments about the need for a National Theatre rumbled away, mostly in private though the central themes were clear enough. The problem was essentially that, up to that point, a 'national' theatre really meant only one thing, a theatre devoted to performing Shakespeare, the one national dramatic icon with any significant public presence. It could be and was argued that England (for this was a wholly English debate) already had two theatres devoted to performing Shakespeare, one inside London at the Old Vic and one outside at Stratford in Warwickshire, the Shakespeare Memorial Theatre which had first been built in 1874 following the success of a festival there on the tercentenary of Shakespeare's birth in 1864.

The subsequent passage of the Shakespeare Memorial Theatre was a microcosm of British theatre. The original Stratford theatre was much mocked as being both small and outside London as well as being financially supported by a local brewery run by the Flower family. The theatre was only used for an annual festival and the company spent the rest of the time touring, an activity which, under the leadership of the redoubtable cricketing actor-manager, Frank Benson, had acquired for the company an international reputation. By 1925, it had received a royal charter and when the original theatre burnt down, a public subscription fund was opened to build another. This was not particularly well-supported in Britain but its overseas touring enabled it to tap funds in the USA from where over half the money ultimately came. Throughout the 1950s, it had vied with the Old Vic as the leading Shakespearean house, in effect for the title of the national theatre of England's national playwright. In 1960, Peter Hall, a twenty-nine year old director, was appointed as Director of the Shakespeare Memorial Theatre

It is unclear whether the governors of the SMT really understood just what they took on in their appointment of Hall, a young man whose public image was almost as flash as that of John Osborne having married a French film-star, Leslie Caron, in 1956 and who was reported as loving fast cars. He was also unusually astute about money having lectured on business finance and management when on national service in the Air Force and was convinced of the need for public subsidy for the theatre. He argued to Fordham Flower, the chairman of the governing board that:

> ...for Stratford to prosper as anything other than a provincial heritage theatre it had to be transformed into a publicly funded, permanent, or semi-permanent, company

> *performing classical and contemporary work, built around a core of artists, with a base in London as well as in Stratford. There were signs that British theatre was beginning to reconnect to its society, having previously failed, in Hall's words, 'to take into account the fact that we have had a World War...and that everything in the world has changed – values, ways of living, ideals, hopes and fears.*

(Chambers (2004))

Hall was also, and most importantly, a showman. He immediately used the theatre's royal charter to change its name to the Royal Shakespeare Company thus acquiring two key icons of national identity. Who needs to be National when they can be both Royal and Shakespearean?

The *de jure* National Theatre had, at almost the same time, acquired its own national icon, Laurence Olivier,[83] a film-star also once married to another film-star, as well as a leading classical actor. Olivier had, rather surprisingly, recruited the critic Ken Tynan, by now well over thirty but still a provocative supporter of a new, radical theatre, as his dramaturge, a post that was literally foreign to the British theatre requiring the adoption of a German word to describe it.

The period between 1959 and 1963, the point at which both Directors were really able to launch their two institutions, was taken up with the Byzantine manoeuvres over funding which were henceforth to characterise the British arts establishment. The basic

---

[83] Olivier formally became Director of the National Theatre in August, 1962 moving from the Chichester Festival Theatre. However he had been anointed some time before and had been involved in negotiating about the conditions of the new institution.

lines were that the NT required a large input of capital funding to build its new theatre are well as continuing operational funding. The RSC under Hall's plan required only operational funding, though on a hugely increased scale for a venture to expand into London from its Stratford base which was opposed not only by supporters of the NT but also by some on its own board. In developing their strategy, the NT was able to rely on the new Chairman of the Arts Council, Lord Cottesloe, and on the general wave of support for public theatre shown by the numbers of municipally-financed houses being planned throughout the regions. It seemed inevitable and proper that at the summit of these new regional theatres there should be an even grander London theatre able to call itself 'national'. As noted above, the support of the local council in London proved to be the crucial link in setting up a financial package for the new theatre. The main problem for Olivier was that he was only a director-in-waiting, able to do nothing concrete until the deals were actually done. Even when appointed, he was tied to the small and conventional Old Vic as a base until the South Bank site was completed.

Hall, on the other hand, had the great advantage of being able to demonstrate in action just what a national company could do. He persuaded Flower to agree to use the financial reserves of the company, accumulated over years of touring, in setting up a London base. This was not easy given the opposition of one of his own board, Binkie Beaumont, to the very idea of a publicly-funded theatre in London. The manoeuvres that Hall undertook to acquire a London base throw an interesting light on the decline of the West End theatre since the early 1950s when, as discussed above, The Group effectively controlled it. Hall wanted to lease the Aldwych, a rather large and grand but dowdy West End house, owned by Prince

Littler's Associated Theatre Properties Ltd. Littler refused to play so Hall turned to his brother, Emile Littler, once a key player in The Group but now, for some fraternal reason, disaffected. He offered the Cambridge Theatre, which he controlled, and a scheme for joint management, neither of which Hall wanted but which could be used as a bargaining chip when he returned to Prince. In the end, Hall got his lease on the Aldwych at the cost of 25% of the gross box-office plus refurbishment of the theatre at the RSC's expense. A key element in the package was the deal struck with Keith Prowse Ltd, the largest ticketing agency in the country, to guarantee roughly 25% of the first season's sales. Beaumont resigned and the skies failed to fall in.

The whole episode was a sign that the old regime in the West End had fallen apart and the first embryo of the new one had come into existence. Yet it was one which contained a clear weakness. Although probably Hall himself, and his associates such as Brook and Barton, would have denied it, the initial founding finances of the RSC introduced a link with the commercial West End which the RSC has never quite broken and would later exploit almost to its own extinction. The 'RSC Stratford Company at the Aldwych' opened in December, 1960 with a production of Webster's *The Duchess of Malfi* which broke the theatre's box-office record. In early 1962, a production of Anouilh's *Becket* transferred to the Globe Theatre, the headquarters of Beaumont's empire.

Hall's efforts to demonstrate the capacity of the new RSC was almost maniacal in its extent. In 1962

> *Hall turned the RSC into what one commentator described as 'the biggest single theatre venture in the world.' By*

hiring the Arts Theatre in London, he expanded the RSC empire to embrace three theatres, in addition to the Studio in Stratford, two West End transfers, a small-scale tour to mainland Europe and an ambitious large-scale tour of the UK presenting challenging Shakespeare and two world premières. Its company of actors and staff numbering almost 500 presented 24 productions in an unprecedented range of classical and contemporary work to some 700,000 people. As if this size of operation were not enough, Hall harboured other ideas for expansion. In order to make the RSC's stages better able to accommodate the free-flowing production of Shakespeare he intended, he embarked on two major building schemes. One, in partnership with Ballet Rambert, was to build in London their own 1,600-seat flexible theatre with a smaller space alongside. The other was to turn the Stratford theatre into a 2,000-seat thrust stage amphitheatre – in Hall's words, 'the most exciting theatre building in Europe'.

(Chambers 2004 p.20)

All this constituted a colossal financial gamble as little of it was self-financing. Hall relied upon creating such an impact that closure as a result of financial constraints would prove impossible. It was a dangerous strategy requiring continuous efforts inside the negotiating corridors as well as blatant manipulation of the media. In the end it just about succeeded. The 'double-bill' of Clifford William's *Comedy of Errors* and Brook's *King Lear* was greeted with critical and popular acclaim and toured abroad to huge success. Just as *Lear* opened, the final decision in the long-drawnout negotiations was announced. In Chambers' summary:

> *At the end of October Cottesloe told the RSC that it would receive a grant and this should be read as acceptance of the RSC operation in London. A week later—before such announcements would normally be made— the RSC was informed of the sum, £47,000 for 1963-4. It was about half what the RSC judged it needed and meant no pay rise for actors, no reopening of the Arts experiment, and no new building for the Studio in Stratford. More worryingly, there was a warning from the Treasury that has haunted the company ever since. It was not issued directly but by the messenger, in this case Sir William Emrys Williams, secretary-general of the Arts Council. He was told to pass on to the RSC the following advice: while the RSC might assume that 'it will be necessary for them to operate on a National Theatre level' the Treasury would not be able to accept 'any wider implications which might be held to flow from any such assumptions.' In other words, the RSC would not receive a commensurate level of subsidy to the NT's even if it performed commensurately. It would always be the poor relation...*

> *...The RSC had won its battle but, as it turned out, had lost the war; it had gained the public subsidy and recognition as a national institution essential to Hall's plan, which meant the London base could be maintained, but it was not sufficient to fulfil Hall's ambitions for the company. Nevertheless, the settlement rankled with regional theatres and remained a divisive issue in the disbursement of the national*

funding cake. From the perspective of state arts funding in Britain, awarding a grant to the RSC represented an act of faith the like of which was not to be seen again that century. However, the sum awarded was arbitrary and nearly three times less than the NT received. This historic imbalance remained a constraint for the rest of the RSC's life. There was never enough money to support long-term experiment or training, or to reduce ticket prices substantially. It also meant in later years the RSC had to do more and different things not always for artistic reasons but to attract necessary additional funds...

(Chambers 2004 p.28)

Thus, in 1963, Britain acquired two national theatres. Neither was in fact wholly new being in effect continuations of the two previous institutions, the SMT and the Old Vic and each had to cope in its own way with this heritage. One was under-funded but became undeniably sexy, the other was apparently funded adequately but saddled both with the image of being part of the old order, despite the presence of Tynan, and with the fact that for some years, it was to be confined to the rather small and out of the way Old Vic, itself a key part of the old way of doing things. Olivier might have seen the irony of that fact that, almost twenty years before, he had been a part of a series of now-legendary Shakespearean productions by the Old Vic company which had actually been performed at the New Theatre in the West End. Now he was Director of the new National Theatre actually back in the Old Vic itself apart from one, unsuccessful effort to recreate the previous success at the New Theatre. In the event, it was to be thirteen years before the NT moved to its new building with Hall as its Director.

In the years until the NT began to move to the South Bank in 1976[84], the two companies continued to roll along the paths which had been set out in these early times. At the Old Vic, Olivier formed what was essentially the pinnacle of the solid regional theatres with a wide-ranging and prolific repertoire[85] based largely on classics with Olivier, himself, taking on regular set-piece star parts[86] despite a series of major illnesses.

Despite Tynan's prominent presence, new work was largely absent apart from Peter Schaffer, whose *Royal Hunt of the Sun* (1964) was followed by *Black Comedy* (1966) and *Equus* (1973), and Stoppards's *Rosencrantz and Guildenstern* (1967) which, overall, set a pattern of rather undemanding fare in a period when new playwrights were dropping like ripe apples in autumn. The only exceptions to this were Arden's *Armstrong's Last Goodnight* (1965), brought in from Chichester, and Trevor Griffiths' *The Party* (1973) whose meaty central part proved irresistible to a dying Olivier. The problem the NT had with new work is highlighted by its great row in 1967 over Tynan's insistence of staging Hochhuth's *Soldiers*. This play, written by a Swiss-German, had as its central theme the morality of the Allies' saturation bombing of Germany with a sub-plot concerning the possible involvement of Winston Churchill in causing the death of General Sikorski, a war-time Polish leader, in an air-crash. Churchill had died only two years before and had been given a state funeral with, memorably,

---

[84] Its third stage, the Cottesloe, did not open until 1977.

[85] In 1963-73, Olivier's period as Director, the NT produced 98 shows, almost ten a year.

[86] *Othello* (1964), *The Master Builder* (1965), *The Dance of Death* (1967), *The Merchant of Venice* (1970), *The Long Day's Journey into Night* (1971) and, finally and the only new piece, *The Party* (1973)

the defunct cranes along the upper Thames wharves being bowed down as his coffin passed. It was the first time a commoner's funeral had been broadcast live since Ivor Novello's and was a lot more theatrical. One member of the NT's board, Lord Lyttleton, had been in Churchill's War Cabinet and he persuaded the board to reject unanimously the production, a decision which Olivier accepted. Tynan eventually engineered a brief run for *Soldiers* (1968) outside the NT and the general critical reception was essentially to wonder what all the fuss was about. It was not until the opening of the new stages on the South Bank and under Hall's direction that the NT began at last to grasp the meaning of being a national theatre by producing new British plays which only it and the RSC could adequately tackle. Brenton's *Weapons of Happiness* (1976), the first play presented on the huge space of the Lyttleton stage (the former board member having by this time been transmuted into an artefact), was the initial example.

The presence of three, contrasting stages enabled areas of performance style to be explored which the proscenium of the Old Vic as well as Olivier's temperament had restrained. This included such as Bryden's promenade explorations *Lark Rise at Candleford* (1978) and a trilogy of *The Mysteries* (1985) adapted by Tony Harrison in the small Cottesloe and the revival of American musicals, which began with *Guys and Dolls* in 1982, and which was to prove an almost annual as well as lucrative venture. The large South Bank building of the NT was not universally liked but eventually its massive presence would become a key feature of a revitalised South Bank, both a tourist centre and a national monument. In the 1960s and early 70s, the relatively conservative image of the NT seemed a throwback to the previous age of solid and hidebound provincial repertory, narrowly class-based and largely irrelevant. However in the new building and under Hall's direction, which was notably less flamboyant than at the RSC, the NT gradually gathered in the aura of a genuine national theatre particularly in times when funding pressure from political forces genuinely hostile to public institutions made it a visible symbol of a progressive country. It was, however, perpetually dogged by funding problems[87] in its new expanded premises and was forced to drop many of its initial ambitions to be a wider theatrical presence than three stages in London. Its lack of any significant touring became a source of constant criticism as was its links with commercial theatre in the West End, seen initially as a source of income for Hall rather than for the NT.

By way of contrast, the RSC began by seeming to be almost wilfully fixed on exploring all possible ways to stage its work and to explore new forms. Spurred by Hall's decisive breakout from the Stratford base, over the almost twenty years until it moved into the Barbican, the RSC restlessly sought new venues. In a sense, whereas the NT set itself up as the peak of solid provincial repertory in the heart of London, the RSC became the pinnacle of the kind of touring theatre which was the most dynamic element of British theatre throughout the 1960s and 70s. The earliest signal of this was Brook's Theatre of Cruelty Season at the LAMBDA theatre in 1964 which, as a club, escaped the still prevailing censorship rules. The Brook season, which led on to his *Marat/Sade* (1964) and *US* (1966) productions at the Aldwych, was in its way a straightforward development of previous *avant garde* theatre, albeit sponsored by a national theatre. Less publicised but in its own way equally important was, first, the founding of the RSC Club with its own

---

[87] Documented at length in Hall's *Diaries*

magazine, *Flourish*, and following from this the founding of a small touring group, originally called, slightly bizarrely, Actors Commando. The inspiration for this seems to have been Michael Kustow, another of the American artistic entrepreneurs discussed above, and certainly there was a strong element in it of his approach. The Actors Commando group developed into Theatregoround with the help of an anonymous donation which enabled it to buy a bus which could carry both personnel and equipment including a mobile stage. The first full play mounted in this way was Shakespeare's *King John* directed by a young woman, Buzz Goodbody, who had previously been a directorial gofer for two years. The production was a perfect example of radical touring theatre; fast, irreverent, politicised and funny. In its sole main-house showing, London critics generally disliked it but the small regional venues where it mainly appeared loved it. So, luckily for Goodbody, did Peter Brook.

In succeeding years, the RSC mounted seasons in various small London venues as well as the Aldwych, including the Roundhouse and The Place, until it finally settled on the same kind of venue as Marowitz had done in the 1960s, a defunct rehearsal space in central London, appropriately named The Warehouse in 1977. On its opening night the roof leaked which seemed about right. The Warehouse continued to present new drama until 1983 when small new productions were transferred to the studio space in the Barbican. In Stratford, a small costume store was changed into a studio theatre, The Other Space, under Goodbody's direction while plans were evolved for what eventually in 1986 became the Swan. In 1977, the RSC started what became a regular season in Newcastle, regular enough for it to be claimed as the third home of the RSC in the 1990s. The company also ran national tours developing its own portable seating for non-theatrical venues and toured at various times in the USA, Japan, Australia and New Zealand.

This restless behaviour was in part a genuine urge to experiment particularly by its younger directors, notably Trevor Nunn, who became director in 1967 following Hall's sudden departure, Terry Hands, who came from the new Liverpool Everyman, David Jones, who ran the Aldwych, and Buzz Goodbody. Money pinched on most things that the RSC did and, although criticised in the early 1970s for extravagance, the company was always able to return to basics throughout most of this period. Nunn's first successful production at Stratford, a revival of *The Revenger's Tragedy*, much praised for its design and costumes, was produced on the bones of an existing set with the black-and-silver costumes made out of old blackout material[88] found in a store and sprayed with silver paint. Goodbody's *Hamlet* with Ben Kingsley in 1975, a key Shakespearean production of the decade, came from the Other Place on a budget that was barely in three figures.

In various ways and, to some extent, self-consciously, these RSC directors were trying to re-create the era when, as noted above, Shakespeare had been a genuinely popular playwright appealing to audiences across the social spectrum. There was a great emphasis on making the plots of the plays clear, for example in the history plays giving the supporters of each side distinctively coloured costumes, and on improving the verse-speaking of actors. The fights and battles were given a real edge, almost literally in the case of the *Wars of the Roses* in which Bury insisted on using real metal blades rather than the metal-edged wood used before. In Goodbody's production of *As You Like It*,

---

[88] Rough cloth hung at windows in the war to stop light escaping.

Charles the Wrestler was played by an actor who had been a professional wrestler and who trained others for the contest. Live music, often composed by Guy Wolfenden, the Director of Music, was used much more extensively. In his *Midsummer Night's Dream*, Brook was happy to turn to elements of circus performance to create a feeling of magic. An element of spectacle, even melodrama, returned. This was not without its negative side. Spectacle for its own sake without genuine relevance to the play could smother rather than illuminate but, overall, the RSC's work in this period not only transformed the way in which Shakespeare was performed but also had much wider reverberations in British theatre.

However, the perambulations of the RSC also had a root in money. Its permanent home remained the Shakespeare Memorial Theatre in Stratford, a large tourist theatre with no real base in the surrounding community, unloved by actor and director alike. Achieving a high occupancy in Stratford with its huge overheads was the basic requirement for the company. This required a relatively high return-rate for the half-dozen or so favourites who would guarantee this, at least in Stratford, something which after some years inevitably produced directorial staleness which in turn meant lack-lustre productions which failed to gain a more demanding London audience for the necessary transfers. *The Wars of the Roses* in one way and Brook's *Midsummer Night's Dream* in another were able to nullify this problem and both went on to lucrative tours. As Chambers notes, in a period when inflation was eating away at the real value of grants, the only way to increase labour productivity in a theatre company is to pound more productions out of the same work-force and this essentially is what the RSC did with four theatres plus touring. There was also a cutback on production size from Hall's original hopes so that when, in 1975, Hands directed the history plays at Stratford, the company size was about half that of *The Wars of the Roses* a decade before.

The RSC had been founded on the cash reserves built up by a decade of profitable overseas tours and throughout its subsequent progress there existed a strong streak of commercial enterprise. The Aldwych acted as an in-house West End transfer so this aspect of commercial linkage never acquired specific prominence until the company moved to the Barbican. However its international touring was primarily a cash cow whilst from 1978, its national touring was sponsored by Hallmark, a greetings card manufacturer. In 1975, it faced a major funding crisis which forced it back upon the basic commercial imperative of the company, to fill the Stratford theatre and transfer successful productions to London.

In this period, when the RSC effectively was *the* national theatre whilst the NT acted as a superior regional repertory, the ambiguity of this role could be most seen in the path of Trevor Nunn, its second Director. Nunn's work at the RSC until his final years was primarily with the central Shakespearean canon which he tackled in two contrasting ways. The first was the big show as seen in his Roman season which attempted to put the five Shakespearean Roman plays into some kind of social order. New stage machinery was installed at Stratford and the company size was increased but the project failed to gain the kind of cohesive lift-off that its ambitions demanded. It would in the end be remembered largely for Nicol Williamson's performance of *Coriolanus* when the production moved to London. The second approach was the small-scale as in his initial *Revenger's Tragedy* but most memorably in a studio-theatre production of *Macbeth* (1976) with Ian McKellen and

Judi Dench, which owed a lot to Goodbody's *Hamlet* and which stripped away the pretentiousness which had begun to envelope much of the RSC's Shakespeare in the previous few years.

Nunn directed almost no contemporary work at the RSC even though through the 1970s this became the most innovative part of the company's work. However he was involved in two projects which illustrate the passage of the RSC as a national public theatre. The first was an attempt to stage a show based on the General Strike of 1926, probably the single most divisive class conflict in Britain in the twentieth century. First given a working script by Hall when he arrived in Stratford in 1965, it was intended to be in the mould of *Oh! What a Lovely War* but had proved beyond Nunn's capacity and was dropped. He returned to the idea in 1970 when the production was to be the centrepiece of a season at the Roundhouse, the converted engine-shed in North London, an essentially public space far removed from the proscenium theatres of the Shakespeare Memorial Theatre or the Aldwych. With directorial input from Hands, Nunn and Goodbody, a fixed script was dropped. Instead the company was asked to develop a show based upon the transcripts of the contemporary debates in Parliament counterpoised to scenes of the Strike based upon company research with music and songs written by Guy Wolfenden, the RSC music director. It was hoped to fill the cavernous spaces of the Roundhouse with fairground rides adapted to act as metaphors for some of the action. A ghost train, for example, might be used as a coalmine. In effect, the production was to some of the techniques developed by Mnouchkine in France and shown off to great success in their production about the French revolution which did crack the space of the Roundhouse in 1971. The production was pulled at the last moment after some months of rehearsal and Nunn returned to classical theatre.[89] The failure of the production was essentially a failure to bridge the gap between the radical touring shows and the set-piece main-house work without losing on the way the energy and political dynamism of the smaller groups.

In the course of the 1970s, the RSC staged some of the most politically conscious plays of the decade including Griffiths' *Occupations* (1971), Arden and d'Arcy's *Island of the Mighty* (1972), Edgar's *Destiny* (1976), Bond's *The Bundle* (1977) and Barker's *That Good Between Us* (1977) to name just some of the most outstanding. The Warehouse in particular for the five years of its existence under Howard Davies direction became a showcase for new writing. However, with the exception of *Island of the Mighty*, whose disturbed genesis is discussed below, these all originated in studio work though *Destiny* did move successfully from the Other Place to the Aldwych. In effect, the RSC fell into a triple-track artistic policy; rather grand Shakespeare originating from Stratford (for example, Hands' productions of the history plays with their conventional nationalistic interpretations in 1975-78); intellectually challenging new work and stripped-bare classics at its two small venues; and, mostly, rather unchallenging middle-brow new work at the Aldwych (for example, Stoppard's *Travesties* (1974) and Nichols' *Privates on Parade* (1977)) which was very much in line with the demands of a standard West End audience.

In 1980, Nunn was faced by another major funding crisis which threatened its London venues, the existence of which had never been fully accepted by

---

[89] A cut-down version of the show was later staged by Wolfenden and David Benedictus under the title *What a Way to Run a Revolution*, a title which sums up its rather light-hearted style.

the Arts Council. It responded by setting up an Aldwych season quite unlike those that which had gone before consisting of another of Barton's mammoth three-part classical adaptations, *The Greeks*, and the idea of adapting a Dickens' book for the stage, something apparently prompted by a trip to the Soviet Union where Dickens' adaptations were very popular. He chose *Nicholas Nickleby* and working with a writer, David Edgar, who was experienced in group collaboration, set about the same kind of company creation that had been tried with *Strike* and had since become a staple of the creative process of touring companies such as Joint Stock. The outcome was a show staged in two parts which was, essentially, the final pinnacle of the RSC's rather submerged role as the leader of radical touring theatre using all the techniques of improvisation, movement and breaking down the boundary between actors and audience which had been developed in such theatre. It was a show that cried out for staging in a venue like the Roundhouse but in the end it transcended the Aldwych and became a huge hit, coming back for a second season and making a pot of money on Broadway as well as being adapted for television. It was, however, a little ironic that after a decade of political subversion, with a writer known for his left-wing views and at the beginning of the most socially divisive decade of second-half of the century in Britain, the message of the play, faithful to the book, was essentially one of the possibility of social renewal and redemption and of benevolent capitalism. The final joyful scene was marred only by the mute reappearance of the unfortunate Smike, the only symbol that perhaps all was not well with the world.

In 1981, Nunn made the first of his forays into commercial theatre when he directed the phenomenally successful musical *Cats* for Andrew

Lloyd Weber followed in 1984 by *Starlight Express*. The financial propriety of this kind of crossover was much debated at the time. Less obvious was the fact that having set up the RSC with the possibility of moving in a new direction, combining the kind of forms used in *Nicholas Nickleby* with its classical roots, Nunn chose instead to effectively abandon subsidised theatre, at least for that decade, and to work with a new form of musical in the commercial sector. It was in many ways the most decisive and important cultural action of any one individual in post-war theatre. Unlike the flamboyant Peter Hall, Nunn has never really expanded on his decision. However two factors are likely to have been involved, both of critical importance in the decades discussed in the succeeding chapter. First, the new impresarios like Lloyd Weber and Cameron Mackintosh opened up the possibility, unknown since the 1950s, of making a very large amount of money out of commercial theatre. The second was the impossibility of operating the RSC under anything other than culturally crippling conditions at its new home in London at the Barbican and the financial rigours of the new Conservative government.

In 1985, Nunn directed *Les Misérables* at the Barbican, probably the most successful and lucrative show of the twentieth century. Essentially an opera sung by actors, in one direction it completed the break with standard forms of classical theatre begun by Hall twenty years before. Along another axis, it provided the key cement between the major national theatres and the West End which was to shape their direction over the succeeding two decades. Like *Nicholas Nickleby*, it would be hard to see in *Les Misérables* much of the subversive intent which had pervaded the RSC since *Wars of the Roses* with the radical elements of the original novel being played largely for spectacle or personal sympathy yet both were 'public' plays in the fullest meaning of the term. The search for national community was not so much abandoned as tied to the shifting ice-floe of Thatcherism, forced to follow its path at least for a while.

Real communities

He [Richardson] believed that theatre should be a meeting pace for a variety of groups both young and old, and wanted the theatre to make a more direct contribution to the life of the community. He used to describe the theatre as a 'social necessity' and himself as a 'community servant'. In particular he recognised the increasing importance of the theatre director's role in the pattern of community life.

G.Vallins describing the first director of the Belgrade Theatre, Anthony Richardson, in 1965. (Jackson p.5)

What I would like to see above all is the theatre accepted as a necessary and useful part of the community—as useful and as necessary as the doctor and the shop on the corner. It shouldn't just be a luxury item for a minority with special tastes.

Peter Cheeseman interviewed in *Plays and Players*, March, 1967

'The impact of ideas' a critic wrote 'was enormous. The impact of the drama in theatrical terms was also enormous.' But she went on to point out that the real importance of the show lay in the context –in the fact that it wasn't presented to an undefined audience in a theatre, but to a particular group engaged in a particular form of social action. We hadn't in any way tried to compromise or tailor a show for this particular audience. We had done and said exactly what we wanted. But we had been

> *aware that we weren't working in a vacuum,*
> *that we were playing inside a social*
> *situation for a sharply defined purpose. And*
> *this situation contrasted strongly with the*
> *absence of such a context in the established*
> *theatre; two years earlier, working with*
> *Peter Brook on US, I had been conscious*
> *that we weren't really talking to anybody in*
> *particular – that the Aldwych audience*
> *would really have no community core to*
> *which our communication could be directed.*

Albert Hunt (Hunt) writing about *John Ford's Missile Crisis* (1970) in 1972

Each of these, nationally rather unknown but in their sphere highly influential, directors placed 'community' at the heart of their activity. For each of them, the word meant something quite concrete; there was nothing 'imagined' about the community to which they were attached. However, each meant something rather different.

The community for which Richardson worked was something specific and geographical, the City of Coventry. As noted above, the Belgrade Theatre in Coventry was the first of the new municipally-funded theatres and it took on its role as a community theatre in an equally pioneering spirit. Coventry was Britain's 'motor-city'; prosperous, unionised, expanding with rings of new council-house estates, it had had its physical heart destroyed in a brief but catastrophic blitz. The impact of that attack went a long way beyond the physical and throughout the 1950s, the local council had prepared plans for the renewal of the city's heart. The word which came, ultimately rather banally, to sum up these efforts throughout the country was 'centre'; shopping centre, sports centre, civic centre, arts centre, leisure centre, aquacentre. It was as if the word summed up the endeavour to create a new form of community, no longer based simply upon a set of neighbouring streets for the combined impact of bombs and slum demolition had by the 1960s often dispersed the tight working class communities defined by a place of residence and nearby work. The new 'centres' were meant to bring people together in other ways than the simply geographic; to shop together, swim together, possibly in the renamed town halls to perform such civic actions as paying rent and rates together. In Coventry, even the new cathedral joined in playing a self-conscious role as a community religious centre.

The new theatres played their own part in this in ways which varied in detail but contained three broad themes. The first of these was simply a desire to open up the theatre as a physical space to be used throughout the day as well as in the evening. The Belgrade showed the way for this by the design features of spacious café and bar facilities as well as a foyer which could be used for other purposes. Most of the new theatres followed this and even those based upon refurbished buildings tried to incorporate some kind of café. Houses which had the space, such as the grand Royal Exchange in Manchester, went one stage further and incorporated shops into an arcade usually focussing on local craft products or some kind of bookshop. The success of this extension obviously varies very widely according to location, competition and management style. The relation between such activities and the cultural purpose of the theatre also varies widely. However, whatever the criteria for success, it is hard to remember now the times when theatres were tight shut during the day, except for matinee performances, unless one visits Shaftesbury Avenue on a Friday afternoon.

The second and more important theme was set by Richardson in 1965 when the Belgrade set up the first Theatre-in-Education (TIE) team in Britain. The general place of drama in education is treated as a separate section and a fuller account of TIE is found there. Children's theatre had had a poor relation status in Britain though it is worth recalling that George Devine's role at the short-lived Old Vic setup after the war had been as director of a children's theatre. The key breakthrough which Richardson made was to establish a professional theatre group tied in partly with the main theatre but also linked directly to the local education authority often being paid their wages by it as teachers. TIE was literally *in* education, inside the classroom rather than performing in theatres in front of more or less willing school parties.

TIE has now become a complicated sector in its own right having spread rapidly through the theatre system in to 1970s before being hit by the public sector cuts of the 1980s. However, it would be difficult to find a publicly funded theatre today which did not have an education department with links to local schools, initiatives which stem directly back to the founding impetus in Coventry in 1965.

The third and most general theme is acknowledgement precisely of the responsibility local theatres have to the local community. Present day examples of this are the 'mission statements' of two theatres, one a large metropolitan house with a national presence, the other a small, rather isolated venue with ambitious but local pretension.

The Playhouse's aims are:

> **To promote** *artistic excellence and, while vigorously making its own region a priority,*

sustain national standing and achieve international standing in theatre productions and arts education programmes in order to feed the cultural life of the city, the region and the country.

To serve a wide range of constituencies and communities within the region, engaging with our audiences and listening to their needs so as to actively develop their interest in and attendance at the theatre.

To offer opportunities for artists to train and develop their work so that they can continue to feed the cultural life of Britain.

To work with artists of international standing in order to extend the artistic horizons of the Playhouse.

To extend and strengthen relationships with other arts professionals and education agencies, especially in our own region, to promote and develop the work and policies of the Playhouse and stimulate artistic debate.

To work in partnership with industry, commerce and political parties in order to promote the Playhouse and increase understanding of the cultural, social and financial importance of the arts.

To engage *in open debate about the role and future of the arts and public subsidy, and to ensure that cultural policy occupies a central place on the government's agenda.*

Mission statement: West Yorkshire Playhouse

...you will find that the Community Company mounts stage productions on the Rep theatre's main stage and in smaller theatres and community venues. This however is only a small part of our work in Dundee. Most of our work is much less visible to those not directly involved and often will not result in a final production on a stage or set.

The Community Company uses creative arts to work alongside other agencies locally in fields such as education, mental health, community development and urban regeneration. Community arts are also used to explore particular issues such as:

- *bullying, in schools or in the workplace*
- *building self confidence and self esteem*
- *health*
- *human rights*
- *equality and social inclusion*
- *racism*
- *regeneration and the environment*
- *gender issues*

This work takes place in a wide variety of settings: schools, community venues, hospitals, sheltered accommodation or at the Rep Theatre itself.

> *The work tends to involve a large degree of active participation. We work with people with the view of bringing about a positive change in their lives, in their community and in broader society.*

Website of Dundee Repertory Theatre

The differences in ambition are plain but there is still a common thread of community presence and obligation. The Dundee theatre is probably closer to the roots of local community than the West Yorkshire Playhouse. The latter sits at the cultural apex of a large city endowed with other theatrical resources whilst the Dundee Repertory is just about all there is theatrically in its isolated spot. Even so they are still relatively close in aspiration. There is a large variation in just how this aspiration is put into practice. Sometimes as at Cheeseman's time at Stoke, community links were expressed partly in the form of productions about the community itself usually its history, but sometimes as with the Shelton Bar closure, about contemporary events. Cheeseman made his motivation for these productions very explicit.

> *I wanted us also to begin to bridge the cultural gap which separates the artist from the majority of the community and which I believe to be a gap created by style not subject matter. I wanted us to begin to develop a popular language, a style of our own which would make theatre livelier and more attractive than the conventional play format."*

(Itzin (1980) p.xii)

There are parallels here with the pattern of old melodrama noted in a previous chapter, that plays in Mile End theatres usually had a Jewish character whilst in Lancashire there was almost a sub-genre of

Lancashire plays. However, whilst these had firmly commercial justification, the new community plays had a wider and decidedly self-conscious purpose of community building. In fact, the conception of community plays developed in the 1960s into a new category of theatre often detached from the physical space of any specific building called a 'theatre'. Ann Jellicoe, a playwright who found initial success with the first wave of new writing at Devine's Royal Court, is the most prominent name associated with this kind of production following her move to the West Country.

All of this added up to a theatre which one way or another tried to place itself within a physical community. In parallel with this, another idea of community developed other kinds of theatre, a theatre concerned with the community of interests.

Just as the word 'centre' acquired a new emphasis in the 1960s, one which was much wider than theatre but which pulled theatre along with it, so too did the word 'community' itself. At around this time, communities emerged which were not just physical locations but which encompassed other kinds of human identity in particular those of gender and ethnicity as well as various kinds of political and social activity. These were not the 'imagined' communities of nationhood but specific forms of identity which were real though sometimes suppressed. In some cases, particularly ethnic identity, this kind of theatre had a clear physical location, for example the Black Theatre of Brixton. However, mostly this area of theatre involved touring around the growing circuit of studio theatres, arts centres and other venues which proliferated in this period.

It is possible to draw up various kinds of classification for such 'identity' theatre but in practice the boundary lines of such schema are always blurred. Thus Joint Stock was a touring group clearly identified as left-wing and adopting innovatory performance and production techniques but still firmly inside the boundary marking 'straight' theatre; 7:84, the touring company founded by John McGrath in 1971 was described as being *"in opposition to bourgeois theatre—a truly revolutionary theatre"* (Itzin(1980) p.120) but which still often played in conventional theatrical venues; North West Spanner, a group set up in 1972 out of a children's community arts project, was a group which specifically targeted groups engaged in local political action such as rent strikes and various kinds of industrial action and which deliberately played in venues where such action was taking place. In 1977, North West Spanner had their entire grant from the North West Arts Association[90] removed on the grounds that they were a "Marxist revolutionary" company and should not receive public funds. (Itzin (1980) pp.291-305) (Their grant totalled some £12,500 at the time). The response to this was interesting. A conference convened in Manchester attracted representatives not only of the obvious groups such as 7:84, Red Ladder, Belt and Braces and other touring political groups but also of every 'straight' theatre in Manchester including the Royal Exchange, Contact, Library and University theatres. The cut was eventually revoked.

The often tumultuous politics of the 1970s provided attractive sites for the development of a form of theatre aimed at illuminating and strengthening the position of specific social groups. Women's theatre groups such the Women's Theatre Group and Monstrous Regiment were founded in the mid-1970s

---

[90] The regional subsidiary of the Arts Council

along with the pioneering and extremely brave[91] gay theatre group, Gay Sweatshop. Support for these along with the overtly socialist groups ebbed and flowed within overall national politics and it is clear that the decline of socialist politics in the 1980s impacted heavily on may such groups. However, the particular patterns of this kind of community theatre should not obscure the fact that it set up a form which has persisted and in a number of ways grown ever since. The 'communities' of drug-users, prisoners, transsexuals, single-parents and many others are now served by theatre groups intended to educate and sustain as well to define their specific existence.

Writers

The second half of the twentieth century and, in particular, the decades of the 1960s, 70s and 80s, were in the words of Martin Esslin *"the most vigorous period of dramatic writing ... since Elizabethan and Jacobean times"*. (Shank p.180) As with several other aspects of the theatre, it is difficult to be very precise about numbers but it seems likely that in this period there were, as Dominic Dromgoole asserts, more good playwrights at work than at any period in history. This marked a shift from the situation immediately after the war, In the early 1950s, there was a dearth of new British dramatists and in 1956 the discovery of new writers was a founding task of George Devine at the Royal Court. The result of this quest was that up to 1962, seven new writers[92] had been produced. If one adds to this list, three writers from Theatre Workshop[93], a couple from the Poetic Drama

---

[91] Physically as well as theatrically given the ever-present threat of homophobic violence at a time when gay men had been given the barest protection against legal action for less than ten years.

[92] Osborne, Wesker, Jellicoe, John Arden, John, Hall and Simpson.

[93] MacColl, Behan and Delaney

movement[94] and a handful who had emerged in commercial theatre[95], then one has largely counted the new playwrights in more than fifteen years from the end of the war up to the early 1960s—perhaps a dozen or fifteen. By way of comparison, in the eight years from 1962 to 1970, Taylor in his survey of the period, makes reference to twenty-nine new writers[96], all male. In their survey of post-war dramatic writing up to the mid-1980s, Chambers and Prior refer to fifty writers,[97] eleven of them female, who had their first plays produced in the fourteen year period 1970-1984. Neither of these books tries to be encyclopaedic so it is likely that some more names could be added to these lists. In the early 1990s, a letter protesting against cuts in subsidy to the theatre was signed by 97 'playwrights', a list which, unsurprisingly did not include some of the more-established writers.

The relative quality of these writers is bound to be arguable but it is perhaps relevant to note that of the twenty-nine writers noted by Taylor only seven failed to be mentioned in Stevenson's survey of the history of English literature in the period 1960-2000 (Stevenson) published in 2004 whilst twenty-eight of Prior and Chamber's fifty failed to be mentioned.

---

[94] Fry and Duncan

[95] The most prominent being Pinter together with Whiting and Ustinov.

[96] Ayckbourn, Barnes, Bond, Brenton, Caute, Corlett, Cregan, Gray, Halliwell, Hampton, Hare Hopkins, Laffan, Mercer, Milner, Nichols, Orton, Pinner, Plater, Selbourne, Stoppard, Shaffer, Shaw, Spencer, Taylor, Terson, Williams, Wood,

[97] Jane Arden, Barker, Berkoff, Bill, Bleasdale, C. Bond, Byrne, Chadwick, Clark, Cox, Churchill, Daniels, Darke, Dorell, Dunbar, Friel, Gooch, Griffiths, D. Holman, R. Holman, Horsfield, Hutchinson, Keefe, Kureishi, Lavery, Lowe, Luckham, McClenaghan, McGrath, Marchant, Matura, Morrison, Page, Parker, Russell, Stott, Thompson, Wandor, Whelan, Whitehead, Wilkinson, Wilcox, Williams, Wilson, Wright,

Does a rise in the 'dropout rate' from 24% to 56% suggest some decline in perceived quality as viewed some decades later? Or is it that the flood of new writers in the 1970s in particular tends to overload any attempt at general critical mapping? Perhaps the basic problem in making any kind of critical assessment of writing for the theatre in this period is that there was a significant shift in the role of the writer in relation to the dramatic process. The end of the nineteenth and the first half of the twentieth century saw a shift in the position of the playwright towards being the key creative agent in this process and towards the elevation of the text as the prime repository of a play's meaning. This process was most clearly spelled out by the critic William Archer who constantly championed what he termed the Greek in the theatre as against the Goth; intellectual stimulation versus the sensual stimulation of 'effect', that is all the components of theatre which arise from the non-textual. (See, for example (Archer)) In the melodramas of the Victorian era, writers occupied a relatively lowly status regarded primarily as constructors of the basic skeleton of a play on to which the key elements of effect and stagecraft were built. This position was reflected in the financial rewards of writing, a lump sum with no royalties for repeat performances. Essentially, a writer normally lost any control over his work once it had been handed over to the theatre manager. At the end of the nineteenth century and, specifically, in the Edwardian era, the playwright acquired a quite different position, most notably in spoken drama but also in musical theatre where the author of the 'book' came to claim almost equal status with the composer of the music. The process whereby this happened is complex and deeply entwined with the shift of theatre towards the elitist art-form described in the prologue. The basic result of the shift was that the writer came to own a play, both legally in copyright terms and also intellectually in the sense that in naturalist theatre the text became almost the sole source of effect within the production. In the work of a writer like Shaw, this sense of ownership provided room for a wide range of impacts, but as the century progressed its constriction became more and more apparent. Priestley has already been quoted on how he struggled against the constraints of naturalism but had always to return to it.

When Devine attempted to revive British theatre, he tried to do so by developing a writers' theatre, initially by approaching established novelists, at the time much the dominant work-group in the hierarchy of writers, to write plays, something which met with little success. Although plays did arrive through other channels and they had their well-publicised impact, as described above, there was in the early part of the 1960s a sense that this impetus had rather petered out. The major new stimulus that occurred from this point on was that in the new state-subsidised theatrical venues, a number of changes were required, notably a toppling of the dominance of the text as the key element in dramatic art. There were a number of strands to this but three stand out—the proliferation of venues in which naturalist drama was, physically, simply not an option; the desire to develop a more popular form of theatre; and, linked to both these as well as fitting with a more general political motif of the times, experiments with various forms of collaborative theatre .

One block throughout much of the twentieth century as to how one became a playwright was the simple weight of investment which hung upon the decision. As the British theatre came more and more to focus on the West End with its trail of pre- and post-London tours, so the choice of text became more and more crucial in the risking of ever larger sums of money. An established playwright could, as Delderfield notes, make a comfortable, even a wealthy, living. But how to acquire that status given that the craft of play-writing was believed to be fashioned over several productions and given the dearth of small theatres where financial success was no criterion? At the Royal Court, Devine attempted to side-step this problem by the Sunday performances in which plays were essentially read without costumes or set but the real breakthrough came when Haynes opened up first the Traverse and then the Arts Lab to all-comers and the subsequent explosion of small performance venues. The physical form of these combined with the minute production budgets meant that writers were forced to experiment with forms outside naturalism using techniques drawn from almost any source other than the conventional theatre. When Brenton in *Christie in Love* (1969) opened by a figure rising up from a 'grave' of crumpled newspapers, he was drawing more on Hammer horror films than on any literary dramatic predecessor as well as being aware of the financial restrictions of his company whilst, as noted above, Roland Muldoon saw the origins of CAST more in Chuck Berry than *Waiting for Godot*.

More than their immediate predecessors, many of the writers in the 1960s set out to entertain and were not too fussy about the techniques they adopted to this end. Most of the new writers of the 1950s seemed to have ambiguous feelings about extending their work to a wider audience. This can be seen even with the key individual in the development of popular theatre in that period, Joan Littlewood, who eventually was unable to cope with the popularity of the musical theatre developed at Stratford East and the way in which this appeared to cut across the initial objectives of Theatre Workshop. Only two of the 'Royal Court' writers, Arden and Jellicoe, really took on board the need for theatre to expand its appeal, Arden by moving to Kirbymoorside and experimenting with local community theatre before moving off in new directions, Jellicoe by turning her back on conventional theatre and dedicating herself to mass community theatre.

In contrast, what Taylor termed the Second Wave of writers were, broadly, in search of ways to entertain wider audiences. Not surprisingly, the most successful were those who took existing forms and moved them on in ways that were unexpected but not threatening. The most successful of all was Ayckbourn who in the Arts Council survey of national theatre in 1985 warranted a unique individually-named category in their list of production-genres as some 6% of all productions in that year were of his plays. His comedies of social life are in some respects close to the boulevard comedies which had frequent, if usually short-lived, lives in the West End in the 1950s. However, their distinctive theatrical edge derives from their origins in theatre-in-the-round, a physical form designed to break up the accustomed assumptions of naturalism in proscenium theatres. It is interesting that Osborne and Pinter, the two most prestigious new writers of the 1950s, were from the start very comfortable in the West End whilst Ayckbourn's work has always been less comfortable there, his enormous appeal lying mainly in provincial public theatres. The adoption by Schaffer of the techniques of melodrama has already been noted whilst Orton took the sexual farce of Brian Rix and allied it to a text which had at least the appearance of substantive content. These three writers, probably the most successful of the 1960s Second Wave in terms of audiences, although quite different on the page, have the common feature of deriving their success from using a production technique, familiar but previously regarded as deviant not to say inferior to naturalism, and then allying to this a text based upon naturalist conventions.

One might add to this the way in which Hall at the RSC was quite prepared to rewrite even the sacred language of Shakespeare and to allow Barton to add in pastiche in order to make the sequential history plays more entertaining. Although not prepared to take quite the liberties of the eighteenth century in altering plots, Hall accepted that the basic job of his theatre was to entertain even at the expense of Shakespeare's text, an approach which at the time scandalised older actors such as Peggy Ashcroft schooled in a much more reverential attitude to the text of the master.

The collaborative approach to writing had been used at Theatre Workshop by Littlewood initially as a way of shaping preliminary scripts during rehearsal notably in their two great successes, *A Taste of Honey* and *The Hostage*, both by writers whose stage experience was close to zero. More experienced writers are said to have been much more resistant to this technique and the final Littlewood show at Stratford, *Oh! What a Lovely War*, adopted the rather different approach of the entire cast developing an initial idea based upon research and experiment rather than a fixed script. Apart from the notorious production, *Lay By*, written in 1970 as a deliberate exercise in shock by five young writers[98] on rolls of wallpaper in the Circle Bar of the Royal Court, collaboration between writers was relatively rare. The partnership between Arden and D'Arcy is the only long-term example though Brenton and Hare collaborated on two important plays in this period.[99] Much more common was a collaborative process between the company and the writer as it

---

[98] Brian Clark, Trevor Griffiths, David Hare, Stephen Poliakoff,
[99] *The Churchill Play* and *Pravda*

became increasingly common for writers to attend rehearsals and for initial scripts to be amended during these. The process of creation adopted by the Joint Stock company of having a writer work with a company on an idea, then preparing a working script which would be re-worked during rehearsal, though much admired, required the existence of a permanent group with long rehearsal time, something which few theatres could afford even with subsidy. However, many new plays of the period went through some more diluted form of this process. Ayckbourn's practice of using a theatre in Scarborough as a home base in which the stage impact of texts would be refined before the show went to wider audiences is a specific example of this.

At extreme of the creative spectrum were the various ways in which plays were created without any specific writer. The best-known of these was the work of the director Mike Leigh in which actors improvised words around a broad story line until at particular point these were frozen to form a written script. Although Leigh was the only person to turn this into a fully developed technique, many other productions, in particular those around a community project or by some of the small touring companies used improvisation of one kind or another.

The only generalisation which can really be made of the new playwrights of this period is that they explored and freed up the language which could be used in the theatre. In part, of course, this new freedom with language derived from the removal of explicit theatre censorship in 1968. This hangover from the eighteenth century was an extraordinary commentary on the cultural and social place of theatre up to the middle of the twentieth century, an archaic mode of control whose archaism was emphasised by the fact that the censor was the Lord Chamberlain, an official at the royal court whose other functions were completely obscure. The feature of this official's work which was then most extraordinary was not so much that it censored sexual references. As the famous trial over the publication of Lawrence's *Lady Chatterley's Lover* in 1963 showed, general obscenity laws were quite widely used in Britain up to the 1960s to prohibit much in the way of sexual reference. This changed quite quickly in this decade and in fact, as Orton shows, by the mid-1960s it was possible to get a quite wide range of sexual expression through the Lord Chamberlain (though not directly to homosexuality). The point was that a much wider range of subjects than sex could be banned including any reference to living people, to royalty and to anything that might be seen as insulting British allies. It was a commentary upon the social position of theatre that until 1968, matters which were routinely published in newspapers, magazines, books and which increasingly could be seen and heard in cinemas and on television and over the radio were often banned from live theatre performance.

The origins of theatre censorship lay in what was seen as the unique potential of live performance for 'inflaming' the masses and therefore in the necessity of applying tight political control over theatres. This was essentially a conclusion drawn in a largely non-literate society and had become obsolete during the nineteenth century. The emphasis of theatre censorship had changed from controlling any tendency to inflame the masses towards preserving the theatre as a proper place for polite society in which such matters as referring to the royal family were breaches of decorum rather than offences against public order. Writers such as Shaw and Barker certainly chafed under the Lord Chamberlain's bonds and some plays, *Mrs Warren's*

Profession and *Waste* for example, had to be produced under club restrictions, the normal get-out for indiscreet material. However, the extraordinary longevity of a mode of direct control long since abandoned in most cultural areas can be only ascribed to the fact that most people, indeed most cultural workers, simply did not care very much about such an absurd control even in the land of free speech. It finally became an issue in precisely the period when theatre did begin to return to a position where people cared about it and then it crumbled almost immediately.

Clearly, the abolition of censorship removed constraints on writers though their ability to refer to any topic and use any language remained constrained by the laws of libel and general obscenity as Arden and D'Arcy were to discover over *The Ballygombeen Bequest* and Brenton over *The Romans in Britain*. However, if one looks at the general flow of material from, say, 1960 through to 1980, it is not immediately obvious that 1968 marks any clear turning point in the language of plays. Ironically, the most celebrated results said to be a result of abolition were productions including *Oh! Calcutta!*, and *Hair* whose most notorious features were physical nudity, moving not stationary, something not covered by the Lord Chamberlain but by the local police whose powers remained the same but who began to interpret the obscenity laws very differently. (Though some parts of the original script of *Hair* were censored by the Lord Chamberlain). Indeed, in a sense it was the resurgence of the Goth over the Greek which did for the Lord Chamberlain. No doubt *Lay By* would have had a hard time with him; it was after all written precisely to test the limits of what could now be done on stage. However, one of its most notorious, not to say unpleasant, features, an act of forced fellatio in its necessarily wordless nature could have passed through the Lord Chamberlain's office literally unseen, though it might have been closed by the police only a few years before. A shift in the sexual content of plays was guided as much by a general relaxation in definitions of obscenity as by the abolition of the theatre censor. The important consequences of this were more to do with the removal of the wider constraints though to a considerable degree these had become unenforceable.

Writers were set free in the 1960s not by the removal of censorship but by the freedom deriving from the broadening of their canvas as naturalism faded. Osborne was the first sign of this. As Chambers and Prior observe *"For Osborne...language is paramount"*. (Chambers (1987) p.126) In *Look Back in Anger*, it is the tempestuous flow of Jimmy Porter's language which carries the play for all its threadbare plotting and characterisation. In future plays, whenever Osborne was able to expand beyond naturalism, as in *The Entertainer* and, most obviously, *Inadmissible Evidence* in which dreams and reality are impossible to separate, his use of language allows the play to work. When he is dragged back to it, as in most of his later work, enervation sets in.

Although the liberation from naturalism offered a greater scope for writers, the shift in their roles meant that for some, recovering control over the texts became an important issue. This achieved some national notoriety in 1972 when Arden and D'Arcy resorted to picketing the Aldwych theatre where their play, *The Island of the Mighty*, was being produced by the RSC, over what they saw as a mistaken emphasis in its direction. This dispute was clouded by the fact that the two writers appeared to be simultaneously asking for control over their text and also extension of democratic control in the theatre to be extended to all workers including front-of-house staff. Such an extreme example possibly obscured the fact that the flood of new writers had been accompanied by a drop in the financial rewards for playwriting as well as loss of control over the performance. In 1975, this led to the formation of a Theatre Writers Group which had by 1977 shifted into being a *de facto*[100] trade union, the Theatre Writers Union. This began by blacking any new plays at the National Theatre unless they agreed to sign minimum contracts which laid down not only money but also certain rights of control over casting and publicity and the right to be paid to attend rehearsals. The improvement achieved financially can be measured by the yardstick used at the time. In 1976, Brenton was paid £350 commission for the first new play at the South Bank theatre of the National Theatre, *Weapons of Happiness*. The new contract agreed in 1977, offered at least £2000 which was then judged to be a reasonable return for six months work.

This professionalisation of playwriting did not by any means end complaints by writers as to how their work was treated. Edward Bond had a long-drawn out dispute with the RSC over the treatment of his *War Plays* whilst Arden and D'Arcy effectively withdrew from British theatre. However the introduction of the minimum contract, which became extended in various forms throughout the subsidised theatre, meant that writers had roughly the same kind of treatment as other workers.

Conclusion

The period discussed here, roughly the two decades from 1964 to 1984, can be broadly defined by three Arts Council reports into the state of British theatre. The first, *Housing the Arts*, in effect forecast the total

---

[100] *De facto* rather than *de jure* because of problems in law of actually defining a writer as a worker.

collapse of theatre unless the state intervened. The second, *The Theatre Today*, focussed its main attention on what essentially was the forecast outcome of *Housing the Arts*— the almost complete withdrawal of the private sector from theatre outside London. The final report, *Theatre is for All*, was published in 1986 following what was seen as a path-breaking reappraisal by the Arts Council of its role, *Glory of the Garden*. Each in its own way reports on a 'crisis' in the theatre. *Housing the Arts* is concerned with the apparently ongoing collapse of the basic fabric of theatre whilst *The Theatre Today* focuses on the terminal crisis of the commercial theatre outside London. By the mid-1980s, each of these had run its course and British theatre had been transformed from a wholly commercial sector into the hybrid public/private form which has essentially continued until the present day. The 'crisis' to which *Theatre is for All* refers is much less tangible, something reflected in the recommendations of the report which are simultaneously too vague and too ambitious (for example a levy upon television revenues) to be taken seriously.

The nature of this last perceived crisis seems to centre upon the uneasy compromise reached in the transforming process of the previous two decades. In terms of audience, theatre had resisted the collapse foreseen in the early 1960s and had achieved what would have been seen as a remarkably wide appeal. Research conducted for the Arts Council at the time showed that, overall, 10% of the population went to the theatre at least once a month compared with 12% who went to the cinema. This rough equality between theatre and cinema audiences would probably have been the most surprising outcome of the use of state subsidy to an observer from the early 1950s when cinema audiences were at their peak and it was believed that the maximum audience participation in repertory theatres would be around 3% of the population. The age split of this audience was significantly different between film and theatre. Only 8% of the age-group 16-24 went to the theatre regularly compared with 34% of filmgoers whilst in the 45-59 range, 15% went to theatre and only 4% to the cinema. This split would continue to worry theatre workers but given the large disparity between film and theatre seat prices was probably inevitable. If anything, the fact that theatre was, and was to remain, so much more expensive than cinema makes its equal popularity the more remarkable.

The gloom that pervades *The Theatre is for All* seems to come from two sources. The first, inevitably, being financial.

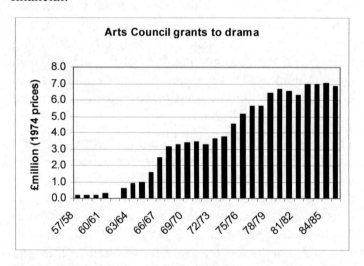

Fig 2: Arts Council funding for drama, 1957-85

Fig 2 shows that central funding for the theatre increased in real terms throughout the 1970s and into the 1980s, reaching a peak of £7.0 million in 1974 prices[101] in the period 1982-85. It began to dip in 1986 and would continue to fall in real terms but, apart from a brief decline around 1981, there had been over twenty years of growth in state funding. This came in two periods, first a steady growth in the 1960s followed by about four years of stagnation[102] with another period of growth in the second half of the 1970s. The consequence of this was that in the two decades between 1964 and 1984, central funding for drama increased in real terms approximately seven-fold. It is not clear whether this pattern had been precisely matched by increases in support from local authorities and from regional arts councils whose funding came in part from municipal sources. Touring companies usually received little support from these but some theatres were heavily reliant on their local council, for example Greenwich which in 1981 received 42% of its income in this way or Coventry which obtained 46%.[103] The problem in working out just how much theatre had become dependent on subsidy and where that subsidy came from is that it varied very widely between theatres. Thus Guildford only received 2% of its income from the council and earned 84% of it through the box-office while Rochdale only obtained 10% in earned receipts. In general, the proportion of Arts Council subsidy was in the range 30-40%, though it could go as high as 92%; local authority and regional arts council support was in the range 20-30% though it could go up to 46%, whilst earned income was usually 30-50% of total costs.

[101] £50.6 million in 2003 prices
[102] This coincides almost exactly with the period of the Heath Conservative government, though unlike the later Thatcher regime, there was no obvious hostility then to arts funding. It was, however, a period when public sector spending was under attack.
[103] Arts Council Archives, ACGB 43/30

Financial pressure on theatres resulted not from actual cuts but from two other factors. First, there was the competition resulting from the rapid growth in the number and size of groups seeking subsidy. At one end of the scale, there was a roughly six-fold increase in the number of touring groups in the course of the 1970s before a peak of around 300 was reached in the early 1980s. Not all of these asked for any funding, nor did all who asked receive, but probably most obtained some support. A new approach to funding by the Arts Council from 1984 onwards meant that a relatively open-handed policy would be drastically pruned but this belongs to a following chapter. At the other end of the funding spectrum, both national companies came under financial pressure in the 1970s and required higher and higher subsidies to maintain themselves. The RSC was particularly stretched given that its ambitious expansions to multiple theatres had never been adequately funded and had sometimes been undertaken in the face of Arts Council opposition. The National had originally been more generously funded but the operating costs of its new South Bank spiralled and needed more and more money. The diaries of Peter Hall in the second half of the 1970s are full of references to the struggle to reduce the costs of the new site, a struggle which in the end resulted in the abandonment of all ambitions to do other than run single venue rather than operate as a genuinely national theatre. (Hall (1983) p.355)

The second factor was that the basic real costs of operating theatres seem to have increased sharply in this period. This was not a new phenomenon—it has already been noted that costs moved upwards after the war. Costs increased in this period essentially because the sudden expansion, in particular of touring groups, had been undertaken on the cheap. Actors were paid very little in many cases. Notoriously the new lunchtime theatres in London usually paid their actors nothing on the grounds that their performances would be showcases for agents and producers. As discussed above, writers were given tiny fees for new work as were designers. It would be wrong to suggest that the theatre became a highly-paid profession during the 1970s but undoubtedly some adjustment was required and achieved. Equity contracts were introduced much more widely, commissioning fees were increased and, in general, theatre became much more organised in a union sense of the term. Peter Hall has presented his clashes with the theatre unions at the South Bank, which at times threatened to close the venue, in rather garish terms but in fact the situation was really no more than reversion to a *status quo ante* in which the specialist theatre unions were organised and well aware of their power to close theatres at short notice causing irrecoverable loss of revenue. The 1970s were a decade in which a form of militant labourism was a dominant theme in the wider economy and the theatre was not left out of this process.

There is a well-known economic theorem which shows that any performing art which has fixed labour productivity (for example, the size of the cast of Hamlet cannot be reduced much nor can their productivity be improved by speaking their lines faster) is bound to become more expensive relative to other commodities as real wages rise. This may have had a further impact on costs but a more immediate force was simply that those involved in the new public theatre grew older and needed to fund mortgages and children.

The second problem was that although British theatre had been pulled back from the abyss, its central cultural problem had not been fully resolved. This chapter began with three crises in theatre; financial, artistic and cultural. The artistic issue had been squarely resolved and so to a degree had the financial. Artistically, the constraints of naturalism had been thrown off. If, in the 1950s, native British theatre had been something of a joke in artistic terms with only such a fringe group as Theatre Workshop able to receive a serious reception on the Continent, by the 1970s, British theatre had become the cutting edge of world-theatre. In fact some touring groups probably had higher reputations abroad than they did in Britain whilst several writers had begun to rely on their foreign royalties as their major source of income. Even British directors were in demand on the Continent following the departure of Brook to Paris. The funding crisis had up to a point also been resolved by a general acceptance that, outside the West End, theatre required public subsidy. The degree of public support remained limited and subject to relentless pressure but the general principle had been conceded. However, the cultural role of theatre, just where this new public theatre fitted as cultural form, remained unresolved.

Public theatre in Britain came of age in a political climate far removed from that in which it was born. The idealistic politics of the 1960s and 70s had been badly brought back to earth in the 1980s and there was very little faith left in the ability of public expenditure to resolve social problems. Broadly speaking, theatres were being sustained by a subsidy level around the 50% level which meant that they were required to exist in a rather hybrid world neither state-financed nor commercial in which it was necessary to work both the increasingly convoluted funding system and also the older devices for maintaining box-office levels. Theatre as a live performance art retained a unique potential for going out into a world outside its fixed buildings but it was a controversial and often unrealised potential. The split which this introduced was expressed obliquely, but accurately, in *Theatre is for All*:

> *There are divisions in the theatre world, given the wide range of "theatre" now provided and a major one is between those whose perception of theatre is community based and those who perceive it in terms of the over-riding importance of a given text and performing in theatre buildings.*

(Arts Council (1986) p.10)

Just how this division developed in the new world of militant conservatism loose in Britain is the subject of the next chapter.

Theatre in a new Britain: the 1980s onward

It took a few years for British theatre along with a large section of British society at large to recognise that the 1980s were the start of a new era of British life. It was only after the Falklands War, abolition of the Greater London Council and the crushing defeat of the National Union of Miners in 1985 that it finally became clear that a Conservative government under Margaret Thatcher, re-elected in 1984 with an increased majority, albeit on a minority of the votes, was intent on reversing the social shifts of the 1970s. In an earlier chapter, it was emphasised that in the early years of the 1980s, the volume of money going as subsidy to the theatre remained virtually constant after the huge increases of the preceding twenty years. The pressure on resources which was perceived at the time came largely from the demands of the two national companies as well as from increasing numbers of groups requesting funding from an Arts Council which had had something of an open doors policy throughout the 1970s rather than actual cuts. However, after 1985 this started to shift into a situation of real financial stringency.

It is unclear just how much of this pressure resulted from any clear idea of curbing unwelcome criticism. Certainly it is true that it would have been hard to find any overt support for Thatcher inside the theatre and there was a relentless stream of productions which were strongly critical to the point of caricature. The Brenton/Hare play *Pravda* (1985) put on at the National Theatre to great critical and popular acclaim might be seen as flagship of such work with its passionate portrayal of a corrupt newspaper magnate not dissimilar to Rupert Murdoch, owner of the *Sun* and *The Times* and a strong Thatcher supporter. But there was more to the shift than simple political vindictiveness. Public subsidy for theatre was, overall, moving up towards the 50% mark though it varied, as we have seen, quite markedly from company to company. At this point, it started to stick and there was a distinct reluctance to go higher. In 1985, the National Theatre had to close its small hall, the Cottesloe, to cut costs and there was no great outcry. The sums of money involved were, as always, tiny in comparison with other government budgets but in the theatre as in most other areas of government involvement, there began the period when the British public seemed above all else to warm to cutting taxes, cutting public expenditure and, generally, preferring private consumption to public expenditure. Around this time there developed a theory that, in society at large, public acceptance of state expenditure dropped sharply when it began to rise above 40% of the national product although it proved to be difficult even for a Conservative government obsessed with reducing state expenditure to pull it down much below this level.

In the theatre, the key voice in this was a report by the Arts Council, *Flowers of the Garden*, which set out its new role as seen by a new, Thatcher-appointed, leader, Luke Rittner. This will be discussed in more detail below but essentially it set out a vision for a theatre in which individual venues would come to be judged in terms of how they could sell themselves both in terms of audiences but also in terms of business sponsorship. In 1985, British theatre emerged as the hybrid it was to remain, neither private nor public but in some indeterminate way a public business.

One of the ways in which this process was undertaken was to re-define the relationship of public theatres with the private theatrical sector and, in particular, with the West End whose revival was one of this periods most surprising aspects. The names associated with this are Andrew Lloyd Weber and Cameron Mackintosh, the two mega-moguls of the period, plus the director, Trevor Nunn, who has made his reputation as a classical director in that most public of theatres, the Royal Shakespeare Company. All their fortunes were closely linked with the new wave of a form, at that time somewhat left by the wayside, the musical.

The West End and the British musical

At the very beginning of this story, the big American musicals starting with *Oklahoma!* were identified as the key living component of British theatre in the late-1940s and into the 1950s. The big West End theatres lived off their annual influx of the latest Broadway hit and the No 1 touring houses outside London made such money as they did on the subsequent tours. However, as noted, by the mid-1960s this sustenance was becoming extremely thin as the American talent for musicals appeared to dry up. Apart from Sondheim, whose work never appealed to a mass public, there was a dearth of new blood and the old blood seemed less and less able to hit the buttons in the right order. The patterns of popular music had changed. As one chronicler puts it:

> It became increasingly rare for a showtune to land on the rock-dominated air waves and pop charts. With almost no income from records and sheet music sales, the most that composers and lyricists could hope for was the two percent of a show's gross allotted to them in a standard contract. As a result, new talent went into the more profitable fields of pop music, television and film. Several

> *veterans like Irving Berlin retired in disgust,*
> *and those who laboured on found that styles*
> *and formulas which had worked for decades*
> *were suddenly unacceptable.*

(Kenrick 1960bway2)

Cabaret (1966) was the last of the old-style blockbusters and even it, a dark masterpiece, played for only 1165 performances on Broadway, well down on the 2000 plus which had become the accustomed run for a successful show and a length needed to accommodate the soaring costs of these spectacular shows. *Hair* (1968) made the most of the mythology of 1967, the Age of Aquarius and all that, and made a triumphant entry to London but it was less of a musical and more of a rock concert and, in style, could not compete with real thing. The fact that it landed in the West End the day after censorship formally ended gave its modest nudity something of a frisson but it could hardly conceal the basic tawdriness of the project.

The West End needed these big musicals to fill its biggest venues like Drury Lane and to provide the basic cash flow to feed into the rest of the commercial network. In the 1970s, this network either fell apart outside London or in the West End meandered, largely disregarded. The decay of the Group did mean that independent producers had a somewhat freer hand and such as Michael Codron and Oscar Lewenstein kept pitching away putting on plays by various new and slightly daring writers including Pinter, Storey, Hare and Simon Gray but the heart was decaying with only the stricter planning rules of the period really standing between the Edwardian theatreland around Shaftesbury Avenue and new commercial development. In the 1970s, there developed a 'Save Our Theatres' campaign which centred around proposals to re-develop the Covent Garden area which could have resulted in the demolition of several theatres.

The ultimate saviour of the West End originated in an unlikely place: the Old Assembly Hall in Hammersmith where the school orchestra and choir of St Paul's Junior School presented a twenty-minute 'pop cantata' as their Easter concert in 1968. It told the story, less improbably than might be seen later given its context, of the Old Testament's Joseph. The cantata's composer was Andrew Lloyd Weber and the lyricist, Tim Rice. The concert was a success and a second performance was arranged at Central Hall, Westminster, headquarters of the Methodist Church but available for suitable secular performance, where the father of the music teacher at St Paul's was organist. Weber's younger brother, Julian—a classical cellist—also performed. Over two thousand people attended, mainly parents and relatives of the children. This amateur show was seen and reviewed very favourably by the jazz and pop music critic of the *Sunday Times* and a third and expanded performance was arranged, this time at St Paul's cathedral. Tim Rice worked at the time with a pop music producer, Norrie Paramour, who arranged for Decca records to release the expanded version as an album which although reviewed reasonably favourably had little commercial success. The collaborators were then offered a management contract to develop more work and in 1971, after release of a successful record, they opened the result of this collaboration, *Jesus Christ Superstar,* on Broadway, where it was a modest success, and then in London where it ran for eight years. When it closed, it had become the then longest running show in the history of the West End. *Joseph...* was picked up in 1972 at the Edinburgh Festival, where the story of the many-coloured coat was finally introduced, and subsequently at the Young Vic in London before transferring to the West End in 1973. In 1968, the copyright of *Joseph* was sold to Novello & Co for 100 guineas. In 1989, Lloyd-Weber's production companion, the Really Useful Group bought it for £1 million. Weber then collaborated with Alan Ayckbourn to write a grim and unsuccessful musical, *Jeeves* (1975) before he and Rice finally hit pay dirt with *Evita* (1978). Again, the stage production was preceded by an album, in this case by as long as eighteen months, and again, as with *Jesus Christ Superstar*, the album contained one hit single. Sung by Julie Covington, better known as a straight actor, *Don't Cry for Me Argentina* became a No 1 hit selling over two million copies and has subsequently had over one hundred cover versions.

There are several interesting features of this remarkable story. One of them is the extent to which Lloyd-Weber's chance arose out of the privileged network of private education and the contacts which come from it. The seemingly effortless move from a school hall to St Paul's cathedral is not something that would readily have happened outside this kind of network. This is not simply a point about class privilege in Britain. The cultural basis of Weber's work was rooted in the relatively elitist world of choral music, opera and classical music which would have been familiar to those inside the circle of private education, much less so outside it especially outside London. Although he flirted with rock music in *Jesus Christ Superstar* to the extent that its touring revival in the U.S.A. in the late-1990s used a heavy-metal rock star, Weber has always been at heart a classical composer writing what he sees as operas, insisting, for example, on dropping the prefix 'rock' in referring to *Evita*. *Jeeves* was a failure precisely because by collaborating with a straight dramatist, elements were introduced which made it too long, too dreary. The book, a key component of the great American musicals, failed to connect. Weber succeeded because he wrote musicals which returned to the elemental basics of nineteenth century opera—orchestral music, raw emotions and a couple of hummable tunes. In the 1970s, there appeared to be only three routes for musicals; rock music like *Grease* (1972) for the 'youth audience'; sophisticated melodic light entertainment for a 'mature audience'; or revivals of old favourites. None were big money-earners. Weber's genius lay in seeing that what was needed was a return to the techniques of Verdi and Puccini and to hell with the probabilities of the plotting and to any connection with social reality. This was the cultural distinction between the new 'British' musical and its American precursors. Whereas the latter had been successful because they always attempted to make some connection with a version of (American) social reality, however distorted, the British musical junked all such links and returned to a version of private human passions and emotion.

If that was Lloyd-Webers' genius then his flair was to see that musicals needed to be marketed in a new way. The link between recording and stage musicals had been set up by *Oklahoma!* (for whose record tie-in, the term 'album' was invented); Weber or his business associates saw that the new music industry required that the tie-in process needed to be reversed. First release the album and the hit single then, on the back of the resultant publicity, produce the show. The shows which came after *Evita* used different techniques but they had a common theme of working the international media to build up excitement before the show actually hit the stage. The key word here is 'international' in two directions. Working from a British base, Weber's ambitions have always been very international right from the fact that his first professional opening was in New York. In a sense, the collapse of the U.K.'s No 1 Touring Circuit with its long-term cash flow had to be replaced with an international equivalent. Secondly, the growth of London as an international tourist centre meant that marketing for London shows required in particular a U.S. marketing dimension so that American tourists would arrive in London with their tickets for a Weber show in the same envelope as their air-tickets and hotel bookings.

After Evita came the three key shows; *Cats*(1981), *Starlight Express*(1984) and, most important, *Phantom of the Opera*(1986). Although the first two have now closed their main runs in London, they can still be seen touring in Britain and at various sites throughout the world. Their statistics are really staggering. *Cats* when it closed in 2002 in London had run for twenty-one years and notched up 8950 performances, a record, whilst on Broadway it ran for eighteen years, also a record. *Starlight Express*, despite its extraordinary mechanical demands (the show is about trains and is skated on a track running round the theatre), was presented in seven countries and has run for fifteen years in Bochum, Germany with world-wide receipts by 2004 in excess of £230 million. Above all others, *Phantom of the Opera* had by 2004 recorded over 65,000 performances worldwide with a box-office in excess of £1.6 billion. It is also possibly the most spectacular live show ever staged with twenty-seven large lorries being required to move the set between theatres. Its producers' publicity states that it has played to 99% capacity in London where, apparently, it will play for ever.

Weber's subsequent work has always strained to match the success of these three shows. *Aspects of*

Love (1989), *Sunset Boulevard* (1993), *Whistle Down the Wind* (1997) and *The Beautiful Game* (2000) have all rather come and gone whilst the three central pieces have, somewhere, continued to pack them in. *The Woman in White* (2004) may or may not buck the trend. It is unclear just where the mix has gone wrong; whether it is public taste, whether the marketing has not been so focussed or whether his choice of subject has not quite lived up to the bizarre and fantastic which exemplified his work before 1990. Perhaps it lies in the choice of collaborator for having parted from Tim Rice as lyricist after *Evita*, Weber made two crucial matches with Trevor Nunn as director of *Cats* and *Starlight Express* and in Cameron Mackintosh as producer of *Cats* and *Phantom of the Opera*.

Trevor Nunn's career in musicals was seen by many as veering sharply away from his role as artistic director of the RSC. However, as we saw in a previous chapter, almost his first assignment inside this august company was to attempt to stage a musical play based upon the General Strike, a project which he returned to in 1970, only have it collapse in the face of production difficulties, not to mention cost, associated with turning the Roundhouse into a fairground. In 1972, he tried without entire success to use complex stage machinery at Stratford in the Romans season, whilst in 1980, he showed a complete grasp of how to direct large-scale ensembles in his version of *Nicholas Nickleby*. The idea of directing a musical based upon poems by T.S.Eliot was really no more than a commercial extension of this kind of work. *Cats* is often criticised as being musically banal with just one memorable song (*Memories*), the standard critique of Weber. What could not be doubted was that given a suitably enlarged budget, Nunn provided a stunning opening twenty minutes and appropriate finales and expertly marshalled his ensemble of cat characters.

Similarly, *Starlight Express* has never been praised for its musical heights but it is an epic piece of directorial vision albeit one directed to a somewhat bizarre end. Nunn completed his own triptych of successful musicals by directing *Les Misérables*, an opera by Schonberg and Blondil which he first directed for the R.S.C. at its London home but which swiftly moved into the West End under the auspices of Cameron Mackintosh. Nunn was widely criticised for this mixing of public and private roles as it was clear that *Les Misérables* had been set up from the start as a commercial venture. Nunn has subsequently acquired a large fortune on the basis of these three musicals, all undertaken when he had a job with the RSC, but he pointed the way to the future in his effortless combination of public and commercial. It is indicative of a shift in cultural perceptions that the first leader of the National Theatre, Olivier, was an actor with a successful film career, whilst the second, Peter Hall, was a devoted opera director with his ventures into commercial theatre being in straight drama. His successors at the National have all been successful directors of musicals. Apart from Nunn, Richard Eyre, who moved his version of *Oklahoma!* in 1982 from its original public home into the West End, earning the National a million pounds, has never disguised his enthusiasm for the genre and directed *Mary Poppins* in 2005 after his role at the National had finished whilst Nicholas Hytner, the current director, directed *Miss Saigon* (1989) for Cameron Mackintosh after Nunn had been asked to step down by Mackintosh.

Cameron Mackintosh, the third of the group, went to the Central School of Speech and Drama but left without showing discernible talent in any onstage activity. He retained a consuming passion for theatre and turned to producing in the 1960s. Of all the inauspicious shows with which he was associated at this time, until teaming up with Weber and Nunn for *Cats*, the most outstanding venture was his work as advertising manager for *Hair* when he invented 'Hair Rail' offering inclusive rail and theatre tickets for customers living near London. The cleverness lay not so much in pricing as in realising that the combination settled anxieties about missing the last train home and offered one simple package. Mackintosh has never been a consistent backer of winners. After *Cats* came such as *Blondel* (1983) and a revival of *The Boyfriend* (1984) before the machine clicked into gear with *Les Misérables, Phantom of the Opera* and *Miss Saigon*. International touring from an established London base enabled these three to generate huge revenues. By 2004, *Les Misérables* had been produced in 223 cities in thirty-eight countries, numbers which far exceeded the old pattern of touring round the No 1 circuit in the U.K. Cloned productions kept costs down whilst clever use of international media allowed success in the key venues of London and New York to be disseminated in advance to Prague, Manila, Buenos Aires, Shanghai and the rest. Les Mis or Phantom 'fever' could be generated as far away as Seoul in the weeks before the show opened and guaranteed the opening night publicity essential to this kind of show.

Some have regretted the loss of the specific cultural form of the classic American musical; Richard Eyre, for example asserts that the big British musicals "*are simply not as **good** as*...[a list of sixteen US musicals]" (Eyre p.344) He continues that "***Les Misérables** and **Miss Saigon** advance on their audiences laden with weighty subject matter, portentous thin-framed machines for giving you generalised rather than particularised feeling, unmitigated by irony. They give the impression, rather than the reality, of feeling, like Victorians scattering water on letters to look as if they'd been written in* *tears*." The problem with this approach is that the cultural form he laments was a specifically American one offering a specifically American 'particularised feeling' and was, moreover, defined by a particular period of American history which ended with the Vietnam war. The British musical (with the interesting exception of Willy Russell's *Blood Brothers* (1983)) has never had a national identity; the key to its success, as Eyre rightly points out, is its very internationalism, that it is understood as easily in Seoul as New York. But as noted above, these musicals were developed from a foundation of opera, a genre which has never rested upon quite such specific national identity as *Paint Your Wagon* or *Pal Joey* to take two of Eyre's sixteen examples; in some genres, international rather than national identity is regarded as the mark of quality.

Like Weber, Mackintosh has never quite repeated his 1980s success in subsequent years. Transfers from public theatre such as *Five Guys Like Moe* (1991) and a revival of *Carousel* (1993) were always going to be only local successes whilst *Martin Guerre* (1996), Schonberg and Blondil's third shot for gold, died in London despite Mackintosh's enthusiastic backing. Even so, both Lloyd-Weber and Mackintosh acquired personal fortunes ranked in the hundreds of millions and allowed both to move into London theatre ownership and management.

After the collapse of The Group in the early 1960s (insofar as the collapse of something so intangible can be charted), theatre ownership and control in the West End had become increasingly fragmented partly into various components of The Group such as the Stoll Moss group and Bernard Delfont's company First Leisure whilst other interests, usually associated with property development as much as drama, had also become involved. Theatres occupy huge pieces of real estate, often in prime city centre sites, and, particularly outside London, had often been targets of property developers. At some point in the early 1970s, public and political opinion had switched from regarding those remaining hulks of the old private theatre as ugly reminders of a past age to viewing them with more nostalgic eye. The closure and subsequent demolition of a classic Matcham[104] theatre, the Glasgow Empire, a 2000-seat monster sitting on Sauchiehall Street in the centre of Glasgow was a symbol of the first; the successful campaign to save the theatres likely to be impacted by the Covent Garden redevelopment of the second. It remained possible to negotiate halfway houses between full preservation and demolition. The containment of the 19th century auditorium of the Lyric, Hammersmith inside an office block is an example of this and there were other variants of theatre demolition with a new auditorium being built alongside commercial buildings. However, broadly speaking, a stricter application of planning laws plus the impact of a major property market collapse in 1974 meant that old theatres had to stay as such or find some equivalent use. These became hard to come by as attendance at cinemas slumped so the standby of the 1930s was no longer viable. Theatres worked as theatres or they went dark particularly in the West End.

Cameron Mackintosh's West End theatre interests began in 1990 when he entered into a joint-venture arrangement with Delfont for the Prince Edward (1643 seats) and Prince of Wales (1100) theatres to which was added the Strand Theatre (1067) in 1991. Subsequent additions included the leases of the

---

[104] Frank Matcham was the best-known architect of late-Victorian and Edwardian theatres noted for his elaborate interiors.

Queens (987) and Gielgud (889) theatres so that by 2005, Delfont Mackintosh Theatres (now owned 100% by Mackintosh) holds five freeholds and two long leases of the forty theatres normally considered to be the West End. Four of these are 'musical' theatres with the Queen's being home to the cash-fountain of *Les Misérables,* but three (Albery (872), Gielgud and Wyndham's (750)) are relatively small and usually stage spoken drama.

Andrew Lloyd Weber's theatre interests also centre around seven musical venues including the London Palladium, (2298) Drury Lane Theatre Royal (2237), Palace (1400), Her Majesty's (1200), Adelphi (1500), New London (1106) and Cambridge (1230) plus the smaller Duchess (474), Garrick, (656), Lyric (959) and Apollo (776) theatres.[105] The size criteria is relative; there are few really small theatres, say below 500 seats, in the West End, only some five or six. It is the continuing existence of so many large venues (fifteen out of forty West End theatres have more than 1200 seats) which really defines its central purpose which has always been the presentation of musical theatre. The constant complaints about the dominance of such theatre in the West End quite misses the point: that most of its theatres were designed for and can only exist financially and culturally by presenting musicals. It is the continuing existence of a smaller number of theatres able to exist, just, on spoken drama which is the West End's most surprising feature given the collapse of such commercial presentation outside London.

The third major force in the new West End, the Ambassador Theatre Group, owns and operates 11 of

---

[105] Such listings are complicated by the fact that some theatres are owned by one group and leased by another. This listing refers to ownership in 2005.

the smaller venues.[106] The group was founded in 1992 and originally owned just the Ambassadors theatre. It has since taken over ten other West End venues as well as a further 12 outside London's centre though mostly on the capital's periphery. The group specialises in small-scale musicals rather than the huge blockbusters of Weber and Mackintosh—Willy Russell's quirky success *Blood Brothers* (1983) is probably the best-known of these—as well as straight drama, often transfers from the subsidised theatre or enlivened with star Hollywood names.

The West End's survival as a coherent theatrical entity owes a great deal to the reinvention of the musical described above and the river of money produced by half-a-dozen huge successes. However even the most recent of these, *Miss Saigon*, was a product of the 1980s and has almost passed into history. The force of these productions lay in the same combination of dramatic power and technical wizardry which kept Victorian melodrama afloat and, as in the nineteenth century but on an accelerated timescale, the rapacious financial and aesthetic demands of the combination may have caught up with it. The financial demands of the genre were seen in Disney's ventures into the arena, first with *Beauty and the Beast* (1994) and *The Lion King* (1997), each of which is reputed to have cost more than $10 million in their original Broadway productions. Each involve extraordinary technical effects which entertain by themselves without providing any great dramatic tension. *The Lion King* has been dismissed as no more than a hugely expensive puppet show and to point this up, its director, Julie Taymor, is co-credited as being both

---

[106] Albery, Comedy, Donmar Warehouse, Duke of York's, Fortune, New Ambassadors, Phoenix, Piccadilly, Playhouse, Wyndhams and Trafalgar Studios.

director and designer. No one can doubt its theatrical impact however. *Chitty Chitty, Bang Bang* (2002) and *Mary Poppins* (2004) with their flying cars and people belong in the same region though they may not repeat the same long-running success. Both were backed by Hollywood film money; *Chitty, Chitty, Bang, Bang* by Miramax and the producers of the James Bond films[107] and *Mary Poppins*, though co-produced by Cameron Mackintosh, by Disney. The spin-off from Disney animations is set to continue with *The Little Mermaid* and *Tarzan* both in the pipeline. The gigantic *Lord of the Rings*, (2006) allegedly budgeted at $25 million, sets new standards in both financial risk and special effects and may suggest that such musicals are beginning to tread a perilous path in the way in which they ramp up expectations in terms of spectacle.

Weber's latest musical *The Woman in White* (2004) is essentially an attempt to return to the melodramatic force of *Phantom of the Opera* and teamed up with his old partner, Trevor Nunn, may succeed in doing so. He has also maintained his marketing flair by hyping his latest adaptation, *The Sound of Music*, (2006) with a BBC talent competition for the lead part. Even so, the initiative for the musicals has to a considerable extent passed out of British hands and with it at least some of the impetus to support the whole of the West End theatrical agglomeration.

The West End has been sustained by two other factors, its relationship with public, subsidised theatre, something which will be discussed later on, and the huge growth of international tourism in London. In the early-80s, international customers accounted for some 12% of West End audiences, a proportion which had grown to nearly 28% in 2003, mostly from North

---

[107] Ian Fleming was the author of all the original novels and *CCBB* seems to have come in a film rights' package.

America (17%). This number fluctuates wildly—32% in 1991, 18% in 1997—largely in response to international incidents. For example, the bombing of Libya by the US air-force in 1984 had an immediate impact on American tourism as had the destruction of the Twin Towers in 2002. The important role of American tourism in particular has had a systematic impact on programming, particularly for such as the National Theatre where there has seldom been a season without a U.S. playwright featuring prominently. The virtual adoption of Arthur Miller by the British stage is probably not entirely unrelated to this.

West End audiences remained relatively static in the final fifteen years of the last century and into the present one. In 1987, audiences to Society of London Theatre (SLOT) venues[108] having moved up quite sharply in the mid-1980s from 8.1 million in 1981 increased only 5% between 1987 and 1997 from 10.88 million to 11.46 million remaining roughly stable thereafter. (Wyndham p.29) However within this total there was a major shift in the kind of drama seen. In the decade 1987-97, modern drama dropped by 29.3% to 1.03 million, comedy by 73.8% to 0.47 million while children's shows and pantomime virtually disappeared going from 0.28 million to 43 thousand. However classical plays (mainly reflecting the role of the RSC and NT in SLOT) rose by 68.6% to 1.35 million and audiences for musicals rose by 43.6% to 7.04 million. In all, audiences to non-musicals dropped by 26%. In this period, the average ticket yield of SLOT theatres rose in real terms by 26.8%

---

[108] Which include the National Theatre, the London venues of the RSC, the Royal Opera House, English National Opera and the Royal Court. Together these account for about 17% of the West End's total audience.

(Arts Council of England) so in total revenue terms, the West End would have seen income rise by a healthy 28%. It is this figure which provides the basis for the wealth created by Lloyd-Weber and Mackintosh given that the fixed asset base of the revenue—the theatres themselves—hardly altered. But, leaving aside the increasing importance of the two national companies, the relentless increase in the domination of musicals meant that the continuing success of the West End would be based more and more on the pipeline of huge spectaculars.

It has also become necessary to undertake significant capital investment in the aging theatres themselves and, although Mackintosh in particular has shown some willingness to do this, there are signs that funds for the smaller venues may be difficult to find. Mackintosh's investment in renovating the Gielgud and Queen's theatres, which involve adding a new venue to the complex, has been described as philanthropy rather than commercial enterprise whilst Lloyd Weber's Really Useful Group has tried to divest itself of its smaller houses.

The West End is thus faced by two threats; the massive scale of the new musicals and their concomitant cost and the increasingly fragile economics of straight drama in the smaller houses.

Public Theatre
Outside London, the importance of public theatre continued to increase. This is not something reflected primarily in subsidy which, as will be seen, dropped but in the way in which commercially operated venues were increasingly taken over by some form of public ownership. Until the early-1970s, when such as Moss Empires decided to close one of their venues—and by 1970, virtually all its theatres were either to be closed or converted to bingo—there was little local reaction.

The Glasgow Empire, for example, now exists only on nostalgic websites. But increasingly such closure was greeted with more or less strident local opposition and there was a greater tendency for planning permission for change of use or outright demolition to be refused. A good example of this is the fate of the Grand Theatre in Blackpool which its owners, the Tower Company, applied for permission to demolish in 1972. The theatre, an ornate example of the Matcham era, was defended by a local *ad hoc* pressure group, the Friends of the Grand, and permission was refused. Lengthy negotiations then followed culminating in the purchase of the Grand by a trust formed out of the council, some business interests and the Friends. It re-opened in 1981 with a production of the *Merchant of Venice* with Timothy West and though it seldom re-visits these classical heights it still operates as a charitable trust receiving a wide range of shows.

This pattern of purchase by a trust funded mainly by public sources, sometimes the Arts Council, sometimes a local authority, and supplemented by private funds collected by an appeal by a group of local supporters. The Sunderland Empire, Birmingham Hippodrome, Manchester's Palace Theatre and Opera House, the Sheffield Lyceum and Newcastle's Theatre Royal are good examples. The venues may later be operated directly by the trust but often they are handed over to a commercial management company, Clear Channel is a prominent example, to run under some general supervision. In such circumstances the fact that the house is, in effect, publicly owned is largely hidden. In general, such venues offer a variety of light musical entertainment supplemented by occasional straight drama though this can vary. The Theatre Royal, for example, has been a northern home for an annual season of the RSC. The common factor is that they operate without overt subsidy though they may receive subsidised productions. The public aspect of the venue is that it is not required to earn any return on capital or show any profit and so, presumably, is able to offer a lower receiving fee to the largely commercial shows who book it than if it was under commercial ownership. An interesting recent example of this form of public ownership is The Lowry in Salford which has two theatres as well as a gallery for the paintings of A.S.Lowry. Built with money from Salford Council and the National Lottery via the Millennium Fund as well as some funds from the European Commission, it operates a wide receiving policy hosting such as Northern Opera as well a plays from both commercial and subsidised sources.

The financial heart of public theatre, however, remained with revenue funding from either the Arts Council or from local authorities. An overall assessment of how this funding shifted in the last twenty years of the twentieth century is difficult as the basis for it shifted several times and consistent statistics are sometimes hard to assemble. The first major shift in central funding came about with a desire in 1984 by, what was then the Arts Council of Great Britain, to devolve spending to English regions. (Scottish and Welsh funding was already devolved). This was largely overtaken by changes in the structure of local government administration at the same time which abolished a top tier of metropolitan councils, in particular abolishing the Greater London Council (GLC) which had a major arts funding responsibility. Then, after the Wilding Report in 1989, the twelve Regional Arts Associations were replaced by ten Regional Arts Boards whilst, in Wales, three Regional Arts Associations were merged with the Welsh Arts Council in 1994. There was a major strategic review of arts policy between 1990 and 1993 and, in 1992, a Department of National Heritage was formed which assumed control over all areas of cultural action by the government. In 1994, a separate Arts Council of England was set up and funding for the arts in Scotland and Wales was moved to the Scottish and Welsh Offices with separate Arts Councils in those countries. Finally, in 1994 arts funding from the National Lottery began, something which transformed, first, capital funding of theatres and later various kinds of revenue funding.

Local authority funding was affected by two major reorganisations. The first and most significant was the abolition of six metropolitan county councils and the GLC in 1986. These seven bodies had taken on significant responsibility for arts funding and their abolition meant that, although various kinds of transfers were made both to government and to remaining councils, overall arts funding did drop. Thus in 1986/87, Arts Council funding appears to increase by £29 million largely because of this transfer of responsibility. What is unclear is the extent to which this adequately compensated for funding previously undertaken by the metropolitan councils. The second reorganisation began in 1996 when various two-tier structures were replaced by unitary authorities. This seems to have had less impact upon arts funding.

There is no consistent and complete source for statistics on local authority funding, only various surveys which are not always consistent. These show that in 1986/87 in England, local authority expenditure on all arts was £140.8 million and that this had risen in monetary terms to £193.7 million in 1997/98.(Arts Council 2000 Table 1.13) Inflation in the period meant, however, that in 1986 prices, expenditure in the latter period was £125 million, a drop in real terms of 11.2%.

This illustrates a central problem with analysing arts funding in this period, the impact of inflation. Between 1984 and the millennium year, prices almost doubled with the bulk of the increase occurring in the first ten years of this period. This means that although national arts funding actually dropped in monetary terms only once (in 1996), the erosion of inflation meant that in real terms, funding did fall at regular intervals and that theatre budgets were under constant pressure. Theatre budgets are very sensitive to inflation as they can achieve very few cost savings or productivity increases and the entire period is characterised by uncertainty and caution. In broad terms, total national arts funding after 1986/87, the year when abolition of metropolitan councils had led to a one-off adjustment to compensate, partially, for their funding, remained relatively constant until 1990/91 when it received a significant upward boost of about 13% in real terms. After this total funding suffered a series of smaller cuts which went on year-on-year for four years and partially reversed the increases of previous years until in 1997/98, the first year of the new Labour administration, it was 9.6% higher in real terms than a decade before. These fluctuations were not uniform. Scotland, Wales and Northern Ireland under what had become separately funded agencies provided significantly higher funding increases than the larger Arts Council of England with real increases over the decade of 24.6%, 21% and 58.9% respectively whilst in England funds increased by only 5.6%.[109] (Arts Council 2000 Table 2.1)

These overall shifts in central arts funding conceal a big shift in what arts were provided with funds, something which had serious consequences for theatre. In 1986/87, direct funding of drama by the Arts

---

[109] All excluding lottery funding

Council of Great Britain formed a third of the total direct funding budget for all arts. In 1997/98, the proportion of the direct funding of drama by the Arts Council of England had fallen to little more than one-fifth of the total budget. This amounted to a drop of 38% in real terms in direct drama funding. This situation did not occur in any of the other three national funding bodies. In Scotland, direct funding of drama rose by 18%, in Wales by 18% and in Northern Ireland by 142%.[110] The large drop in drama funding in England was partially compensated by an increasing share of money disbursed by Regional Arts Boards after 1991 for which no statistical breakdown is available but, given that drama was also being hit hard by the drop in local authority funding discussed above, there is no doubt that the period from the mid-1980s until towards the end of the 1990s was one of serious cutbacks in all public theatre. Given that, even in England, there was a small increase in real funding over this period, there had to be some major beneficiaries from the shift in emphasis. These were the visual arts, which increased its funding in real terms by 62% though from a low level, dance which went up by 31% and music, including opera, which increased by 20%. Dance and music took up 40.7% of the ACGB budget in 1986/87 and 53.9% in 1997/98 of the ACE budget.

This was by any standards a major shift in cultural perception by what can be loosely termed the cultural establishment. Classical music and, in particular, opera were very much minority cultural forms in the mid-1980s. Attendance surveys show that in 1986/87, about 5.3% of the population of the U.K. attended opera, that is some 2.4 million people, that slightly more (5.7%) went to the ballet whilst 23% went to the

---

[110] Northern Ireland funding is statistically combined with dance.

theatre. (Arts Council 2000 Table 6.1) In the subsequent ten years, funding for the opera and ballet increased substantially and attendance increased somewhat, up 29% by 1996/97 for opera and by 15% for ballet whilst attendance at the theatre remained effectively constant. The reasons for this shift in the balance of funding are difficult to explain. It was clearly not just an increase in funding to the old claimant, the Royal Opera House whose revival had so concerned the arts establishment after the war. There is little doubt that in this decade there was a conscious, and to a degree successful, effort by companies such as English, Welsh and Scottish National Opera's and the regional companies such as Opera North to widen the appeal of opera by introducing innovative productions which related classical opera more to modern themes as well as by developing touring circuits. Ballet also tried to extend itself beyond the classical tradition to take on board more modern dance. As a consequence, going to the opera and to dance acquired something of the cultural 'buzz' that theatre had had a decade before at a time when theatre itself tended to stagnate culturally. As discussed above, the most successful show produced by the RSC in the 1980s was, in effect, an opera. There is however a chicken-and-egg problem here. The Arts Council pushed money into both opera[111] and ballet, at least in England for as we have seen neither Scotland nor Wales prioritised music and dance over drama, whilst systematically cutting back drama funding. This would certainly have given opera companies greater scope for innovative programming, which might of itself have provided the basis for the cultural momentum acquired by opera at least amongst the small

---

[111] It is not possible to fully separate support for opera and for classical music in this period but opera always took the lion's share of this budget line.

metropolitan group who continued to provide its main support. What remains unclear is just why the Arts Council in England acquired such a massive indifference not to say hostility to the theatre.

In 1983, the Arts Council acquired a new Secretary General, Luke Rittner, an appointment seen at the time as very controversial. Rittner was only thirty-six and his main claim to fame was of having founded in 1976, the Association for Business Sponsorship of the Arts (now renamed Arts and Business), something which cut right across the then-prevailing grain of public sponsorship of the arts. It did however fit in with the new business-orientation of the government under Margaret Thatcher busy at the time in cutting down such bastions of socialism as the G.L.C. and the miners' union. Rittner undertook a wide-ranging review of the operation of arts funding which resulted in 1986 in the publication of, the report which formed the base for his policies.

The Glory of the Garden was written considerable haste given that it claimed to be the only comprehensive review of Arts Council policy for forty years. It begins with quotes from Rudyard Kipling and Thomas Jefferson and concludes after a scant thirty-eight pages with lists of those groups which will either cease to have central funding or will have to rely upon regional funding to survive. In between it sets out what are essentially three main areas of change. The first is that arts subsidy was too London-orientated with subsidy per capita several times larger than that of regions outside the metropolis. It hoped to redress this imbalance by focussing on eleven major urban conurbations to which are added Plymouth and Norwich given that their omission appears to mark out East Anglia and the South West as cultural deserts. The second is that previous Arts Council practice in choosing clients to support had become spread too thin with too little discrimination between the worthy and the unworthy. To rectify this, a list of fifteen criteria was developed to judge prospective clients including:

- quality of artistic product;
- actual and potential creative strength in relation to both new and established work;
- the extent to which stated aims and objects are realised;
- the fullest practicable use of facilities and the widest provision of the arts to the community;
- education policy in relation to the artistic programme;
- the employment and other opportunities extended to members of ethnic minority groups;
- overall value for money, including any success in extending audiences through other media;
- box office and attendance returns;
- the company's success in raising local authority and other income;
- the efficiency shown in using available resources and the accuracy and control of budgeting;
- the urgency and nature of any fundamental financial problems;
- the adequacy and security of tenure of premises;
- the balance of provision between London and other regions;
- the Council's existing declared policies, particularly the emphasis which it places on full-time professional work.

Finally, it concluded that the balance of funding needed to be shifted away from some fields which had too great a share of the budget, notably opera, and towards other which had too little, notably drama, dance and the visual arts. This posed a problem in a period when its total grant was static, even falling in real terms, so proposed increases in funding to these areas required cuts in others. One of the aspects of the report which created most discomfort within the theatre was that, although a vague commitment to increase drama spending by some £2 million was included, this was balanced by very specific savings of £1,404,000 in the allocations made the previous year to drama. These included dropping ten building-based clients, mostly in London and the south-east, and five touring companies. The fact that one of the latter, Temba Theatre, was one of the very few black companies aroused especial ire given the general commitment to supporting ethnic communities. It also did not pass unnoticed that three of the five touring groups chopped were explicitly left-wing in their approach.

Two out of these three objectives failed rather dismally at least from the theatrical perspective. Despite a basic alteration in the structure of the Council in which far more responsibility was handed to Regional Arts Board, who effectively spent their own annual grants, the amount of money sent to London remained essentially static. In 1991, it was 1.72 times the national average of £2/capita, a number only derived by excluding the national companies[112] whose main work was in London. If these are included then the figure rose to an astonishing 12 times the national average. By 1996, the ratio was 1.71 and 13.4 if national companies are included. The hope expressed in *The Glory of the Garden* that at least one of the capital's five symphony orchestras could be

---

[112] The National and RSC in theatre but also including the Royal Opera and Ballet and the English National Opera.

persuaded to move to East Anglia remained unfulfilled. The balance of funding far from shifting in favour of drama, in particular regional theatres, actually moved in the opposite direction in real terms as detailed above. Funding for the other priority areas of dance and the visual arts did move up but, overall, theatre suffered both because it was the immediate victim of real funding cuts and because of the way that opera funding actually increased.

The final objective of the three, the use of a multi-variate scheme for assessing clients did, however, come into force and shifted, fundamentally, the whole mode of operations of the Arts Council. Until the mid-1980s, review of grant applications was in principle largely done by assessors using the single, rather vague criteria of artistic value. In practice, other factors played a large part including that of simple sticking power; that is once a building-based company or touring group acquired a grant it was seldom removed though it might be altered up or down. Ironically, it had been the smaller touring companies which had protested most about this system, arguing that the single criteria of artistic worth was inadequate at best and often irrelevant to groups pursuing specific targets, for example children's theatre or inclusion of disabled actors. How could, it was argued, a group attempting to bring a version of Shakespeare in a tent to children in an area with no theatre on a budget of £10,000 annually seriously be compared in artistic worth to a large regional theatre with a budget of millions? In practice, the innovatory nature of the work of many small groups in the preceding decades together with sympathetic assessors had meant that their artistic worth was usually accepted within the context of their work. In principle, the lengthy list of criteria developed by Rittner should have assisted such work by providing other criteria than simple artistic excellence. However, in practice it plunged them increasingly into a new world of funding proposals with business plans, target formulation and completion, and mission statements becoming as important as developing new work. Many adapted, learning how to push the right buttons at the various funding agencies which they now confronted. The new flow of funds from the National Lottery although, at least at the outset, aimed only at capital projects, provided both new opportunities and new complexities in fund-raising. There was a new emphasis on obtaining private sector funds though this remained illusive for most groups, seldom moving above 5% of total income.

The problem of tracking drama funding after the mid-1980s when the reorganisation of local authorities caused big shifts in their funding has already been noted. Other changes in the 1990s made the situation even more complex. Three in particular are of key importance.

First, after 1994, the Arts Council of Great Britain was fully broken up into separate Arts Councils for England, Scotland, Wales and Northern Ireland. Each of these received individual grants, initially from the central Treasury then, after devolution, from the new national assemblies for Scotland and Wales. Figures for each are presented in slightly different ways. Arts Council Wales has recently been threatened with complete abolition by the Welsh Assembly although this was finally rejected, although funding of the major cultural centres in Wales has been taken-over by direct funding from the Assembly.

Second, also after 1994, the arts begin to receive significant amounts of money from the National Lottery. The sums produced by the Lottery are huge even when broken down into constituent parts. In the ten years up to 2005, the four Arts Councils had together received almost £2.5 billion, the bulk going to Arts Council England —£2.05 billion. The use of Lottery money was originally directed towards capital projects but over time the distinction between capital and revenue funding has been progressively eroding so that, for example, in 2004/5, Arts Council Wales disbursed £9.2 million in Lottery funds of which £4.6 million went to revenue funding and £3.6 million to capital plus £1.0 to film. The accounts of the other Arts Councils are not so explicit about this breakdown which, in any case, is not always very clear-cut. To take a major example, using Lottery money to wipe out the accrued deficit of the RSC, as was recently done, could be seen as both capital and revenue funding in some unknown proportion. However, it is clear that revenue funding from Lottery money is common practice. The impact of capital funding from the Lottery can be judged from a survey undertaken in 2004 by the Theatre Trust which showed that out of 160 respondent theatres, 42% had already received some capital grant whilst no less than 76% intended to apply for funds in the succeeding five years.

Thirdly, the major funder, Arts Council England, has ceased to provide any breakdown of its disbursement by category providing only lists of recipients whose cultural focus is often unclear. This means that only total funds can now be compared with earlier years.

With these reservations, the broad pattern is fairly clear. Expressed in terms of 1974 prices, as noted above, national funding effectively stagnated from 1984 until 1990 when it received an upward boost to reach a peak of around £40 million. (Though this disguises a hit from declining local authority subsidy). Thereafter, central funding dipped in real terms throughout the 1990s and including the first two years of the Labour administration elected in 1997. In 1999, central subsidy was down to no more than £35 million in 1974 prices, back to the level it was in the mid-1980s and minus a chunk of local authority money. However after this, Labour's spending increased rather sharply so that by 2004/05, total national grants to the four Arts Councils had reached £473.4 million, equivalent to £64.1 million in 1974 prices. Add Lottery funds and it is clear that central subsidy increased sharply in the first few years of the new century.

The impact of this can be seen in estimates made for drama funding in England since 1986 using a more recent price base:

Year	Amount (£)	Amount (£2004)
1986/87	29,765,000	57,207,812
1989/90	36,029,000	57,268,044
1994/95	45,559,000	58,857,895
1998/99	27,128,000	31,230,483
1999/00	29,987,000	33,785,364
2000/01	29,946,700	33,352,554
2001/02	30,288,800	32,896,338
2002/03	74,629,940	78,372,141
2003/04	89,566,873	91,481,813
2004/05	95,601,602	95,601,602

Source: Select Committee of Media, Sport & Culture, 5th Report, 2005

The big increase in theatre funding in 2002 followed on another review by the Arts Council of England (ACE) into the theatre which had painted a bleak picture of a sector barely hanging-on in the face of declining funding with poor morale and little creative development. The appeal for more funding had, providently, coincided with a big increase in general public spending by the Labour government following four years of sticking rigidly to its predecessor's harsh limits. It also produced a *National Policy for Theatre* in 2000 which set out aims for the theatre which emphasised its wider social role. This emphasis can be seen ACE's statement of aims produced in 2005:

The National Policy defines theatre in a broad sense, while focusing specifically on the following priorities:

- *circus*
- *new writing*
- *street arts*
- *work for and by children and young people*
- *experimental theatre*

We will work to see that cultural diversity is addressed in each of these areas and in theatre as a whole.

The National Policy is built on six key aims. We expect all funded organisations to deliver the first two, and expect that the remaining four will inform the thinking of everyone working in subsidised theatre, though we do not expect everyone to give them equal priority.

1 A better range of high-quality work: *We will invest in artists and arts organisations across the country who show a real commitment to creativity and innovation.*

2 Attract more people: *We expect funded theatre to have audience development at its heart.*

3 Develop new ways of working: *We will invest in organisations and practitioners who embrace a culture of innovation and support a wider range of forms and traditions.*

4 Address diversity and inclusion: *Theatre must engage with audiences and artists from a broader, more diverse range of backgrounds.*

5 Develop the artists and creative managers of the future: *Theatre must improve the working environment and provide better pay and conditions for artists, technicians and managers.*

6 An international reputation: *We expect the theatre community as a whole to develop work of international quality and bring the best world theatre to England.*

This omitted, however, two other aspects of the 2000 Policy: education and regional

The basic status of public theatre changed very little in the two decades after 1985. The fluctuation in subsidy throughout the period with periods of freeze and fall followed by upward shifts provide a constant tension and tended towards a more conservative approach to production. There was a much greater number of joint productions between regional theatres and houses which had previously maintained a constant flow of in-house material came to use touring productions. Lottery funding from 1994 onwards provided opportunities to refurbish facilities which after twenty or thirty years had become careworn or to add on new premises. The greater complexity of funding tended, if anything, to cement the role of most theatres in relation to local communities with wider use of theatre buildings and various kinds of outreach programmes. It became necessary for touring groups to sharpen their focus in terms of what were their target audiences and their cultural objectives. The main shift was towards becoming public businesses responsible to a variety of groups including funding bodies as well as the continuing necessity of maintaining audiences. There was also a greater use made of the West End to provide additional revenue. Such new plays, both straight and small-scale musicals, as were put on in the West End tended to have had tryouts in the subsidised theatre. The extent to which this shifted the commissioning of new work is unclear partly as one of the consequences of the cuts in subsidy was a drop in new work. There was less excitement but at least there was survival. Public theatre had survived its most fundamental challenge and emerged, if not unscathed, then certainly toughened.

Theatre and education

In 1947, George Devine's role in the triumvirate which took over management of the Old Vic was to start a children's theatre, a venture which appears to have been effectively still-born. It is not clear just why he took on this project but one can surmise on the reasons for its failure. Theatre at the time was a grown-up affair. A pantomime at Christmas was for most children the closest that they would get to a theatre. Schools commonly organised an annual school play but drama as a separate subject in any form was unknown. The situation in universities was little better for although most had active dramatic societies, the study of theatre was almost unknown outside those dramatists, principally Shakespeare, whose work as literature was accepted into course on English literature. Until 1894, the Vice-Chancellor of the University actually retained the legal power to ban all professional performance in the town though it is unclear just when or if he used it. Bristol University did open a drama department in 1947 but it only began to issue single-honours degrees in 1968; to that point only joint-honours, often with a foreign language were allowed. (Rose M.)

In 2005, the role of drama in education had been transformed. Drama as such had become an integral part of the secondary curriculum. In 2005, slightly over 100,000 pupils sat a G.C.S.E.[113] in Drama forming about 12% of all those who took these exams whilst in the same year, drama along with expressive arts formed 2.3% of all A level G.C.E.[114]

---

[113] General Certificate of Secondary Education
[114] Advanced General Certificate of Education

examinations, some 7% of all examinees.[115] For comparison, French formed 2.1% of the total and Information and Communication Technology, 2.4%. At degree level, there were 5775 entrants to courses in 2005 to one of the 96 institutions offering courses in some form of drama. This can be compared with 3464 entrants in Chemistry, 2927 in Physics and 5445 in Economics. At a specialised level, 17 institutions offered courses in Theatre Design and no less than 44 awarded degrees in Acting.

In theatres themselves, it would now be hard to find a publicly-funded venue which did not have some kind of educational outreach programme. The main funding body, the Arts Council of England, in 2000 placed education as one of its eight 'priority areas' in the following terms:

> *We expect most forms of funded theatre to place education at the heart of their work. Involving young people in theatre is key.*

> *The Arts Council recognises the importance of working with the education sector: with schools colleges and higher education. We will work with the education sector to influence the role of drama in the curriculum, seeking to maximise teachers' appreciation of the value of theatre as an educational resource and to fund more theatre in educational contexts.*[116]

(Arts Council of England 2000(b) p.5)

---

[115] English GCSE examinations are usually taken by 16-year olds; A levels are taken by 18-year olds effectively as entrance examinations for university.

[116] Arts Council of England's National Policy for Theatre in England, July 2000, p.5

Arts England had formed its own Education and Learning Department and had produced a detailed review of the role of drama in education. (Arts Council, 1999).

The process by which this shift occurred effectively began in the Belgrade Theatre, Coventry in the mid-1960s, the moment when publicly-funded theatre began to develop its position as a community rather than a commercial resource. The formation of the Coventry Theatre-in-Education (TIE) team was a step-change in how drama and education were perceived as connecting. Instead of school trips to see a show, a team of actors took a show to a school and not just a show, a theatrical intervention into the process of education. The Coventry TIE group were funded by the local education authority to develop theatrical programmes which linked with education. An early Coventry programme involved taking a party of children into rural parkland on a walk which intersected with staged actions by the team involving, for example, colonisation or violent confrontations. The children were encouraged to engage with these and to develop their own ideas as to what was the story which they were seeing. Other, more conventional, programmes took place wholly inside schools but all retained this element of interaction between the actors and the children. The children did not just see a play but were engaged inside a play. The work of TIE was literally the use of theatre to educate not just as form of drama education but a technique which could be used to teach physics as much as history though the latter probably predominated. One of its key points was the employment of the actors by the local authority on pay-scales similar to conventional teachers.

Coventry TIE developed rather rapidly to centres such as Bolton and Glasgow and then to a wide range of groups, some directly linked with local authorities, some functioning as separate groups which presented shows to children and young people both inside and outside school. By 1975, one survey (Chapman) suggested that there were 22 TIE groups in existence, a further 6 groups with direct local authority links plus 28 children's and young people's theatres plus 22 community theatres which claimed to have an educational branch or purpose, in all some 78 groups though clearly with varying commitments to education. The average size of the specifically educational groups was around six actors and, although this varied quite widely, a typical group would have perhaps half its funding from local councils with half coming from regional arts associations plus various charitable trusts.

The timing of a shift towards recognition of drama as a component of higher education had much the same timeline. The first university to open a drama department was Bristol in 1947. It was not until the 1960s that other universities followed Bristol, first Manchester (1961), then Birmingham (1964), Bangor (1965), Glasgow (1966) and Exeter (1968). By 1975, 18 universities offered degrees in drama with an equal number of polytechnics and other institutions offering externally validated drama degrees. (Martial) In all these cases, it appears that the courses were not aimed at providing professional qualifications in theatrical skills, specifically acting, though practical activity formed a part of the curriculum to a greater or lesser extent. One general feature of the period was that university education was being expanded rapidly with both new foundations and expansion of the existing. It was common for the new facilities to include performance venues of some kind, often available for public performance. Examples include the Northcott Theatre at Exeter University and the Gardner Arts Centre at Sussex University.

Theatre-in-Education originated at a time when there was both a surge in interest in new educational methods associated with a switch towards inclusive comprehensive education rather a selective tripartite system and also a general rise in left-wing ideas. It was inevitable that TIE would be heavily involved in both. It is doubtful if any TIE team of the period was other than of the left and the programmes produced tended to reflect this. The mode of involvement with the children and the room allowed for children to move the performance in different directions fitted with the more radical ideas education of the time.

By the 1990s, the place of drama in education had become almost a separate academic topic with its own journal (*Research in Drama Education*), its own funded research and international conferences (Somers). This in a period when the practical side of the topic was undergoing the most severe financial crisis of a sector in which such crisis was the norm of everyday life. A combination of local authority re-organisations and financial stringency and the real cuts in the budget of the Arts Council synchronised with a general shift in view towards the role of experiment in educational practice and a reaction to the generally left political position of virtually all TIE groups. The national curriculum developed in the 1990s to standardise and regulate schools had, at first, little place for drama as a separate topic, relegating it instead to a subsidiary part of English literature. A number of TIE groups closed whilst all had to re-organise their relationship with the educational sector. In 1993, it was still possible to count about 30 groups whose work centred around TIE and a further 50 who undertook some TIE as part of their overall activity. (Jackson (1993) p.5) so there had been little shrinkage in actual numbers since the mid-1970s though there was probably some attrition in the succeeding five years. The major shift appears to be one of scope and of performance style. The whole-day programme with the TIE workers taking on the role of teachers has been largely given up and replaced by either performance directed towards drama as a subject studied by the pupils or by performance around specific social issues, for example drugs or sex-education. However, balancing this contraction in TIE groups as such, most secondary schools had gained specialised drama teachers, sometimes several, whilst many new schools were built with specific performance facilities.

There is no quick summary possible of the ways in which theatre and education have impacted upon each other over the last forty or so years, the period in which there has been serious focus on the issue. One obvious fact is a huge expansion in the number of children, particularly adolescents, engaged in some form of performance. This can stretch from private schools focussing on singing and dance through the thousands of amateur dramatic groups which have youth wings and theatres which have performance workshops to a national bodies like the National Youth Theatre and National Youth Music Theatre which have nation-wide auditions and semi-professional ambitions. There are no numbers available but it would be no surprise if theatrical performance was not as popular an activity as any organised sport.

Second, the role now played by drama as a specific educational activity must act to strengthen the audience base of professional theatre. Only a small fraction of those one-hundred thousand 16-year olds annually taking drama for the their GCSE will ever become professional performers. Even the nearly six thousand who annually begin studying drama at degree level will mostly go into jobs outside performance. But whatever their ultimate position, it seems probable that they will retain a greater interest in seeing drama in the theatre than otherwise. Simply put, there is an increasing number of people who have received a basic education specifically in drama and who are likely to be receptive to new ideas and modes of presentation.

Third, the use of drama has a mode of education and training has expanded way beyond schools and colleges. There is hardly an area of social concern which does not have at least one drama group working in it whilst businesses use the techniques of theatre to train staff in all areas of work. It is likely that theatre, seen as some kind of performance, is now more integrated into general life than in any previous era.

Writers

Writing does not alter overnight. However, if a new wave of drama can be said to emerge in 1956 with *Look Back in Anger* then, in a negative way, 1985 can be seen as a watershed in new drama in Britain. As noted in the previous chapter, the decades of the 1960s and 70s produced a mass of new playwrights with perhaps eighty or ninety first plays being put on under the new regime of public subsidy. However, the mid-1980s saw many of these either fading from wider view, moving to other forms or simply giving up. Two of the major writers of the 1950s and 60s, Osborne and Arden had already effectively abandoned the theatre by this point. Osborne's last piece, apart from the odd *Déjàvu* (1991), a kind of sequel to *Look Back in Anger*, was *Watch it Come Down* in 1975 whilst John

Arden's last British production with Margaretta D'Arcy was *Island of the Mighty* in 1972 leaving *The Non-Stop Connolly Show*, (1975) which his biographer, Albert Hunt, regards justifiably as a masterpiece, still languishing with a single amateur performance in Dublin.

Two other prestigious writers from roughly the same period were also in trouble by the mid-1980s. Edward Bond, still only fifty in 1984, had probably acquired the greatest international reputation of any British playwright with 24 plays written between 1962 and 1985 when his trilogy *War Plays* was produced by the RSC. Bond had demanded more and more control over his work and had previously had broken with the National over *The Woman* (1978). Peter Hall's view of this production is that it was *"a superb play superbly done"* (Hall 1983 p.368) but there is no doubt that Bond, who directed it, perceived several problems in working with the National. He also directed *War Plays* but ran into some serious conflicts with the RSC. One historian of the RSC is inclined to blame this on an inexperienced co-director and insufficient rehearsal time for a demanding text (Chambers 2004 p.137) but in any event Bond withdrew from the third play. As he had already broken with both the National and the Royal Court, the other main supporters of his work, this meant that he had serious problems thereafter in staging new plays under conditions he found satisfactory. He has not stopped writing; there have been ten new plays since 1985 but almost entirely for youth and amateur groups. Bond's work has always been controversial and sometimes obscure. Despite having command of an immense variety of work including musicals, light comedy and open-air agit-prop, he never courted popularity and at times the strength of his emotions seemed to overwhelm the intellectual content of some plays. However, there is little controversy about the enormous power of his main work and he probably commands a greater international respect that any other British playwright. However, since 1985 he has been effectively absent from British theatre.

Arnold Wesker faced a different problem in staging his work—it simply fell out of favour to the extent that since *Caritas* in 1981, which was produced by the National, he has had difficulty in finding a British stage, sometimes having his work premiered outside Britain where he also still retains a considerable reputation.

This means that by 1985, the four of the five writers who had characterised the new turn of British drama twenty-five years before had all effectively left the British stage. All were in their fifties in 1985, an age when in previous eras playwrights were in full flow but which in a youth-focussed age might have provided some reason for their falling from grace. Only Pinter, who had written almost a play a year since 1957, remained centrally active but even his output dropped to the extent of writing only eight plays since 1985, some hardly more than squibs. It is also apparent that other, younger though still established, writers found the going much harder after the mid-1980s. An obvious example of this is Howard Brenton, who wrote twenty-six plays between 1969 and 1985 but has only had seven produced since. His early work, starting with *Gum and Goo* (1969), was for small stages but in 1976, his *Weapons of Happiness* was the first new play at the Barbican complex of the National whilst in 1985, *Pravda*, written with David Hare, was probably the hit of the season at the same theatre, both on its biggest stage. He did have a new play presented at the National in 2005 (*Faith*) but only for a short run in the smallest stage in the complex. Other writers whose productivity showed a sharp decline after 1985 include Trevor Griffiths whose *Comedians* (1975) is one of the most important plays of the entire period of this book but whose new work, since 1986 and his *Real Dreams,* has struggled to find venues and who has written only four further pieces. Barrie Keefe (thirteen plays up to 1985, four since), Claire Luckham (nine up to 1986, three since) and Peter Flannery (ten up to 1985, one since) are other examples of theatre writers who have largely faded after some years of success. These and others have not stopped writing. Like Hanif Kureishi (nine plays up to 1985, one since) and Sue Townsend, who wrote nine plays before 1985 and the success of Adrian Mole, they have often switched their efforts to other forms such as television, cinema and novels. An outstanding example is Poliakoff, now seen as an outstanding television dramatist with his earlier stage work almost forgotten. But there is no doubt that after the mid-80s, many of the prolific writers of the previous two decades had their output drastically curtailed.

An obvious and well-publicised reason for this was the lack of money. As the public money allocated to drama dropped, one casualty, particularly in regional theatres, was the closure of the studio theatres which had often show-cased new writers and a drop in the money spent on commissioning new work. This meant that *"production of new plays generally declined in number later in the century, from about 12 per cent of work staged in London and regional theatres between 1970 and 1985, to around half that figure by the early 1990s."* (Stevenson p.390) By the early 1990s, the situation had reached the point where eighty-seven playwrights signed an open letter to the press protesting the situation. It had little effect as new writing continued to feel the pinch to the point where in 1999, the London *Evening Standard,* the closest to a local newspaper possessed by London, failed to find any new play worth an award in its annual theatre presentations. Television, whilst offering many fewer slots for one-off drama, had developed various forms of series ranging from the staple 'soap' to extended crime or hospital dramas which all offered reasonable pay for relatively undemanding work and this occupied the talent of a number of erstwhile playwrights.

Clearly, however, money was not the only reason why, in particular, some established writers failed to find outlets or left the theatre whilst others went on to achieve further success. Hare, Stoppard, Ayckbourn, Bennett and Frayn are examples of writers much of whose major work lies after the mid-80s. In the previous chapter, the development of the 'public' play was emphasised alongside the growth of public theatres. The scope of such work was much wider than what Peter Hall in 1984 rather condescendingly called *"the 'whither Britain' school of drama"* (Appleyard p.9). A great deal of it was concerned with various aspects of community, whether geographical or personal. However by the mid-80s, concern about community was being driven underground by the ferociously individual-orientated ideology of Margaret Thatcher whose denial of the existence of 'society' neatly condensed the view that nothing should be allowed to mediate between the individual and the working of the market. It was not so much that playwrights ceased to be able to present left-wing plays—only one of the five named above could in any way be regarded as a supporter of Thatcher—but that the social context within which plays were written shifted significantly.

The extent of this shift can be seen in a rather exaggerated form in the most significant plays presented in 1985 and then in 1986. In 1985, the National opened Hare and Brenton's *Pravda* and a complete cycle of the Harrison/Bryden *Mysteries*; the RSC opened Edward Bond's last troubled production on a major stage, the *War Plays* trilogy and *Les Misérables*; whilst the Royal Court produced Frank McGuiness' exploration of Ulster community history *Observe the Sons of Ulster Marching Towards the Somme*. In 1986, the RSC opened Christopher Hampton's *Les Liasons Dangereuses* and the Royal Court produced Jim Cartwright's *Road*.

Road, according to one writer " *the most exciting play of the decade in Britain*" (Griffiths p.51), marks a turning point. A somewhat formless piece, it is essentially a series of monologues by men and women driven to personal despair by the economic depredations of the period. There is no 'wither' to this Britain; the journey has already been done and it has led to a set of personal cul-de-sacs of misery and hopelessness so intense—*"forcing the brains out of their heads"*—that the future has ceased to have any coherent meaning. This is the key point; that writing public plays about communal issues ceases to have any great purchase when not once but twice by 1985, the electorate had voted a party into power which appeared set on reducing Britain to a mass of individuals interacting not in communities but by markets. Howard Brenton showed his particular awareness of this by first expressing doubts about the possible extent of influence of radical culture in *Bloody Poetry* (1984) using Shelley as a historical example then, after a third Conservative electoral victory, consigning national change to an unspecified utopia set in an indeterminate future in *Greenland* (1988).

Brenton had in fact never been particularly optimistic about Britain's future. In *Weapons of Happiness* (1976), the eastern European socialist comments about Britain *"Nothing will change in England. Decay, yes. Change, no"* whilst in the marvellous ending of his most complete play, *The Romans in Britain* (1980), suggests, presciently, that utopian myth may be the best that is on offer. Two cooks wander in post-Roman Britain and one decides to become a poet, a trade for which, optimistically, he concludes there will always be a demand. He invents a poem about a king:

> *1ˢᵗ Cook: Actually he was a king who never was. His Government was the people of Britain. His peace was as common as rain or sun. His law was as natural as grass growing in meadow. And there never was a government, or a peace, or a law like that.*
>
> *His sister murdered his father. His wife was unfaithful. He died by the treachery of his best friend.*
>
> *And when he was dead, the King who never was and the Government that never was — were mourned. And remembered. Bitterly.*
>
> *And thought of as a golden age, lost and yet to come.*
>
> *Morgana: What was his name?*
>
> *1ˢᵗ Cook: Any old name dear [to 2ⁿᵈ Cook] What was his name?*
>
> *2ⁿᵈ Cook: Right. Er — any old name.*
>
> *Arthur?*
>
> *Arthur*

The passage of writers through this time is best illustrated by the work of the great survivor of the heroic decades of public plays, David Hare. Hare had never seemed fully at ease with simple left nostrums for change nor with Brenton's style of epic theatre though their collaboration *The Churchill Play* (1974) is one of the best examples of what this can achieve. His interest has constantly been drawn to the impact which great events have upon personal life, an impact which he invariably considers to be negative. As he put it in a lecture[117]:

> *We are living through a great, groaning, yawling festival of change — but because this is England it is not always seen on the streets. In my view it is seen in the extraordinary intensity of people's personal despair that as a historical writer I choose to address myself time and time again: in **Teeth 'n' Smiles**, in **Knuckle**, in **Plenty**.*

Pravda, for all its popular success at the National, proved to be his last attempt at moving outside this frame. In *The Secret Rapture*, (1988) he has adapted to the new times moving into essentially private worlds which dominate even his notable trilogy of plays about the British institutions of the Church of England, the judiciary and the Labour Party, *Racing Demon*, (1989), *Murmuring Judges* (1991), and *The Absence of War* (1993). Although sometimes referred to as 'state-of-the-nation' plays they are fundamentally different from such as David Edgar's *Destiny* (1976) or even Hare's own *Plenty*, examples of this rather loose genre from the 1970s. Hare's trilogy is really about how individuals can exist within these institutions taking their existence, albeit under changing circumstances, for granted. They are not uncritical of the institutions, Hare's version of left politics has never been

---

[117] Printed as an appendix to the published text of *Licking Hitler*.

concealed, but they are in a sense contained within them rather than attempting any kind of transcendence.

David Edgar survived the transition of the 1980s by extending his work into a kind of 'whither and whence Europe' in plays such as *The Shape of the Table* (1990), *Pentecost* (1994), *The Prisoner's Dilemma* (2001) and *Playing with Fire* (2005). These all suffer from a common problem however; they are worthy rather than gripping, indeed *The Shape of the Table* is hardly more than a debate round a table. Something had been lost between these and *Maydays* (1985), put on as the first main-stage production of the RSC in their new home in London, the Barbican, which contains scenes set between 1945 and 1985 as diverse as a moving train and a gate at Greenham Common.[118] *Maydays* is, explicitly, an elegy for a lost politics of dissent whilst with hindsight it can also be seen as a last hurrah for this kind of play on the big national stages.

Only two of the established playwrights from the 1970s really attempted directly to face the shifted realities of the 1980s. Caryl Churchill had stretched the boundaries of conventional drama further than any other dramatist of the period in plays such as *Light Shining in Buckinghamshire* (1975), *Cloud Nine* (1979), *Top Girls* (1982) and *Softcops* (1984). Churchill should in fact be located, chronologically, alongside Bond and Pinter as her writing dates back to the early 1960s though it was largely for radio, a form which attracts many female writers possibly because its lesser demands on involvement with the production process make it more compatible with raising children.

---

[118] Then an American air-force base and the scene of a protest against nuclear weapons by women who maintained a presence there for several years.

She only began writing seriously for the theatre in 1972 (*Owners*) when she was thirty-four, a decade older than most other new writers of the time. Her work is characterised by complex structures and shifting time-patterns; the language is not obscure but it often takes time to understand what it is about. In 1987, she wrote *Serious Money* about the life of city traders. Written in rhyming couplets as a kind of Jacobean farce, it was intended as a frontal assault of the mores of a wholly selfish and materialistic culture. It was a great popular success, initially at the Royal Court and then in the West End, and, ironically, made Churchill some serious money herself after years of small-scale theatre. But the crowds of city-traders who block-booked the stalls suggested that its assault was not taken very seriously. After this, Churchill withdrew from the straightforward, if often complex, analysis of social formations into the much more experimental mode of *Mad Forest* (1990). She still deals with specific issues, for example ecology in *The Skriker* (1994) or human cloning in *A Number* (2002) but with an allusive, rather poetic language which contrasts with the direct, almost aggressive, language of her earlier work.

Trevor Griffiths also attempted in *The Gulf Between Us* (1992), about the first Gulf war, and *Thatcher's Children* (1993) to stage direct attacks on the politics of the Conservative government. But it was symptomatic of the times that he struggled to find venues for these even though *Comedians* (1975) was accepted as being the classic play of the 1970s. Like Edgar, he had written his own elegy for lost hopes in *Real Dreams* (1986), written initially for an American audience, with its haunting ending in which, after a group of radical American students spend a night fitfully squabbling over tactics to respond to an illusory attack, one comes front-stage and says, wistfully, *"you must remember that these too were real dreams"* about their lost ambitions for political change.

It was only in the early 1990s, that new writers emerged who seemed able to respond with any degree of passion to the altered social and political situation. They did not do so with any direct political comment. Dominic Dromgoole, director at the small Bush Theatre in the period, characterised them as containing *"no politics, no naturalism, no journalism, no issues. In its place, character, imagination, wit, sexuality, skin and soul"* (Dromgoole p.241) The epitome of this is the work of Sarah Kane and Mark Ravenhill. Kane's *Blasted* (1995) was created with huge outrage at the scenes of explicit violence which it contained to the extent that the writer had to go into hiding. Kane wrote four other plays[119] before she committed suicide in 1999, an act which has to a degree prevented a proper evaluation of her work. She had clearly embarked on a journey which in many ways seems similar to that thirty years before of Edward Bond another writer who also had *"no politics, no naturalism, no journalism, no issues"* explicitly apparent in his work. Bond's *Saved* (1965) was savaged for the random and unnecessary violence of the scene in which a baby is stoned to death in its pram and Bond was ridiculed for claiming that it was essentially a moral play. Kane's violence is a degree more extreme but it can be seen in the same way as Bond's and much the same comment can be made about it.

> *The point is not that babies are habitually stoned to death in London parks and that this is truth that is kept from us. What Bond is*

---

[119] *Phaedra's Love* (1996), *Cleansed* (1998), *Crave* (1998), *4.48 Pychosis* (2000 presented posthumously)

> *saying is that the defences of morality in contemporary society are weaker than we might care to acknowledge and that this is the truth that is kept from us. It is statement by implication not analysis and the justification is clearly social rather than aesthetic.*

(Chambers 1987 p.158)

Kane's later plays began to contain a poetic rather abstract style which lessened the explicit violence in a way which to some extent follows Bond. But, unlike him, in some way she was unable to carry on the journey.

Mark Ravenhill is the other writer usually bracketed with Kane in the new writing of the 90s and he, too, is not dissimilar to a writer contemporary with Bond, Joe Orton though with the sexuality of Orton suitable heightened. Ravenhill is essentially a writer who mocks and satirises though his view of social life is clearly a good deal bleaker than Orton's. In his first play, *Shopping and Fucking* (1996), which made him almost as notorious as Kane, the character Mark's extended monologue on engaging in cunnilingus in a club's toilet with a woman dressed as a policewoman who is gradually revealed to be Princess Diana who is then joined by Sarah Ferguson, Duchess of York[120], is a comic joy which essentially undercuts the basic social commentary. Ravenhill's *Mother Clapp's Molly House* (2001) presented at the National essentially confirms his place as an Ortonesque social satirist.

Kane and Ravenhill stand out from new writers of the 1990s though several other have flashed across the stages of the Royal Court (which remains the main

---

[120] In a subsequent production in Leeds, after Diana's death, the roles are reversed with Diana's identity as the second woman never quite revealed. Even in 1997, taste did draw some limits.

national venue for new writing) or one of the smaller London venues outside the West End. However, none really seem able to develop as major dramatists. In a way, British theatre has moved back several decades with regard to new writing. There are a number of established but mostly aging writers including Ayckbourn (born in 1939), Bennett (1934), Hare (1947), Stoppard (1937) and Frayn (1933), who float along at a level which guarantees their increasingly infrequent plays a production at a major public stage and usually a West End transfer. It is something of a shock to note that apart from Hare it is difficult to name a writer born after 1940 who falls into this category. There are a number of major writers from the 1980s who have almost entirely dropped out of sight and there are a number of younger writers who struggle to move beyond their first two of three plays mostly on small stages. One or two, Ravenhill is an example, have started to claim the status of an established stage presence but they are few in number. All this is in sharp contrast with the situation twenty years ago in which it would have been easy to name twenty writers with some kind of established position and a further half-dozen making an initial impact.

The obvious reason for this sharp decline is that the cuts in funding which took place from the mid-80s onward made an especially heavy impact on the commissioning of new plays especially by regional theatres and touring groups. The two largest national companies also cut back on new work though not to the same extent. In the 1980s, the RSC commonly produced somewhere between five and nine new plays every year. In 2000 this fell to only one despite occupying seven venues and, subsequently, their record has been patchy. Such new work as was commissioned tended to be smaller in scope in terms of cast and design and may have been less interesting to new directors wishing to make their reputations. Whereas many directors in the 1960s and 70s had a firm commitment to new work this is much less obvious from the 1980s onwards. Directors like Hytner, Mendes and Warner focussed almost exclusively on Shakespeare, Greek tragedies and other standards such as Chekhov, even Priestley as Stephen Daldry found with *An Inspector Calls* in 1992. Reworking of these classics, which offered considerably greater scope than the diminished horizons of new plays, provided better chances of achieving visibility which in turn could lead to lucrative work on musicals or film as each of these have done. Writers found it considerably easier to turn to television, film scripts or novels as a way of earning money than to pursue a diminishing number of commissions. A particular example of this is the generation of new women writers who emerged at the beginning of the 1980s including, for example, Debbie Horsfield, Louise Page, Sarah Daniels and Sue Townsend whose output for the stage was prematurely curtailed in favour of other media.

There exists a real problem here for the development of theatre. It is not simply the lack of opportunity it is also the curtailing of ambition and of horizons. Cramped into small casts by budget constraints, the style of much new work has become very similar to the style of television soaps: dialogue between two characters, scenes which last only a few minutes, constantly shifting focus. Dromgoole's *'character, imagination, wit, sexuality, skin and soul'* can be seen as epitomising a good soap particularly as *'issues'* are largely eliminated. It is possible to sustain this with some vigour given a strong plot at least for an hour or an hour-and-a-half. But few recent writers seem able to write scenes with several characters or plays which can unfold over two or three hours. Length or a long cast list are not prerequisites of great plays but they offer possibilities which a short two or three handed play finds it hard to replicate.

This lack of writers able to carry through the ambitions of the previous generation is probably the biggest problem facing British theatre today. There has been some sign that, for example, the new head of the National, Nicholas Hytner, is trying to reverse this. But with new commissioning fees being as low as £6000, equivalent to about two half-hour soap scripts, it is hard to see this being widely successful.

Epilogue

One view of British theatre in the last half of the twentieth century is that it has become state theatre. (for example Shepherd & Womack p.306) to suggest how the cultural status of theatre has shifted in that period. Well, up to a point. What is clear is that in 1945, British theatre was an almost solely commercial enterprise with only a handful of venues receiving any form of subsidy and that forming only a small part of their revenue. Private sponsorship, the saviour of a few provincial repertory theatres in the inter-war period, had almost collapsed whilst the numbers of commercial theatres were diminishing rapidly. This situation persisted well after the war with theatre closure continuing apace until into the 1960s and subsidy being extended only gradually and that to a handful of venues mostly preserving a classical repertoire. The cluster of commercial West End theatres managed to preserve themselves in something like the form of their golden years of the Edwardian era but the cartel which had preserved them crumbled through the 1950s as television, like cinema before it, lured theatre investors away to a new and much more profitable medium.

British theatre was saved by state subsidy, that much is obviously true and, initially, there was a clear intent to save it by preserving what was seen as its culturally valuable elements in much the same way as classical music and opera were preserved by subsidy. The plan set out by the Arts Council in 1960 when faced with the effective extinction of theatre outside London amounted to little more than a dozen centres of high culture. This plan not so much went wrong as it was overtaken by events wholly outside the control of the Arts Council or any possible government body. The first of these was a wave of enthusiasm by local authorities to modernise and expand in a burst of post-war reconstruction. Borne along with a wave of sometimes well-conceived but badly-executed slum clearance programmes and town centre rebuilding there arrived dozens, ultimately hundreds, of new performance venues, sometimes full-scale and rather grand theatres, sometimes arts centres with little to distinguish them from the sports centres with which they might share buildings. Just where cultural values lay in this rush for reconstruction is unclear and local authorities were less open-handed in their subsequent funding of these centres. But what is certain is that performance venues proliferated in parts of the country previously considered as no-go areas by such as the Arts Council. One consequence of this rapid expansion was that ongoing operational subsidy seldom matched the initial enthusiasm for construction with the result that most of these new venues had to rely on box-office for most of their support.

The second and even greater shift was the expansion of British cultural and political horizons in the 1960s and 70s. This was first seen in music but by the early 1960s, the theatre suddenly saw an influx of creative talent across the whole board of theatrical enterprise, the most important of which were various kinds of joint-group in which writing, directing and acting were seen as inter-changeable and to a degree over-lapping variations on the same job. This shift can be seen all the way across from TIE groups in schools to lapping at the doors of august institutions such as the RSC. This shift was only political in the widest meaning of the word; Jim Hayne's Arts Lab was only political in the sense that the Beatles were. However, by the end of the 1960s, theatre was overtaken by the same leftward swing which resulted in a state of various forms of semi-mutiny in Britain throughout much of the 1970s.

In the face of this cultural spasm which was, literally, being acted out in the new performance venues, the suggestion that the Arts Council was engaged in some kind of state-control of theatre is absurd. An odd intervals, various kinds of funding or even direct censorship control raised its head, more often through local authority representatives on theatre boards than from the Arts Council, but they were rather few and even less effectual. The point about much of this explosion of theatrical enterprise is that it was just that—a kind of theatrical DIY, cheap, innovative and capable of being done almost anywhere, above all else enterprising. Like much household DIY, it produced results which were often surprising and sometimes short-lived but also essentially uncontrollable. The Arts Council, not to mention local authority funding sources, throughout this period mostly seem to be floundering behind an expansion in the form and content of theatre which they find difficult at times to understand let alone control. The simple proliferation of calls on resources as shown by the number of evanescent touring-groups is a major sign of this.

The effective freezing of funding in the early 1980s under Conservative governments followed by a period when theatre funding suffered both from a sharp shift away from drama towards other cultural forms and an attack on local-authority funding undoubtedly had an element within it of political revenge on left-wing theatre (though the assault on local authorities had its own and greater source of political animosity). The same can be said of the re-organisation of central funding overseen by the business-orientated Rittner at the Arts Council. However, at the same time it should be acknowledged that the basis for funding, whether solely on some definition of artistic merit or using wider criteria, needed sorting out. The merits of the Rittner system, if it can be graced with the term, can be debated. Its tendency towards box-ticking is obvious and has been, if anything, accelerated by the managerial bent of the Labour administration in power since 1997. One of the major shifts in theatrical practice over the last twenty years has been the absorption into all theatre groups of a kind of business orientation which sometimes sits uneasily with artistic ambitions. This is a consequence partly of central direction from funding agents but also of the absorption of a general market-orientation which has become the hegemonic ideology of the period. Subsidy levels vary widely but it is clear that they are unlikely to rise much above the 50% level achieved in the 1970s except for special cases with some very specific social function.

What has really emerged since 1960 is not so much state-theatre as public theatre with 'public' being interpreted along a number of dimensions. Clearly, one of these is that most theatres are in receipt of public funds and are in some way accountable for these not to shareholders or investors but to a some public body as well as to their 'market' however this is defined. The mechanism for such accountability is complex but one feature of it is that theatres are, broadly, required to have some public role in addition to simply an artistic presence. Just how this works out in practice varies very widely. Its simplest measure is also the one which shows up the shift from private to public most sharply; most public theatres are open most days, sometimes for limited activities connected with drama, sometimes for quite wide recreational activity. As noted, the single most obvious aspect of the path-breaking Belgrade Theatre was that it had a café open during the day to shoppers in the nearby shopping centre. There is not always any clear purpose associated with this public role. Symbolic of this was the completion in 2006 of a building in West Bromwich called The Public built at a cost of £52 million of public funds and containing a range of performance and gallery spaces. It remained empty, however, at least for a while for lack of anything actually to inhabit its spaces. But most of these public theatres did find their way to various forms of wider public service.

There have been numerous efforts in the decades since public theatre became common to control it. Sometimes these have been local and censorial, sometimes national and managerial, once in the last years of the 1980s there does seem to have been an effort to bring the whole yawling monster to heel and limit its radical impact as a small part of a strategy to limit the radical autonomy of trade unions and local authorities. The problem for all such efforts, small and large, is that most theatre-workers have been ready to embrace their version of public responsibility; very few have retreated into any 'art-for-arts sake' ghetto. Along the way there have been many casualties; Joan Littlewood, John Arden and Edward Bond are only obvious examples of those who were pushed into retreat for their ideals. Theatre is a hard and remorseless profession with limited rewards outside the few who can break into the West End commercial setup. It remains difficult for women in particular to maintain any kind of family life and it sustains its own gender and racial barriers. Even so its transformation from a private, enclosed and dying cultural form into a public and expanding one has to be exemplary. This can be seen in the numbers studying drama at various levels as well as in the numbers who go to the theatre. Just how far it has come in fulfilling Peter Cheeseman's hope that *'theatre should be accepted as a necessary and useful part of the community—as useful and as necessary as the doctor and the shop on the corner. It shouldn't just be a luxury item for a minority with special tastes'* can be debated. What is certain is that a lot of people have tried.

Appendix I: West End theatre in 1967

"Some tangible evidence that the West End theatre is in a bad way...We see no sign of the decline, both financial and artistic, being arrested and it is significant that no less than seventeen West End theatres would either have already made a change or would do so in the immediate future if an attraction was available...The cost of putting on and taking off a Theatre production has approximately trebled in the past ten years.

Letter from Peter Saunders, 21 July 1967, to Arts Council Enquiry into the state of British theatre

Survey of Non-subsidised West End Theatres as of 21 July 1967

Theatre	Play	Comments
Adelphi	*Charlie Girl*	A moderately successful musical
Ambassadors	*The Mousetrap*	A success of course, but even in this tiny theatre not playing to anything like capacity
Apollo	*Spring and Port Wine*	Owing to losing money gave notice to leave the Apollo. Transfers under new management to New Theatre on a popular price policy
Cambridge	**Closed**	Has been shut for two months and has nothing in view until October or November
Comedy	*A Day in the Life of Joe Egg*	Opened yesterday following the disastrous two and half weeks run of a musical
Criterion	*Loot*	Finishes its run shortly. It has never played to more than mediocre business
Drury Lane	*Hello Dolly*	Playing to under 30%

		capacity. Is only there because the theatre cannot get another attraction
Duchess	*Wait Until Dark*	Losing money each week, is only there because the theatre cannot find another attraction.
Duke of York's	*Relatively Speaking*	Supposedly one of the hits in town, but after nearly four months, this 4 character play still has not got its production costs back
Fortune	*The Promise*	A modest success making a small weekly profit
Garrick	*Brian Rix Theatre of Laughter*	A cataclysmic financial disaster
Globe	*There's a Girl in My Soup*	A big hit but still well under capacity
Haymarket	*The Rivals*	Doing well
Her Majesty's	*Fiddler on the Roof*	A great big, enormous smash hit, and the only one in town
Lyric	*Cactus Flower*	Ticking over, but will never recover its production costs
New	*The Constant Couple*	Financial catastrophe but as the theatre can find no new production, they are producing 'Spring & Port Wine' at popular prices with a new cast at lower salaries and the author and director taking a share in profits if any and no royalties
Palace	*The Desert Song*	Following the ghastly financial catastrophe of '*110 in the Shade*' the emergency production of this touring production is ticking over
Palladium	*Doddy's Here Again*	Making money but not comparable with the normal season
Phoenix	*The Last of Mrs Cheyney*	Almost as many people on the stage as in the audience
Piccadilly	*Oliver*	Two separate shows were contracted here but each withdrew because of lack of capital. The management had to bring back 'Oliver' at cheap prices as an emergency measure.

Prince of Wales	*Way Out in Piccadilly*	Losing money at the moment but the theatre cannot find a replacement until the autumn
Queens	*The Odd Couple*	Staying on at no rent only because the theatre cannot find another attraction
St Martins	*Closed*	The closure follows a disastrous repertoire season followed by the failure of a transfer from the Nottingham Playhouse
Saville	*Closed*	For some months this theatre has been reduced to having some odd pop groups sometimes on a Sunday. They have apparently given up all hope of finding a show for this very important theatre
Savoy	*Closed*	The last two shows were a complete disaster but because no other show was available they had to take in a thriller with no names but of which they had grave doubts
Shaftsbury	*Big Bad Mouse*	Although it started well, it is now playing to under 30% capacity but the theatre cannot find another attraction
Strand	*Getting Married*	This star-studded revival is on the verge of getting its costs back, but has to come off shortly because most of the stars won't stay on longer.
Vaudeville	***As You Like It***	Terrible business. The theatre cannot find another attraction
Victoria Palace	*The Black & White Minstrel Show*	A success of course but nothing like what it used to be
Westminster	*Our Country Jack*	Short run, finishes on 22 July
Whitehall	*Come Spy With Me*	After a 'successful' run of more than a year, is being withdrawn at a vast loss
Wyndhams	*The Prime of Miss Jean Brodie*	Has been a big success but now only ticking over. Management looking for a new attraction.

Source: ACGB/38/36(1)

Bibliography and Referenced Books

Allsop, K, **The Angry Decade: A Survey of the Cultural Revolt of the Nineteen-Fifties**, Peter Owen Ltd, London 1958

Amateur Theatre in Great Britain, Kemble Press, Banbury, 1979

Anderson B., **Imagined Communities**, Verso, London, 1983 ISBN 0-86091-059-8

Ansorge P., **Disrupting the Spectacle** Pitman, London, 1975

Appleyard B., **The Culture Club: Crisis in the Arts**, London, Faber & Faber, 1984

Archer W., **The Old Drama and the New**, Heinemann, London, 1923

Arts Council England, **Drama in Schools**, Second Edition, Arts Council England, London 1999

Arts Council England, **Digest of Arts Statistics and Trends in the UK**, 1986/87-97/98 Arts Council of England, London, 2000

Arts Council England, **National Policy for Theatre in England**, Arts Council of England, London 2000

Arts Council of Great Britain, **Plans for an Arts Centre**, Lund Humphries & Co, 1945

Arts Council of Great Britain, **Housing the Arts**, Arts Council, London, 1959

Arts Council of Great Britain, **The Theatre Today**, Arts Council, London, 1970

Art Council of Great Britain, **Theatre is for All**, Arts Council, London, 1986

Bishop G., **The Amateur Theatre Dramatic Yearbook 1928-29**

Booth, M.R., **English Melodrama**, H.Jenkins, London, 1965

Booth, M.R., **Theatre in the Victorian Age**, CUP, Cambridge, 1996

Bradbrook, M., **The Rise of the Common Player: a Study of Actor and Society in Shakespeare's England**, Harvard University Press, Cambridge MA, 1962

Bull J., **New British Political Dramatists**, Macmillan, Basingstoke, 1991

Chambers C. & Prior M., **Playwrights' Progress**, Amber Lane, 1987

Chambers, C., **The Story of Unity Theatre**, Lawrence & Wishart, London, 1989

Chambers C., **Inside the RSC**, Routledge, London, 2004

Chapman, C. & Schweitzer P., **Theatre in Education Directory**, TQ Publications, 1975, ISBN 0 904844 013

Cook A.J., **The Privileged Playgoers of Shakespeare's London**, Princeton University Press, Princeton, 1981, ISBN 0-691-06454-7

Craig, S. (ed.), **Dreams and Deconstructions: Alternative Theatre in Britain**, Amber Lane, Ambergate, 1980, ISBN 0 906399 19 X

Darlow M., **Terence Rattigan: The Man and His Work**, Quartet Books, London 1999

Devine G., *Encore*, March/April 1959

Dobson's Theatre Year-Book 1948/49, London, 1950

Dromgoole D., **The Full Room: An A-Z of Contemporary Playwriting**, London, Methuen, 2000

Elsom, J., **Post-War British Theatre**, Routledge & Kegan Paul, London, 1976 ISBN 0 7100 0168 1

Eyre, R. & Wright, N., **Changing Stages: A View of British Theatre in the Twentieth Century**, Bloomsbury, London, 2000, ISBN 07475 4789 0

Fox J., **Eyes on Stalks**, Methuen, London, 2002

Findlater R., **The Unholy Trade**, Gollanz, London, 1952

Goorney, H., **The Theatre Workshop**, Eyre Methuen, London, 1981, ISBN 0 413 47510 3

Griffiths T.R., **The Theatre Guide**, A&C Black, London, 3rd Edition, 2003

Gurr, A., **Playgoing in Shakespeare's London**, CUP, Cambridge, 1987

Hall P., **Peter Hall's Diaries**, Hamish Hamilton, London, 1983

Hall P., **Making an Exhibition of Myself**, London, Sinclair-Stevenson, 1993

Hall P., **Cities in Civilisation**, Wiedenfeld & Nicholson, London, 1998, ISBN 0 297 84219 6

Hall, S & Whannel, P, **The Popular Arts**, Hutchinson Educational, London, 1964

Harbage, A., **Shakespeare's Audience**, Columbia University Press, 1941

Harbage, A., **Annals of English Drama**, Philadelphia1964

Haworth, G, **A Year in the Theatre, 2004-05**, Broadfield Publishing, Manchester, 2006 ISBN 0 9543450 2 9

Hoggart, R., **The Uses of Literacy**, Harwondsworth: Penguin, London, 1957

Hunt, A., **Introduction, *John Ford's Missile Crisis***, Methuen Young Drama Eyre Methuen, London 1972

Hutchinson, R., **The Politics of the Arts Council**, Sinclair Browne, London, 1982

Itzin C. (ed.), **British Alternative Theatre Directory**, John Offord Publications, Eastbourne, 1979.

Itzin C., **Stages in the Revolution**, Eyre Methuen, London 1980

Jackson, T.(ed.), **Learning through Theatre**, Manchester University Press, Manchester, 1980

Jackson, T. (ed.), **Learning through Theatre**, Routledge, London, 1993, ISBN 0 415 086 094

Jellicoe A, **Community Plays and How to Put Them On**, Methuen, London, 1987 ISBN 0 413 42150 3

Kamen, H., **The Iron Century: Social Change in Europe, 1550-1660**, Weidenfeld & Nicholson, London, London, 1971

Kenrick J., **www.musicals101.com**

Kershaw B., **The Politics of Performance** Routledge, London, 1992

Knapp R., **The American Musical and the Formation of National Identity**, Princeton University Press, Princeton, 2005, ISBN 0 691 11864 7

Lacey S., **British Realist Theatre**, Routledge, London, 1995

Lewis P., **The National – A Dream Made Concrete**, Methuen, London, 1990

Marowitz, C. (ed.), **New Theatre Voices of the Fifties and Sixties**, Eyre Methuen, London, 1981

National Curriculum Council, **The Arts 5-16, a Curriculum Framework,** Oliver & Boyd, Harlow, 1990

O'Connell M., **The Idolatrous Eye**, OUP, Oxford, 2000 ISBN 0-19-513205-X

Osborne, J., **A Better Class of Person,** Penguin, London, 1982

Pick, J., **The West End: Mismanagement and Snobbery**, John Offord, Eastbourne, 1983

Pick, J., **The Theatre Industry**, Comedia Publications, London, 1985

Rebellato, D., **1956 and All That: the Making of Modern British Drama**, Routledge, London, 1999 ISBN 041518938 1

Rendle A., **Everyman and his Theatre** Sir Isaac Pitman and Sons, London, 1968

Rose, J., **The Intellectual Life of the British Working Classes**, Yale Nota Bene, Boston, 2002, ISBN 0 300 08886 8

Rose, M., **The Development of Drama in Higher Education 1946-78**, King Alfred's College, Winchester, 1979

Rosenfeld, S., **Strolling Players and Drama in the Provinces, 1660-1765**, Octagon Books, London, 1970 ISBN 0 37496935 3

Samuel, R., MacColl, E and Cosgrove, S., **Theatres of the Left 1880-1935**, Routledge & Kegan Paul, London, 1985

Shank T.(ed), **Contemporary British Theatre**, Macmillan London, 1994

Shepherd S. and Womack, P., **English Drama: A Cultural History**, Blackwell, Oxford, 1996, ISBN 0 631 16812 5

Sidnell, M., **Dances of Death: The Group Theatre of London in the Thirties**, Faber & Faber, London, 1985

Sinfield, A, **Literature, Politics and Culture in Post-War Britain**, Continuum, London, 2004, ISBN 0 8264 7702 X

Slater, M., **Two Classic Melodramas: Maria Marten and Sweeney Todd**, Gerald Howe, London, 1928

Smith J., **Melodrama**, Methuen, London 1973

Somers J.(ed.), **Drama and Theatre in Education: Contemporary Research**, Cactus Press, Ontario, 1996, ISBN 1 895712 88 2

Stevenson R., **The Last of England: Vol. 12 Oxford English Literary History**, OUP, Oxford, 2004

Steyn M., **Broadway Babies Say Goodnight**, Routledge, London, 1999

Taylor, J.R., **Anger and After**, Harmondsworth: Penguin, 1966

Trussler, S., **British Theatre**, CUP, Cambridge, 1994 ISBN 0 5214 1

Wardle, I., **The Stages of George Devine**, Eyre Methuen, London, 1979

Weight R., **Patriots: National Identity in Britain 1940-2000**, Macmillan, London, 2002, ISBN 0 333 73462 9

Weimann, R., **Shakespeare and the Popular Tradition in the Theater**, John Hopkins University Press, Baltimore, 1987

Wesker A., **The Trilogy**, Penguin, London, 1973

Williams, R., **The Long Revolution**, Harmondsworth: Penguin, 1975

Wyndham Report, Society of London Theatres, 1997

Index

Hills. See Boyle
Hobson,H 156, 157, 158, 190
Hochhuth, J 222
Hoggart, R 135, 136, 177, 206, 327
Hotel in Amsterdam, 144
House Un-American Activities Committee, 188
Housing the Arts in Great Britain, 174, 180
Howard & Wyndham, 174
Hulbert, J 105
Hunt, A 136, 192, 222, 234, 301, 327
Ibsen, H 16, 29, 74, 76, 78, 80, 109, 128, 150
Imagined communities, 208, 211
Inadmissible Evidence, 144, 145, 252
Inter-Action, 202, 203
International Ladies Garment Workers' Union, 120
Ionesco, E 116, 150, 152
Ionescu, 116
Island of the Mighty, 230, 252, 301
Itzin, C 172, 190, 202, 203, 239, 241, 327

Jack Drum's Entertainment, 44
Jeeves, 266
Jellicoe, A 133, 150, 151, 153, 240, 242, 247, 327
Jesus Christ Superstar, 265, 266
John Bull Puncture Repair Kit, 199
John Ford's Missile Crisis, 234, 327
Johnny Noble, 156
Johnston over Jordan, 110
Joint Stock, 11, 208, 231, 241, 249
Jones, D 226
Jonson, B 13, 34, 43, 51
Journey to the Surface of the World, 199
Jumpers, 191
Kane, S 310, 311
Keefe, B 243, 303
Keith Prowse Ltd, 218
Kenny, S 160
Kern, J 120, 121
Keynes, J 23, 131, 138, 139, 141, 142, 162
King John, 225
King Lear, 16, 57, 219
Kiss Me Kate, 123
Knuckle, 11, 307
Kott, J 194
Kureishi, H 243, 303
Kustow, M 205, 225

Dreams and Reconstruction